Personal Power through

Creative Selling

Personal Power Through Creative Selling

ELMER G. LETERMAN

COLLIER BOOKS

Macmillan Publishing Company

NEW YORK

First Collier Books Edition 1962

ISBN 0-02-080990-X

20 19 18 17 16 15 14 13 12

This Collier Books Edition is published by arrangement with Harper & Brothers. Macmillan Publishing Company, 866 Third Avenue, New York, N.Y. 10022 Collier Macmillan Canada, Ltd.

Macmillan books are available at special discounts for bulk purchases for sales promotions, premiums, fund-raising, or educational use. For details contact:

Special Sales Director
Macmillan Publishing Company
866 Third Avenue
New York, New York 10022

PRINTED IN THE UNITED STATES OF AMERICA

FOR BILLY

Preface

MY BUSINESS is selling insurance. I am not a writer. Why, then, have I written this book?

I have written it for three reasons. I hope that its pages will prove the sincerity of my purpose. I trust that its message will serve the intentions I have for it.

1

My first reason is to speak a good word for the American way of life which has given me my opportunity to achieve the career I have been fortunate to enjoy.

I have a special reason for saying this. I was born in Charlottesville, Virginia, where the great name is that of Thomas Jefferson. The countryside I knew as a growing boy was full of memories of him. On the hills nearby were not only his house but also those of James Madison and James Monroe, his friends and successors in the Presidency. As I grew up in the shadow of this magnificent man and his friends, I dreamed of America as he saw it, the greatest land of freedom in the world.

My father owned a department store in Charlottesville, and, later, sold insurance in Norfolk, Virginia, where my two brothers, Herbert and Jack, are still selling insurance. Ours was a modest American home in a historic American city. The University of Virginia was our neighbor. The story of Lewis and Clark was part of our town's heritage. Legends and stories of American heroes fed my imagination from every side.

In a way it is dangerous for a boy to dream such dreams as I did. Life can sometimes rob a boy of his dreams, disillusioning him, and making him bitter. I am grateful to America for the fact that it has never let me down.

I long ago left Charlottesville, but my faith in my country has grown with every year. Whatever I have been able to do has come out of the fact that I have lived and worked in a land which gave a boy a chance. My life has proved one thing. Those of us who are privileged to be Americans live in a land offering greater opportunity to its people than any other in the world. I learned as a boy to love the American past. Now, as a man, I have unbounded faith in America's future. I have written this book to bear testimony to this faith.

2

My second reason for writing this book is to record my deep gratitude for the friendships which have enriched my life.

My work has rewarded me with material success. I would be less than honest if I did not say that I enjoy this. But I would be unfair to myself and my friends if I let that stand as the whole story. The friendship of my customers, and their confidence in me, have brought me the most cherished satisfactions of my working life. Financial success is only one side of the coin of gratification. The other side is human and warm. I cherish my friends as being beyond money and price.

When I first came to New York I was a woolens salesman for ten years. Before I was twenty-five I was making $25,000 a year—and those were days when a dollar was a dollar. Then I decided to sell insurance. This was when a great friend proved what a friend can do.

A. E. Lefcourt, then the great real estate man of New York, the William Zeckendorf of his day, gave a dinner to launch me on my insurance career. His guests eventually took $1,200,000 worth of insurance with me. I have never seen a year since when I have sold less than a million dollars worth of insurance.

Mr. Lefcourt not only gave this dinner. He also insured with me every structure he built. And, as the buildings went up, he listed among the credits, "Insured by Elmer Leterman."

As I write of men like Lefcourt and Zeckendorf, I think of friendships with men established in great fortune. But, alongside them, I think of friendships with men whom I knew before they reached success, and in whose rise I have rejoiced over the years.

The friendship which has been the most constant I have known began when I was starting out and met another man starting out in his own way. We were boys with no money and the world before us.

Many an evening in those first days of our friendship, Milton

Biow and I pooled a quarter to share coffee over which we told each other of our hopes and plans. Today he is a unique figure in the modern world of advertising which he has done as much as any other one man to create. I have insured him and his company for millions of dollars. But when I think of him, I am grateful first and most for a friendship which the years have neither weakened nor tarnished.

A few years after I started my insurance career at Mr. Lefcourt's dinner, I formed a partnership with Arthur Stebbins, nephew of Nicholas and Joseph Schenk. Our friendship is still unbroken. He introduced me to the worlds of show business and sports. It was during my partnership with him that I insured Jimmy Durante's nose and Betty Grable's legs. Those were the years of "the era of wonderful nonsense," and we adapted our selling methods and publicity to the mood of the times.

Jack Dempsey was then the heavyweight champion of the world. His heart was as big as his fists. We became friends. I sold him the first big insurance policy he ever bought. He has never ceased to be grateful. Today, I count him as good a friend as any man could hope to have.

The roaring decade of the 1920's ended on the tragic note of the depression. I asked myself what was the future of insurance to be. My judgment pointed me in one direction. I foresaw a big future for group insurance in the economy ahead. Accordingly, I personally withdrew from other types, organized a group insurance department in our company, and concentrated on that. In 1930, a year when business in general was at its lowest point, I sold $58,000,000 worth of group insurance for the John Hancock Company alone.

One experience stands out of those first days. I shall never forget how my knees knocked when I first came face to face with the great John McGraw, Manager of the New York Giants Baseball Club. I was there to persuade him to become the first man in major league baseball to buy a group policy for his club. He took the policy, but, being McGraw, had to dramatize it. So, one afternoon, I found myself out on the Polo Grounds in front of stands packed with fans waiting to see a game. Alongside me stood McGraw. He signed the contract to thunderous applause. And I made my only appearance at a big league game.

Arthur Stebbins, fifteen years after our partnership began,

decided to go to live in California. I carried on alone, still keeping to group insurance. In one banner year, I sold over $250,-000,000 worth.

It was during these years that I discovered Hawaii for myself. When I talk about it, I wish I were a writer. I cannot do it justice. I have visited it more than twenty times. In my office in New York I have one room fitted out as the Hawaii Room. The islands are a second home to me. More than that, they are a never-ceasing source of pleasure, a continuous inspiration, and the home of friendships I cherish beyond measure.

I put high on my list of Hawaiian friends Duke Kahanamoku, the magnificent athlete of other days, now the hero of the islands and sheriff of Honolulu. He is a man of extraordinary personality and gifts. I have found one of the greatest satisfactions of my life in helping him to organize the manufacture and merchandising of the Kahanamoku shirts. They are proving profitable, and offer him security for the rest of his days.

One unique outcome of my association with Hawaii has grown out of my discovery of Macadamia nuts. They grow only in Hawaii. I introduced them into the United States, where they are making their own market. They will prove, I believe, to be a valuable addition to the economy of Hawaii.

After some years of being a "lone" operator, I reorganized my business in 1948, and took a partner in the person of Norman Gortz, C. L. U. He is a young man who represents the new era in insurance. He is as technically trained for his profession as a doctor, as expert in his field as an engineer. Gone are the days when insurance was a refuge for people unsuccessful elsewhere. Today, it calls for men who can measure up to standards and ethics as high as those of any established profession. My partner is of this caliber. Our association is more than a partnership. I learn something from him every day. I have unlimited confidence in his skills. I enjoy his friendship.

My path has been paved with friendships at every step. I am grateful for them all.

3

The third reason I have written this book is to encourage young salesmen into whose hands it may come.

I would like to say to each of them: "Young man, your future lies in a world offering greater opportunities than any mankind has hitherto seen. Only one thing can limit your achievement and success. That is yourself."

I know there are plenty of prophets of gloom and doom around. I do not believe any of them.

I have lived in stirring times. I have had a wonderful life. But I say in all sincerity that I would like nothing better than to be starting out fresh and young again this morning. If I were given the chance to make one wish, it would be this: I wish I could see the next fifty years unfold. I believe they are going to be the most productive, the most amazing, and the most exciting ever seen. To be a young American facing them is to be the most favorably placed youth in history.

I hope that what I have written about my own experience in my own day will encourage every young man in Charlottesville or Kalamazoo or New York or San Francisco or Painted Post or Putnam Corners to believe in himself in his day.

Dream your dreams. Realize that the first step toward making dreams come true is to wake up. Get up and plan. Take your plan on the road and work it. Love your fellow men as you serve them. The heights of tomorrow are waiting for the young men and women who have the faith, the courage, and the friendship to start climbing toward them today.

ELMER LETERMAN

Acknowledgments

AT EVERY turn in my career, friends old and new have played a vital part. My relationships with them have helped me, encouraged me and inspired me. I should like to say "Thanks" here to some of these friends. I realize that it may look like a cold list of names. But it is not. These are friends, and I ask myself how I can possibly be thankful enough for a life which has brought men like these to my side.

My life is fuller because I know such men as Milton Weill, an old friend who is now President of the Arrow Manufacturing Co.; Arthur Morris, founder of the Morris Plan Bank; William Hedges, Vice President, National Broadcasting Company, Inc., and President, New York Rotary; Alfred Lyon, Chairman of the Board of the Philip Morris Co.; Walter C. Hill, Chairman of the Board of the Retail Credit Co.; A. vander-Zee, Vice President of the Chrysler Corp.; Robert Lehman, President of Lehman Brothers; Harry Gould, President of the Aldine Paper Co.; John H. Ballard, President of the Bulova Watch Co.; Emmanuel Katz, President of the Doeskin Co.; Hal Boyle, Associated Press correspondent; Jack Goldfarb, President of the Union Underwear Co.; Abraham Scheffres, textile converter; Stanley Marcus, of Nieman-Marcus; Ralph Williams, President of Faber, Coe and Gregg; W. Henry Belk, of the Belk Stores; Oscar Hammerstein, song writer and playwright; Joe Vogel, President of Loew's Inc.

There is no way of putting a price on the friendship of such people in public affairs as Jim Farley, Gael Sullivan, Arthur Godfrey, Eric Johnston, Floyd Odlum and his wife, Jacqueline Cochran, Arthur (Red) Motley, Tex McCrary and Jinx Falkenburg, Leo Cherne of the Research Institute of America, Hugh Gallagher of the Matson Navigation Company, James O'Neil of the *American Legion Magazine*, Harry White of the New York Sales Executive Club, Jack R. Cominsky of the *Saturday Review*, William Morris of Grosset and Dunlap, Bruce and Malcolm Forbes of the Forbes Publishing Co., and Irving Manheimer of Macfadden Publications and Publishers Distribution Corp.

In my own profession I am proud to have the friendship of such great insurance men as Paul Clark, President and Chairman of the Board of John Hancock, Joseph Bryan of the Jefferson Standard Life Insurance Co., Peter Fraser, Chairman of the Board of Connecticut Mutual, Horace W. Brower, President of Occidental Life Insurance Co., Frederick D. Russell, president of Security Mutual Life Insurance Co., Henry Levine of Security Mutual, and Lester Schriver, Executive Secretary of the National Association of Life Underwriters.

I give a special place among my friends to Jo Copeland, the famous couturière, who happens also to be my wife's sister. She has given me ideas and constructive criticisms which I have found invaluable. She is a constant reminder of the unique gifts which American women are bringing to the world of affairs.

In business we have seen the rise of such leaders as Jacqueline Cochran, Helena Rubinstein, Dorothy Shaver, Elizabeth Arden, and Anna Rosenberg. In public affairs we have watched the emergence of such women as Mrs. Eleanor Roosevelt, Mrs. Clare Boothe Luce, Senator Margaret Chase Smith, and Congresswoman Frances P. Bolton.

This development as a double significance. On the one hand, it speaks for the power of our democratic faith which has triumphed over ancient prejudices. On the other hand, it speaks for the health of our free enterprise system which has opened the doors of opportunity to all talent equally. These women hold their places because of their ability. They give a new impetus to industrial, economic, and social progress.

For fifteen years I have sat regularly at the Algonquin Hotel Round Table. Ben Bodne, owner of the Algonquin Hotel, has continued the great tradition of Frank Case. He is the perfect host for its clientele of writers, dramatists, actors, and artists. At the Round Table I have not only eaten the excellent food of the Algonquin, but have feasted on the stimulating talk of Louis Nizer, the great trial lawyer; Martin Quigley, publisher of *Motion Picture Herald*; Conrad Bercovici, story writer and novelist; Harry Hershfield, wit and raconteur; Frank Kingdon, philosopher and writer; and others like Quentin Reynolds, Eric Johnston, and Jesse Lasky, who visit the table when they are in town. Association with such men has been to me an education I could not have gained in any university.

I am sincerely and humbly grateful that my business has brought me such rewarding friendships. I want every young man in America to know that he has a chance to string for himself a chain of friendships which can enrich his life.

I have reserved till last the crown of all my friendships—my wife Billy. Keen of mind, trained in business, wise with experience, candid in judgment, understanding in spirit, she is my partner in all I do. This book reflects and reports her as well as me, for what I am is what in all important respects our life together has made me.

Introduction: *The Salesman's First Sale*

THIS IS a book for salesmen. It is a book for the man who can definitely say: "I have made up my mind to be a good salesman," and who says it with the same conviction with which another man says: "I intend to be a doctor."

A prospective medical man knows that he must go through years of grueling training. He does not stop with the daydream, "I wish I were a doctor," or linger over the hope, "I would like to be a doctor," or settle down in the illusion, "I will hang out a shingle and buy a little bag and be in the doctor business."

He says: "I realize that I must give up seven years of my life to prepare myself for medicine. And I know that even then I must keep on studying and learning the rest of my life. But this is the life for me, and I am prepared to pay the price for it in energy, time, and money. Medicine is to be my life work."

Salesmanship, too, is a life work. It has its own body of knowledge and information, its own techniques, and its own skills. It demands the same firmness of purpose to assure success as medicine or any other calling. Nobody should choose it for his profession who would be happier doing something else or who is not prepared to put into it everything he has.

This brings us to a straight question requiring a straight answer. Ask yourself: "Have I definitely made up my mind to make selling my life work?" If you are not sure enough to answer "Yes" at once, put this book down and have a heart-to-heart talk with yourself, facing questions along these lines:

Am I looking for an easy way to make a living? Am I turning to selling because I can't think of anything else to do? Am I selling because I think it's one field somebody without preparation can enter? Am I just going to give it try and see how it works out? In my heart of hearts, would I rather be doing something else?

You will not be ready for success as a salesman until you can look at yourself and the world and say: "The one thing I would rather be than anything else is a salesman, and I intend to be the best salesman in my field."

The first sale every salesman must make is to sell himself that salesmanship is to be his life and his life work.

Never mind what others may think about it. Never mind the jokes about salesmen. Ford turned the jokes about his Model T into a billion-dollar business. Never mind the arguments about higher prestige or satisfaction from other professions.

Let others be what they want to be. You intend to be a salesman. As far as you are concerned, one conviction stands against and above all others. Selling is the activity which offers the most satisfying way of life to you.

Once settle that, and you are ready for the next step. Salesmanship is a profession. The man who intends to be a salesman must first, last, and all the time be a student of selling.

Don't be confused by woolly thinking about "everybody is a salesman." You will run across people who think they are making a great point when they say: "A baby is selling his mother on changing his diapers when he cries," or "A politician is selling himself when he campaigns," or, "A teacher is selling ideas when he teaches," and so on, ad infinitum. These are catchy lines for a speech, but they are dangerously misleading. Salesmanship—professional salesmanship—is not a universal tool that everyone uses instinctively. It is a tool the salesman is trained to use expertly.

You can get the point of this by thinking about another woolly saying, "Everybody is a showman." This has enough basic truth for all of us to get the point, but it does not mean that everybody is a professional showman. The professional showman has skills unique to his craft. Milton Berle is more than a joker; he is a student of what makes a joke a joke, and has a file of thousands of jokes to draw upon. Jack Benny has an infallible sense of timing. The professional showman knows what effect he is going to have when he goes through the routine he has prepared for his public.

The professional salesman needs to be as much of an expert as the professional showman, and know his job as well.

You have made up your mind to be a professional salesman. How do you go about it?

Let us begin with the simplest possible picture of a sale. It consists of two men facing each other with words passing between them. Here you have the three elements of a selling situation:

1. The salesman.
2. The prospect.
3. The words they use to communicate with each other.

No matter how big the sale or how impressive the interests the two men represent, these are the three essentials of every selling operation. The prospect may sometimes be represented by a board or a committee consisting of several men, but the picture remains fundamentally the same. If a salesman masters the elements of the basic situation, he can apply its principles to all kinds of combinations of these elements.

Within these three essentials, one is central.

The salesman is central because he is the active agent who has brought the situation into being.

He has created it because he wants a definite result from it. He will gain this result only as he knows all he possibly can about all three elements involved. This provides a common-sense approach to a study of the profession of the salesman.

The salesman's job falls into three parts. Each part can be stated simply. But each part involves techniques and skills which must be understood and mastered. These three parts are:

Part I. Know Your Profession.
Part II. Know Your Client.
Part III. Know Words and How to Use Them.

The three parts into which this book is divided correspond to these three essential elements of any sale.

Contents

PART III   KNOW WORDS AND HOW TO USE THEM

PART I

KNOW YOUR PROFESSION

Chapter 1

Set Your Sights

THE BEGINNING of any journey is deciding where you want to go. The beginning of making the life you want is deciding what you want to be. This is the first step in making a success of your job.

1. Decide what you want to do.

How? Let me tell you with an illustration. Ever since I first opened the sports section of a newspaper I have been reading articles on this question: "Will anyone ever run a four-minute mile?" For decades the answer was "Maybe somebody, somewhere, sometime will do it. Maybe." Roger Bannister asked himself: "Will anyone ever run the four-minute mile?" and he answered: "Yes, I will." He proceeded to turn his knowledge as a medical student into training himself. He sat down and mapped the four-minute mile almost step by step. He secured a devoted friend with almost as good a pair of legs as his own to pace him. He organized every resource he had to accomplish his one purpose. When he was convinced he was ready, he ran the first mile under four minutes in the history of the track.

The one indispensable prerequisite of success is the will concentrated on a single goal.

That is quite a mouthful but well worth remembering. The most important word in it is "will." A man's will is his key to accomplishment. Until it takes command he has no place to go.

On Boston's Commonwealth Avenue is a statue of William Lloyd Garrison, the great abolitionist, which carries this quotation from his first editorial in *The Liberator*:

"I am in earnest—I will not equivocate—I will not excuse—I will not retreat a single inch—and I will be heard."

I was a boy in Virginia when I first read those words. I memorized them. I have used them as a motto. What they said to me was: "Set your goal and drive for it—through every obstruction—past every discouragement—over every temptation to turn aside into some other way."

Decide where you want to go, and get going.

The minute you say "I will" and mean it, a threefold combination clicks inside you. You pull yourself together—your powers are no longer at loose ends but are tightened into one unified driving force. You are stabilized—you are no longer uncertain and unsteady but sure on your feet and set in your direction. You are energized—your will turns the key in the motor of your personality and you hum with power.

Roger Bannister was a whole man concentrated on one achievement. "A whole man concentrated on one achievement" will stand as the description of every man who has ever been an outstanding success in any field, whether sainthood or salesmanship.

What are you going to concentrate on?

Look your field over. Make your decision once and for all. Set your face to your chosen road and do not let your eyes wander. "A man may write at any time," said Dr. Johnson, "if he will set himself doggedly to it." A man may succeed in any ambition, we may add, if he will set himself doggedly to it.

"I will be a successful salesman," you say. Very well. You have met the first requirement for a career. You have chosen your life's work. This brings us to the second step.

2. Learn all you can about the job you have chosen.

I will let Alexander Hamilton tell you exactly what I mean by this. Ponder what he wrote:

"Men give me some credit for genius. All the genius I have lies in this: When I have a subject in hand, I study it profoundly. I study it in all its bearings. My mind becomes pervaded by it. Then all the efforts that I make are what people are pleased to call the fruits of genius. They are the fruits of labor and thought."

Many men miss their goals not because they are blind, but because they do not use their eyes to study their road maps.

When you have decided where you want to go, you take the next sensible step. You get out your maps and plan your route.

Once you have decided what is to be your life's work, you exercise the same kind of sense, and devote yourself to learning the ways of success in your job.

Every successful salesman knows what Hamilton meant when he said that his mind was "pervaded" by a subject in hand. It was with him night and day. He could not forget it. Everything he saw or read or heard converged on it. Your curve of success will rise in direct proportion as you yourself are absorbed in what you are selling.

There is a proved reason for this. Knowledge of your product is not something you acquire merely to have a story to tell your customer. It is more than that. It is the source and stimulus of your own enthusiasm, that spark which electrifies any sale.

You may write this in your book: The more anybody knows of any subject the more excited he can get about it. You may see a picture of a gentleman chasing butterflies with a net and ask: "How can anybody spend his life studying insects?" But you will never hear a student of entomology asking that question.

And that reminds me of a pertinent story. I used to know a salesman named Appleton in Michigan whose line was insecticides. He was good, but he used the same pitch so long that it began to bore him, and naturally to bore his customers. One morning, as he was driving from Detroit to Lansing, a bright idea hit him. He decided to find out all he could about insects. He read books. He mounted some cases in the cellar of his home for specimens, and became a first-class amateur collector. He took some of these specimen cases with him on his trips. He always had something new to say. I have seen the whole family of one of his customers come into the store when he arrived. The kids loved to hear him tell about his bugs. Of course, his sales jumped.

One of my best clients is in the carpet business. He had a salesman who apparently had all the qualifications for success, but who was not getting the results his personality seemed to promise. My friend studied him. What was missing? One day he hit on the answer. He took the salesman off the road and put him into the factory. He kept him there for three months working at all kinds of jobs. The salesman helped to make carpets. He got the feel of the web into his fingers. He got the smell of the factory into his nostrils. He grew enthusiastic about carpets. He read up on the history of carpet-making. He studied carpet designs. He became an authority on the subject of carpets. He was proud of his own carpets. He knew why. And he was proud to sell them.

He went back on the road with a new sparkle in his eye and a new ring to his voice. He hit the selling level my client expected, and now is sales manager for one of the big Eastern regions of the company. He succeeded because he was enthusiastic, and he was enthusiastic because he had learned really to know his product.

This is an infallible rule. Get the feel, the taste, the smell of your product into your system and you will get its romance into your selling.

A geographer might call a certain well-known spot on the earth's surface "an island off the West Coast of Europe," but Shakespeare called it:

> This royal throne of kings, this scepter'd isle . . .
> This other Eden, demi-Paradise . . .
> This precious stone set in the silver sea . . .
> This blessed plot, this earth, this realm, this England.

The contrast is between a man with a cold fact and a man with an enthusiasm. Shakespeare lived, breathed, dreamed, and hoped England. This kindled his genius to make him the most eloquent spokesman for his country that any country ever had.

The more you know about your job the more it will take possession of you, and the more it possesses you the more your enthusiasm will ring and sparkle in every word you speak of it.

But you never truly know what you learn until you begin to practice it. So we come to our third step.

3. Practice what you learn.

You have decided where you want to go. You have studied the route. Now you take the next sensible course. You get out on the road. You have chosen your job. You are learning all you can about it all the time. Now act on what you learn.

There is a proverb as old as China which says: "The longest journey begins with a single step." That first step! I wish I knew some word that would say "decisive" three times all at once. It is the step which says: "I am on my way."

The first step is difficult because it is the one by which a man picks himself up. No one of us has half as much trouble getting a load off our feet as we have getting the load of ourselves on to them. We can always find an excuse to stay put but it takes an act of will to get moving.

This inertia in us corresponds to inertia in the physical universe. Scientists tell us that all things in the universe tend to inertia. The only reason the physical world does not run down to a stop, they say, is that one body's tendency to inertia runs into another body's tendency to inertia, and this creates movement, through mutual attraction and repulsion.

Like the universe, human nature keeps going only in so far as human beings overcome their natural inertia. Some do not. These end up whittling sticks with their backs against the trees. The men who make our world go round are those who have mastered inertia and swung into action.

There is no magic formula for this. The way to get started is to start. But once you are on your way, the job is already half done.

You say to the little woman: "I ought to mow the lawn," and then you yawn and go back to your paper. Inertia has stopped you. You say to the little woman: "I'm going to mow the lawn," and then you get up and go out. You have overcome inertia, and the lawn is already as good as cut.

Now a strange thing happens which is worth thinking about.

As soon as that lawn-mower begins to go "clickety-clack," you begin to feel good. You get into the rhythm of the thing. You know the satisfaction of tearing into a job that has been bothering your conscience. The first thing you know you are saying to yourself: "I'm going to cut this lawn so that it will be the best goldarned looking lawn in this town."

We human beings are like automobiles. We start in low, but once we get purring we step easily through second into high gear.

What applies to a little job like mowing the lawn applies equally to the biggest sale you will ever make. The decisive moment in it will be the one when you close your own door behind you and are on your way.

Two little words will stand you in good stead in this connection. They are:

Start now.

A young fellow just starting out asked me the other day what I would do first if I were beginning my life work over again. I told him that I would have these two words, Start Now, printed in big letters and pasted on the seat of my chair. Then every time I started to sit down I would have to tell myself why sitting down at that minute was more important than being out selling.

Maybe you are now saying to yourself: "That is all right for a man who is naturally active and has a big drive, but I'm not like that. I'm the slow type. I don't know why it is, and perhaps it would be better some other way, but I might as well face the fact that I'm a man who has to take his time to get started." If you have any such idea in your head, let me tell you this. There is not one living man of exceptional achievements who did not begin his life with the same tendency to postpone and delay that you have. He is where he is because he overcame it.

You can overcome it.

There is no secret about how to do it. You overcome inertia by self-discipline.

You may be surprised by what I am now going to say.

The people who have taught me most about self-discipline are famous performers in show business, many of whom I have had the good fortune to serve in my business. These people have talent. There is no doubt about that. But what has struck me most about them as I have come into contact with them is their rigorous, yes, even harsh self-discipline. They work harder than ditch diggers and longer hours than night watchmen. I went to see a star on the stage one evening. She is world-famous for her voice and diction. In this particular performance she had no dancing to do. Yet that very day, trying to make an appointment with her, I had tracked her to a ballet lesson, a singing lesson, and a speech class.

I have on occasion had lunch with one of our great comedians. Every time he has chosen his diet with almost professional care. At an after-theatre party last week an actress excused herself early with the remark: "Have to get that old eight hours' sleep, you know." Behind every glamorous career that has lasted is a star who has let nothing interfere with the strenuous discipline of keeping himself—his body and his mind—in perfect shape.

Every one of us knows how to do more than he does. Every one of us knows how to do what he is doing better than he is now doing it. Every one of us has brain power which he has not tapped.

The average human being in any line of work could double his productive capacity overnight if he began right now to do all the things he knows he should do, and to stop doing all the things he knows he should not do.

Self-discipline is self-management. And you can literally bet your life on this. If you don't manage yourself, somebody else will manage you, and you will spend the rest of your life working for him and not for yourself.

Does this sound harsh? Don't let it scare you. It has a silver, or perhaps a golden, lining.

Self-discipline develops good habits, and good habits of work lighten the burden of work. They take care of routine work almost effortlessly, leaving you free to concentrate on creative work.

Take a simple example. You decide you are going to begin your day at 6:30 A.M. Your alarm clock awakens you every morning with its startling ring. You hate it and growl at it. But you still set it every night. After a while you begin to wake up on your own at 6:30. You turn off the alarm before it gives its harsh and unwelcome ring. Your body adjusts itself to the 6:30 hour. Perhaps you get so that you can wake up in the morning at any hour on which you decided the night before. You awake rested and ready for the new day. Now you can throw the alarm clock into the ashbin.

Development of good working habits through self-discipline will rid you of one annoying detail after another in just this way.

In the beginning we make our habits. In the end our habits make us. Deliberately training ourselves to good habits calls for an act of the will, but it eventually reduces the wear and tear on the whole personality.

Watch your little son trying to tie his shoelaces, and think of how easily you tie yours. Cast your mind back to when you were learning to drive a car, and compare it with the automatic way you now drive. Estimate, if you can, the number of hours and units of energy you have saved by developing the right habits for the handling of these two simple day-by-day operations.

You can handle a hundred details of your job just as satisfactorily by following the same procedure with them. It has two parts:

Learn the rules.

Discipline yourself till you act on them automatically.

Make yourself keep up your prospect list, and the day will come when you will be automatically prospecting as regularly as you open your eyes. Force yourself to keep good records, and you will arrive at a time when you keep them as efficiently and economically as you shave. Drive yourself to be punctual, and you will soon be keeping your appointments on time as naturally as you eat three times a day.

What basic training is to a soldier, self-discipline is to a salesman. It reduces routine to habit and sets him free to put all his reserve strength into the good fight.

This brings us to the fourth general approach to the job.

4. Reappraise continually what you practice so as to correct faults.

You have chosen your destination. You have read the maps. You have charted your course. You are on your way. What do you do next? You keep track of the signs to make sure you are continuing on the right way. Apply this horse sense to your job. Make regular reappraisals of your work to be sure you are going ahead.

Don't kid yourself that you are on the road when you are only in a rut.

Reappraisal consists of three parts—examination of the record, reflection on it, and resolution.

Take time to examine what you have been doing—analyze it, compare it with past accomplishment, be brutally frank about it.

Take time to reflect on what your analysis discloses—get to the bottom of it.

Resolve to correct at once what your analysis and reflection reveal as your weak points.

In all reappraisal, be ready to talk to yourself like the well-known Dutch uncle, and be equally prepared to listen to the advice of the man who knows more about your job than you do.

The talk you have with yourself is the most important talking you do for one clear reason. You are not as interesting to anybody else as you are to yourself. Nobody else is going to devote to your problems the same degree of concentrated thought that you can. This is what Cicero meant when he said: "Nobody can give you wiser advice than you can give yourself." You are the only person alive to whom your success is the one dominating interest.

But quickly add this: Get all the advice and help you can from senior associates. Take it when it is offered.

Practice is good. Self-appraisal is priceless. Help from a pro is indispensable. There is not much sense in practicing your golf swing if all you are doing is perfecting your slice. The odds on your correcting your slice on your own are all against you. The pro can take one look at you and tell you where the trouble lies.

Seize every chance you can get to have the pro in your business look over your record with his experienced eye. Ten minutes with him may be worth hours on your own.

The only good salesman is the salesman getting better day by day. The job worth having is the job that grows on you as you grow in it.

Decide what you want to do.

Learn all you can about it.

Practice what you learn.

Reappraise regularly what you practice so as to correct your budding faults.

Chapter 2

Salesmanship Is Work

THE DICTIONARY *is the only place where success comes before work.*

The four guideposts in our first chapter are positive. Each calls for effort—an effort of the will, an effort of the brain, an effort of the body, an effort of judgment. Effort is work. We have begun with a fourfold definition of work.

Work is the beginning, the middle, and the end of success. He who does not work will not sell. He who sells will produce sales in direct proportion as he works. He who works will demonstrate how seriously he wants to succeed by how much he works.

Three little words sum up what has lifted most top men above the crowd—"And then some." They did all that was expected of them—and then some. They did as much as anybody else in the same line or the same outfit—and then some.

The soldier who gets the decoration is the one who performs "above and beyond the call of duty." He is a good soldier—and then some. The rewards of the market place go to the men in peaceful pursuits who display the extra that in a soldier makes the hero.

Many fail to recognize opportunity because its favorite disguise is hard work.

"I never did anything by accident, nor did any of my inventions come by accident," said Thomas Edison. "They came by hard work."

The following story will illustrate just what Edison meant.

The Edison and Bell interests were once locked in a tight competitive struggle in England. Edison had the transmitter rights for a telephone system and Bell had the receiver rights. Neither could move without cutting the other's throat. There had to be a consolidation, but who was going to control it? As a practical matter the Bell interests had the advantage in the situation. Accordingly they presented a consolidation plan which would bring them the bigger share of the profits. Edison's English agent, at his wit's end, sent this agreement to Edison with a recommendation that he sign it.

Edison went into action: He cabled his agent: "Do not accept terms of consolidation. I will invent new receiver and send it over."

"Then," said Edison telling the story afterward, "I set to work."

In three weeks he invented the new receiver. It was better than Bell's. In a few more weeks he had six hundred made. He put them, along with a body of men trained to make and handle them, on a fast liner. They started to install them immediately on their arrival in England. This brought Bell around. Edison and Bell were consolidated on equal terms soon afterward.

The answer Edison gave to a situation that apparently had no answer was "Then I set to work." It is the password that answers every challenge of every sentinel guarding every road of opportunity.

The climb to the top is a walk-up never a walk-over.

There are no elevators in the House of Accomplishment. There are only stairs leading from one floor to the next. You walk up them one by one, and you get stuck where you stop climbing.

Let me give you two statistics on salesmen to bring out how this applies full force to them. Twenty insurance companies were asked to state the distinguishing good qualities of their 400 most successful salesmen. The answers put good character at the top of the list. But immediately after that, second, was "willingness to do a full day's work." Alongside that put this story dealing with all kinds of salesmen. The members of the Chicago Sales Executive Club were asked to answer a questionnaire about their hiring and firing practices. Their replies showed that of 624 salesmen discharged by them, one out of every three got his walking papers for "lack of industry." In plain words, he did not work.

The man who is content to get by is the man who will be passed by.

You can meet him in every office and on every sales force. He has been sitting in the same chair and covering the same customers for forty years. He does just enough to keep his job. He has watched his juniors rise above him year after year. He has finally accepted the fact that he is a mediocrity, and has settled down to live the rest of his life as Johnny Treadmill.

He has learned how to get by, but not how to get on.

He never really grasped the meaning of the old salesman's motto: "You gotta see a lot of people, and you gotta see 'em often."

Eddie Wilson down in Vermont lived by this motto: He sold electrical appliances. He knew all about them, and he could talk about them to his Yankee customers. He made such a name for himself that he was asked to talk to a Montpelier sales convention on "How I Tripled My Quota." Eddie was a country boy without much schooling who had found his way into the electrical business because he liked to tinker with tools. When he found himself on a dais with an audience in front of him, he got more and more scared. To bolster his courage he began to take a nip from a handy bottle. As he felt the dread moment of his introduction coming nearer and nearer, he reached more and more often for the bottle. At last he stood up. The speech he had prepared had long since taken wings for parts unknown. All he could stammer out was: "See the people, see the people, see the people." It was enough. It told the whole story of his success.

The man who told me this story was there. He is now the New York sales manager of a big Vermont manufacturer. He closed the story by saying: "I was a young man then, and that speech of Eddie's made more impression on me than any other I ever heard. It was what really gave me my start."

Beginning with Eddie's sentence, we can build the six steps of salesmanship:

See the people.

See enough people.

See the right people.

Apply your product to your people's needs.

Tell its story.

Close the sale.

We shall elaborate on these steps later, but here I am emphasizing that everything begins with that first step. It reminds me of a recipe for rabbit pie that appeared in an old English cookbook: "Rabbit Pie. First, catch the rabbit. . . ." The recipe for salesmanship has just as plain a first step: "Salesmanship. First, find a customer."

The only way to catch a rabbit is to get out into the fields. The only way to find a customer is to get out and make calls.

Contacts sprout contracts.

Make calls. Make more calls.

Let me give you a formula. I will build it around the most famous formula of our time. $E = mc^2$. That is the equation of Einstein which led to the splitting of the atom and the opening of the atomic age. It means that energy equals mass multiplied by the square of the speed of light. We can accept that on the authority of the scientists and leave it to them.

Now, let us take that same equation and apply it to a salesman. $E=mc^2$ means for a salesman that efficiency equals the man multiplied by the number of his calls, and that his sales will always eventually square with those calls.

I have been a salesman and have watched salesmen for a good many years. My experience and observation have brought me to four very definite convictions:

1. There are a few men born with a natural flair for salesmanship—they start out with an advantage.
2. Making a lot of calls will do for the average salesman all that his natural flair does for the born salesman—and a whole lot besides.
3. An ordinary salesman making an extraordinary number of calls will make more sales than an extraordinary salesman making an ordinary number of calls.
4. The supersalesman is the natural-born salesman who makes an extraordinary number of calls.

These conclusions bring me to a special word for two kinds of salesmen—those who think they are natural-born salesmen, and those who are afraid they are naturally inferior salesmen.

First, to the man who thinks he is naturally superior:

The easier it is for you to be a good salesman the harder you will have to work to be a great salesman.

A great talent is a natural invitation to laziness. Why? Because a brilliant man can meet ordinary competition without effort. To lift himself to a higher level he not only has to overcome the natural inertia which we all have to overcome, but he also has to overcome the extra temptation to ride along on his talent. The greatest handicap a fluent man has to overcome is the gift of his own fluency.

When wise old Aesop wrote his fable of the hare and the tortoise, I would not be surprised if he had in mind two salesmen of onions in his home town. One of them was brilliant enough so he could afford to take a long siesta every day. The other was so dull he could only take time out for lunch. The bright one, as Aesop knew him after many years, was still charming customers clustered around his stall in the market place, but he was buying his onions from the dull one now in the wholesale business.

The bright man who cannot curb his own brilliance will find it running away with him, and throwing him in the ditch. The fluent man who gets drunk on his own eloquence will end with himself for an audience. The handsome man who expects to get by on his face will eventually fall on it.

One of the most gifted speakers in New York found himself a few years ago with fewer and fewer invitations to speak. Less eloquent men were supplanting him in popular favor. Then one day he did get an invitation to speak at a dinner honoring Mrs. Eleanor Roosevelt. He decided to make an unusual speech. He worked on it as he had not worked on a speech for years. It won him an ovation. Mrs. Helen Reid, the remarkable woman who has made the *Herald Tribune* what it is today, stepped up to him after the dinner to say:

"That was a great speech. You are undoubtedly the best speaker in New York—" here she hesitated, and then added— "when you take the trouble to prepare."

He got the point. He had been loafing on his talent. At first, people had been excited by his pyrotechnics, but they had found out that, like any fireworks show, they left nothing afterward but a lot of empty litter. He was smart enough to put himself on a regular working schedule, and he is now in demand again.

It is not much of a trick for some people to look like geniuses at sixteen. It takes all the work in the world to stay a genius until sixty.

My observation of people who started out to be world-beaters and ended up disillusioned is this: Disillusionment in nine cases out of ten is the daughter of idleness.

When Marshal Ney, flushed with pride in his own brilliance, once brought a report of a great victory he had won to Napoleon, the Emperor listened, and when Ney was finished asked one question: "What did you do the next day?"

There are two kinds of people who do not get much done today. One of them is the man who admires what he did yesterday so much that he spends today congratulating himself on it. The other is the man who is going to do everything tomorrow. No matter how brilliant you are, neither yesterday nor tomorrow can do today's work.

If you are a naturally brilliant salesman, be grateful for your inborn gift, but recognize that it can trip you into the error of believing that you can get by on less work than the next man. The greater your talent the harder you will have to work to get the most out of it.

Now, let me turn to the fellow at the opposite extreme—the man who fears that he may be naturally inferior as a salesman. I have one important message for such a man.

A man's greatest strength develops at the point where he overcomes his greatest weakness.

You may be saying: "I am shy. I am tongue-tied. I am not good-looking. I am unsure of myself."

Here is good news for you. What you now think is your greatest handicap, work can change into your greatest asset. This may sound to you like whistling in the dark. It is not. Work can change an original imperfection into something near perfection.

We have a beautiful illustration of this in one of the great men of our time. Winston Churchill started out in life with a speech defect. He knew he could never have the career he wanted unless he corrected it. He concentrated on it. Precisely because he gave this weakness of his greater attention, and handled it more carefully than any other one detail of his life, he developed such skill in speaking that he is universally hailed as one of the great orators of our day. Where he was inferior he achieved his greatest superiority.

I feel so strongly about this changing of weakness into strength through work that I made a hobby of collecting examples of it. You can guess the reason. When I started out in life I had the will to be a salesman, but I had no college education, I had no illusions about being handsome, I was no natural charmer. I needed encouragement. I found it by studying examples of people who turned their weaknesses into strength. I got my education from them. I made a point of having people with brains around me. I studied the good manners of people at ease in the world. I applied to my work everything I could learn from everybody.

Here is a short run-down of some of the men who have inspired me—men who have demonstrated that greatness consists in overcoming natural weaknesses and handicaps.

Demosthenes, the Churchill of ancient Athens, began life with a stammer. Homer, the poet of a sunny world, was blind.

Both Frederick the Great and Napoleon, commanders of men, were small and unimpressive in build. Socrates and Michelangelo, exponents of beauty, were both ugly in appearance. Byron, the romantic poet and lover of perfect form, was lame from birth.

Above all, I have found encouragement and inspiration in the life of Abraham Lincoln. He had less than eighteen months of regular schooling. He grew up tall, gangling, and homely-looking. At twenty, he was a rough-looking Midwesterner splitting rails. Who, seeing him then, would have prophesied that he was to become the most beloved character in his country's history? He had so much to overcome, and worked so hard at so many handicaps, that he became the only all-round American worthy to stand on equal terms beside George Washington.

Yes, every great man is greatest at the point where he mastered his most outstanding weakness.

If you have the will to be a salesman, but feel some sense of inferiority holding you back, don't run away from it. Face it. Don't be afraid of it. Spell it out. Go to work on your weakness. Keep working on it. There will come a day when you will be strongest where now you think yourself most likely to fail.

Whether he is extraordinary or inferior, one truth applies to every man in his job: There is no substitute for work, and work can solve any problem.

Never mind yesterday. Never mind tomorrow. Do today's work today.

Effective work has two facets—quantity and quality. We shall have a good deal to say later about how to improve the quality of what you do, but here we emphasize once more the first and unavoidable principle that there can be no success at all without work, work, and more work.

A pamphlet came to my desk the other day which bore the title *The Ten Commandments of Success*. It pictured a salesman's day in ten stages from getting up to receiving a gold cup at the end of the day as the Number One salesman. Under the first nine pictures was an identical caption: "Work Like Hell." Under the tenth was printed: "Keep On Working Like Hell."

Assuming, as all the evidence justifies us in doing, that hell never rests in its effort to get men going its way, this was good advice. It may not have contained the whole truth, but we can say this for it: It presented the essential first truth a salesman must learn—a truth without which everything else he learns will be like so much mustard without any beef.

A prize fighter is finished when he is out on his feet. A salesman has not begun until he is out on his feet. Shoe leather is his one expendable item.

You remember Zeke the storekeeper who had no urge to get out of his chair when his customers came in. One customer ventured to remonstrate: "Why don't you get up when I come in?" To which Zeke replied: "Why don't you come in when I'm a-standin' up?"

We need no preacher to point the moral of that story. Zeke was in very truth a store*keeper* and not a goods *mover*. The man who does not move himself will never move his goods, and the man who does not move his goods will not even keep his store for long.

Out of the wisdom of the gypsies comes a wise saying: "The dog that trots about finds a bone." The salesman on the go makes the sales.

You may be saying to yourself that I have been saying the same thing over and over again in different ways. I have. And I would go on repeating it in other ways if I were sure to do so would clinch it in your mind.

You want to make more sales?

Make more calls.

Do more work.

"By the sweat of thy brow," says the greatest of books, "shalt thou earn bread." It is not the lot of man to avoid sweat. The salesman who is afraid to sweat will never sell.

One of your goals is to make the money which will assure you the life you want. There is no sense in camouflaging this. Mr. J. P. Spang, Jr., president of the Gillette Company, said to a convention of tobacco distributors recently: "Some people seem to think it is an awful word. 'Nice' people—even 'nice industrialists'—don't use it much any more, I am told . . . The word I refer to is—'profit.' " He said it out loud. Profit and loss are at the core of our American system. Success in it is an ambition calling for no apology from anybody.

I saw the Empire State Building erected. Today when I look at it I am thrilled by its glorious mass and lofty tower, but I never forget the long months the builders took to dig into the rock of Manhattan to lay its foundation. Twice the weight of the building was removed in rock before the building began. Once the foundation was slowly and painfully laid, the superstructure rose relatively quickly. What the foundation was to the Empire State Building the *amount* of work he does is to a salesman. It outweighs all other considerations put together two to one.

What I shall say in the rest of this book does not change this estimate one bit. All I am going to discuss is how to make all you do produce the most profitable results. Skill is not a substitute for work. Skill is applying proved techniques to work. A lot of work done efficiently produces maximum results.

The rest of this book is a supplement to this chapter. It will discuss how to add quality to quantity for full efficiency.

We turn now to the techniques of salesmanship.

Chapter 3

Know-How Turns Effort Into Profit

How A MAN does *what* he does determines whether he will get out of it maximum results with minimum waste.

The *how* of work constitutes its techniques.

Technique may be defined as the method of procedure essential to expertness in a given line of work.

It is know-how. What a difference it makes we can illustrate with a familiar baseball story.

When Frank Frisch, then manager of the Pittsburgh Pirates, came back from training camp one year, he reported: "We have a kid up at Albany who can bat a ball seven miles." That kid came out of military service in 1946, was signed by the Pirates, and at once began to make a name for himself. Every baseball fan was talking about Ralph Kiner. He hit 23 homers in his freshman year. But his batting average was only .247. Then Hank Greenberg joined the Pirates. He and Kiner roomed together. Greenberg took Kiner in hand. That year Kiner hit 51 homers and had a batting average of .313.

That is what technique means—getting superior results out of using the same amount of effort more skillfully.

Go to bat as often as you can but know what to do when you get to the plate.

What makes sense for the ballplayer makes sense for the salesman.

Every job can be reduced to a comparatively simple pattern of basic activities, just as we can say that every human body is supported by a skeleton which corresponds in essential details with that of every other human body. For example, a street cleaner takes a broom to a certain place and proceeds to sweep. A painter prepares a palette, sets up his canvas, arranges his brushes, and proceeds to paint.

In this sense, selling also has a clear pattern underlying all sales. The skeleton of salesmanship may be reduced to five essentials:

1. A salesman knows his product.
2. A salesman knows his prospect.
3. A salesman meets his prospect and arouses his interest.
4. A salesman convinces his prospect to buy.
5. A salesman closes his sale.

These five essentials may be called the bare bones of salesmanship. What makes the difference between one salesman and another is what flesh the individual puts on these bones.

All human bodies have similar skeletons, but some put on muscle and some put on fat. All street cleaners perform the same operations, but one handles them in such a way that he is soon foreman of the gang. All painters follow the same patterns of activity, but a few become masters. The five bare bones of salesmanship are the same for everyone who makes a sale, but the career of every individual salesman is the result of what he builds on them.

We begin with the bare bones, however. No matter how good a salesman may be, he cannot avoid the routines of his work. Nor can any other worker. It is said that Michelangelo used to groan all the time as he worked on his statues, but, groan as he might, and genius as he was, he knew that there was no way for him to get a masterpiece out of a block of marble except to chisel away at it one blow at a time. Routine is the necessary putting of one foot ahead of the other, and repeating this process endlessly, which gets us from where we are to where we want to arrive. The man who shirks routine may dream of accomplishment, but he will wake from his dream to find himself sitting in the same chair with nothing accomplished.

There is no avoiding routine—but this is not the last word in the matter. There is another word to be said, and it is this. We can make routine exciting by keeping alive the sparks of curiosity and ambition within ourselves.

Doing the ordinary can become an extraordinary experience producing extraordinary results. Every successful salesman has learned this. He has climbed out of the ranks of ordinary salesmen in one of two ways: (a) he has done the ordinary thing with extraordinary enthusiasm, or (b) he has introduced into the ordinary some unusual thing which bore the stamp of his unique personality. Let us take a look at how these two aids to selling may be developed.

1

What turns the ordinary into the extraordinary is the extra you put into it.

Men fail not because they do not know but because they do not get excited enough about what they know. Nothing—literally nothing—worth accomplishing was ever achieved without enthusiasm.

The minute you find yourself saying that your work is dull, take a look at yourself. It is you who are losing your shine. It is you, not your work, that is dull. Make no mistake about it. The moment you begin to be bored with your work is a personal crisis. Unless there and then you give yourself a polish you will have no brightness inside or out. You cannot make gold, but you can polish it.

One first step toward successful selling is this: Find something to sell about which you can be enthusiastic, and then be enthusiastic about what you sell.

I get a kick out of the story of the department store floorwalker who, after a few years on that job, left it to become a policeman. After he had been on the force for a few months a friend asked him how he liked his new job. He replied: "I like the uniform. The hours are not bad. I have security even though

I don't get too much immediate pay. But, boy!—I like one thing best of all: the customer is always wrong!"

For him, being what he was, that was the right job. He could be enthusiastic about it. I imagine he ended as commissioner.

To balance that, here is a story more applicable to a good salesman. It was told to me by an Amsterdam trader in precious stones who was a fellow passenger on a transatlantic crossing.

A rich Amsterdam merchant was anxious to buy a diamond of certain specifications for his collection. Word got around, and Harry Winston called him to say he thought he had found the stone he wanted. The collector came to see it, and was met by the salesman assigned by Winston to greet him.

The salesman exhibited the exquisite stone, describing and explaining it with expert exactness. The customer listened, and praised it, but eventually turned away, saying: "It's a wonderful stone, but not exactly what I want."

Winston, who had been watching the interview from a distance, stopped him on the way out. "Do you mind if I show you that diamond once more?" he asked.

The customer agreed. Winston took the stone in his hand. He did not repeat anything the salesman had said. He talked about it as though he were just releasing into words his own genuine admiration of it as a thing of beauty.

The customer changed his mind. He bought the diamond. While he was waiting for it to be brought to him, he turned to the owner of the store. "Well," he said, "you sold it to me, but tell me this. Why did I buy it willingly from you when I had no difficulty saying no to your salesman?"

Winston answered: "That salesman is one of the best men in the business. I have no hesitation in saying that he knows more about diamonds than I do. I pay him a good salary for what he knows. But I would gladly pay him twice as much if I could put into him something which I have and he lacks. He *knows* diamonds but I *love* them."

What transforms routine into excitement comes from within.
This brings me to a point which I cannot make too strongly.

Perhaps you are now saying: "Of course enthusiasm helps. Anybody can see that. But enthusiasm is an emotion. This chapter is about techniques. How can you talk about techniques in connection with emotions? You can't turn enthusiasm on and off like a light, or train it as you develop muscles."

Enthusiasm is subjective, it is true, but that only means that we have to find a technique for handling ourselves. Enthusiasm can be fed and developed by anyone who is prepared to follow its rules as rigorously as a professional strong man does his exercises.

The first rule we have already stated:

1. Choose as the product or service you are going to sell something about which you can get enthusiastic.

In Chapter One was suggested and illustrated the second rule:

2. Keep learning all you can about what you are selling.

Nothing sustains enthusiasm like a lively curiosity kept active by knowledge. The process of learning is a process of living. As long as you are learning, what you learn will come to life for you and in you. Every morning you will wake up expectantly, looking forward to the new fact, the new insight, the new idea that day will bring you. Every time you hit on a new facet of your work which interests you, you will refresh yourself.

This does not mean that you will have to tell all you know every time you open your mouth, but it does mean that everything you know will automatically add weight to what you say. You will speak from depth. You will carry the authority of your reserves. It is one of the mysteries of conversation that we know immediately from the way a man speaks whether he is spilling his words from a shallow knowledge or whether he is drawing them from a deep understanding. You cannot know too much about your job. Every word you utter will carry extra persuasiveness for every new fact you know.

I have already given you illustrations of this in the stories of the carpet and the insect powder salesmen. Now I would like to carry it to the next step.

The more you know about your product the prouder you will be of your association with it. This brings us to the third rule of enthusiasm.

3. Take pride in your product.

In Radio City, where I have my coffee, Charles De Zemler operates a barber shop. It is one of the most unusual barber shops in the world. He has collected from all parts of the world all sorts of interesting items relating to the history and practice of tonsorial art. His shop is full of objects from oil paintings and cartoons to mugs and razors. It constitutes what is probably the most nearly complete private museum of its kind anywhere.

What it says, to the people who see it, is as plain as though Charlie had a recording machine reciting it, and much more convincing. It says: "Here works a barber proud of his calling and full of enthusiasm for it."

A friend once laughingly remarked to me: "Charlie is nuts about barbering." What I should have replied, only I did not think of it in time, was: "The salesman who is nuts about what he is selling already has the kernel of good salesmanship in him."

Here, then, are the first three rules for feeding enthusiasm:

1. Choose something to sell you can be enthusiastic about.
2. Keep on learning all you can about it.
3. Take pride in it.

I have repeated them because they fall into one class. The fourth is of a different kind. It is very practical, not so self-evident, and, at first glance, may not seem to make sense. But here it is:

4. When you find yourself losing your enthusiasm, work harder—drive yourself to make more calls.

The way not to grow cold is to get hot.

As a matter of practical psychology, a lot of people are turned around on what is cause and what is effect in the relationship of feeling and work. They say: a man has his low days when he does not accomplish much because he doesn't feel like work. The practical truth is this: a man does not feel like work on certain days because he does not drive himself to work.

A man is like an automobile engine in this respect:

The only way to warm up the engine is to start the motor running.

What you do determines how you feel. How you feel does not determine what you do. Action awakens interest and enthusiasm. Your hands at work will rouse your heart to back them. The one and only sure answer to lethargy is labor.

As a cure for being fed up, work is better than whiskey.

I know this is true in my own experience, and I was intensely interested when a friend of mine told me that William James, the famous Harvard psychologist and philosopher, had stated it formally. According to James, whenever we get into a piece of work calling for effort, we come sooner or later to what he called a "fatigue point," a point where we want to quit, when we think we cannot go on any longer. He maintained that the only way to meet it is to work through it. On the other side of the fatigue point, said James, is a second reservoir of energy of which we shall never be aware, and which we never tap, until we go through the hard place and need it.

When my friend told me about James's theory, my memory went back to a talk I once had with David Marr, who was a well-known long-distance runner in his day. I asked him whether he ever had a "stitch" while he was running his marathons. He laughed and said: "Of course I used to have them. Every long-distance runner has them. You just have to keep on running until they pass away and you get your second wind. Then you can keep going forever."

The "I-don't-feel-like-working-today" feeling in a salesman is his fatigue point, or his stitch. The cure for it is to go to work. Work will carry him through to a new reservoir of enthusiasm, to his second wind.

There is another side to this also. I can best illustrate it by describing an Air Force practice. When a flyer cracks up his machine but not himself he is sent back into the air immediately. Why? Because action will do more than anything else in the world to drive away any psychological fears which his accident might stir in him. If he gave way to them he would always thereafter be a poorer flyer. The sure antidote is to get him back at the controls at once.

The salesman who gives way to lethargy once will find it twice as hard to overcome the next time.

Work itself feeds the enthusiasm by which it is itself improved.

This brings us by a natural step to our fifth rule:

5. Act and talk enthusiastically.

Put all you've got into everything you do. Whatever is worth doing at all is worth doing well. Or, as the Good Book puts it: "Whatsoever thy hand findeth to do, do it with thy might."

The surest way to get all the things done that you want to do is to put all of yourself into doing only one thing now.

The only moment you can fill with accomplishment right now is this one. Fill it to the brim.

Jack Harrison, who is salesmanager of a department in one of New Jersey's great stores, told me how one of his sales girls brought this lesson home to him.

He watched her make a sale to an old lady who looked as though she did not have enough money to buy anything. The sales girl was animated, smiling, and attentive throughout the sale which took a full fifteen minutes. At last the old lady walked away with her package, and Jack moved over to the counter. "How much did she spend on what you sold her?" he asked the sales girl. "Two ninety-eight," the girl replied. Jack said: "You sure put a lot of effort into that two ninety-eight sale." The girl looked at him with unsmiling eyes. "While she was here she was the only customer I had," she said. Jack said he moved away a bit uncomfortable, but he kept his eye on the girl. Before long he noticed that she was getting a following of her own, customers who waited to buy until she was free to serve them. Her sales rose, not spectacularly, but consistently. As soon as there was an opening, he promoted her. She is now his special assistant.

She began by making every minute carry its own accomplishment. She was enthusiastic about every sale, great or small. It became a habit with her. It put an extra spark in her work.

Get yourself warmed up before every call. One of Pennsylvania's boxing commissioners told me this story about Joe Louis's second fight with Max Schmeling.

Joe felt doubly humiliated by his defeat at the hands of Schmeling in 1936. He felt personally humiliated by it. And, he felt that he had let America down when he let a Nazi hero beat him. His own explanation of his defeat was that it took him so long to warm up that Schmeling got to him early. Consequently, in 1938, just before he entered the ring for the return bout, he went through four rounds with a sparring partner in his dressing room. He then entered the ring thoroughly warmed up and on fire to destroy Schmeling. The rest is history. He knocked Schmeling out in less than two minutes with a punch that sent him to the hospital.

A champion puts all he has into every punch.

A successful salesman throws all of himself into every sale. By acting enthusiastically he kindles his own enthusiasm.

The sixth rule flows logically from this:

6. Expose yourself to enthusiasm.

The two most infectious expressions of the human face are a yawn and a smile—keep your face in good company.

Yawn and the world yawns *at* you.

Smile and the world smiles back.

Cultivate the company of people of good cheer.

Let me illustrate with two experiences I had in one day.

That noon at the Algonquin we had the company of three outstanding newspapermen: Quentin Reynolds, Martin Quigley of *Motion Picture Herald*, and Michael Stern of *Argosy*. Mike Stern got into a description of how he tracked down a murder story which had come out of Rome, where he lives, and which had threatened to have international complications. It had been put on all the wires, but he was skeptical about it. His perception was right. The story, including the names of the principals, was made up out of whole cloth. Mike exposed it, and foiled the plans of those who had released it for their own purposes. His account was so vivid, and the story itself so good an example of a great reporter in action, that they aroused Reynolds and Quigley to a high pitch of professional enthusiasm. I could almost feel an electric current run around the table. Everyone there was thrilled by it, and we left the table stirred and excited. We had been exposed to enthusiasm and were tingling with its contagion.

That same evening I was watching Edward R. Murrow's "Person to Person" program. All of a sudden it was transformed from an excellent program into a superb one. Lillian Gish, whom he was interviewing, broke through the conventional boundaries of an interview to plead for a national Department of Fine Arts. There was no doubt about her enthusiasm. Her deep passion for the theater and her love of the arts gave her voice a new and moving power, and lighted her natural beauty. We were listening to somebody who believed with all her being in what she was saying. Her belief made all belief seem more justifiable and wonderful. The idea she was advocating was certainly debatable, but she was inspired and inspiring. Her spirit struck fire on ours as one stone produces fire when struck against another.

This is the miracle of enthusiasm. It enlists hidden impulses in all exposed to it. It wins its own kind of response in an excitement answering back to it.

The successful salesman treats himself to the company of enthusiastic people. To be with them is like living in the sun.

Enthusiasm is the mysterious current which flows from seller to buyer and sparks consent.

The first way to rise above the crowd is to do the ordinary thing with extraordinary enthusiasm.

The six rules for feeding and developing enthusiasm are:

1. Choose to sell something you can be enthusiastic about.
2. Keep on learning all you can about it.
3. Take pride in it.
4. When enthusiasm lags, work harder.
5. Work and talk enthusiastically.
6. Expose yourself to enthusiastic people.

Now we are ready to consider the second way to give your work the distinction that will make it outstanding.

2

He who follows others is always behind; have the courage of your own originality.

There is not much difference between you and everybody else, but that little difference is *you* as distinct from everybody else. And what is distinct can become the beginning of distinction. You as a unique individual have never been duplicated in all the billions of people who have preceded you on this earth, and you will never be exactly reproduced in all the billions who will follow you.

I like to think about it this way. Every face in the world is made up of a forehead, two eyes, a nose, two cheeks, a mouth, two ears, and a chin. A child can draw a face which everyone will recognize as a face because all faces have so much in common. Yet the amazing fact is that no two faces are exactly alike. Your face, for better or for worse, is yours, and when people see it they call you by name. It is not much different, but it is different enough to be unique.

You, yourself, are unique in the same way that your face is. *You* are your only exclusive.

Be yourself.

Have the courage to do the unusual thing with the stamp of your own personality on it.

A few years ago some authors began to write books "debunking" our national heroes. They dug up all kinds of gossip and stories to show how the great men were only human like the rest of us. Their favorite target was George Washington. They took a fiendish glee in recounting all the things they could find in his career which showed he had weaknesses like the rest of us. They reminded me of little boys taking potshots at a man in a top hat. I shall never forget a comment which one of my best friends, Dr. Frank Kingdon, made on this. He said: "Sure, George Washington was ninety-five per cent like the rest of us, but this is not the important thing about him. The important thing is the five per cent in which he differed from us. Instead of trying to show that Washington was like us, these fellows would be better employed if they could show us how to be like him."

It is the little area of our own private difference which makes each of us an individual. It is where we are individual that each of us can put a unique touch into salesmanship.

I have three enthusiasms outside of my love of my family and my country. They are my friends, my work, and Hawaii. For many years I have visited and revisited Hawaii. To me it stands for beauty, pleasure, and charm. It is my second home. If you visit my office the receptionist ushers you into a waiting room lighted and decorated to bring into it a bit of the sun and color of Hawaii. There is not another room in the city like it.

I had the room fixed this way because I myself wanted it like this. It reflects a unique enthusiasm of mine. But, though I did not do it for this reason, I have found this unique effect a great asset in dealing with people. The sunny atmosphere at once lifts the spirit of my visitors. They come into my private office smiling, their mood sunnier than the one with which they got out of the elevator. They want to talk about the room. It breaks down their reserves. It establishes a warm relationship between them and me immediately.

My reception room illustrates a truth worth cherishing. The

unusual thing which truly reflects you serves as an introduction which fixes you in the other fellow's memory. Not only do my visitors respond to the room while they are in it. They talk about it outside to their families and acquaintances. Every time they do so they mention my name.

The unusual is memorable. A few years ago the Baltimore *Sun* covered its whole editorial page, except for one column of explanation, with dots. Newspaper men tell me that they estimate that only eight per cent of a newspaper's readers read editorials, but I'm confident that less than eight per cent passed that page that day without taking a second look to see what the dots were all about. The idea the *Sun* was trying to get across was that every dot represented a Federal employee, of whom, in the paper's opinion, there were too many. Whether you agree or don't agree with their position, you will never forget their original way of putting it over.

I once ran across a case where a man with the courage of his own originality did something so outrageously wrong that it turned out to be right. I was walking down a San Francisco street when I saw this sign in a shoe-shine parlor: "Pedal habiliments artificially lubricated and illuminated with ambidextrous felicity for the infinitesimal remuneration of twenty cents."

That sign broke all the rules about avoiding overflowery language. But I had a funny experience with it. I copied it down as an illustration of the wrong way to use words, and my intention was to say that "Shoe Shine, Twenty Cents," told the story better. Then something happened to me. As I started to walk away I suddenly realized that it was the only advertising sign of any kind that I had taken the trouble to copy in all San Francisco. My curiosity was aroused. I had an irrepressible impulse to meet the man who dared to be so wrong. The outcome was that I went back to the parlor for a shine I did not need.

Thinking about this afterward, I came to this conclusion. The shoe-shine man knew what he was doing. He violated the rules consciously. Because he was conscious of what he was doing, it worked. The violations that kill us are the ones of which we are not conscious.

Another sign I remember for its originality I saw in Detroit, in, of all places, a pawnbroker's window. It read: "I'm here to help you—see me at your earliest inconvenience." That is a good sign. It automatically calls up a picture of a man totally apart from our ordinary stereotype of a moneylender.

Your originality, properly channeled, can become your trade mark. Take a few examples:

You may be anything but an expert on English kings, but you know about Henry VIII, the only one to have six wives.

You may not be much for remembering the faces of American authors, but you can recall Mark Twain with his shock of white hair.

The vice-presidents of the United States may be hazy in your mind, but you know that there was once a Vice-President Marshall who broke into the solemnity of a Senate debate with the quip: "What this country needs is a good five-cent cigar."

You probably do not specialize in the political leaders of India, but you remember Gandhi in his loincloth.

Unsuccessful presidential candidates may not be your strong point, but you have no doubt about who Al Smith in his brown derby was.

Most trade union leaders may be just names to you, but you have a definite opinion about John L. Lewis with his booming voice and bushy eyebrows.

Women in public life may be something you manage to know little about, but you know who Mrs. Roosevelt is, and would not be surprised to meet her on any plane, train, ship, bus, subway, street, or escalator on which you might find yourself.

Be original enough to impress people without being eccentric enough to scare them: eccentricity is the prerogative of only the old and the rich.

We can summarize this chapter in two sentences: You can be a top salesman by doing the usual with unusual enthusiasm. You can set yourself apart from the crowd by doing the unusual thing which truly expresses you.

Doing either or both involves two activities: *thought* and *action.* The chapters that follow will deal with these in turn.

Chapter 4

The Three Whys of Selling

The first thing to do with any enterprise is to beat the "why" out of it.

I learned this from one of the greatest living publicists, Herbert Bayard Swope. He was at a meeting considering the advisability of issuing a manifesto on a matter of public interest. The man who had started the idea explained his interest and read the statement he had prepared. There was some discussion, and then Swope intervened. He said:

"Now let us get back to the beginning with the first three questions we have to answer. First, why do it at all? Second, if we agree we should do it, why do it now? Third, assuming we agree to do it now, why do it this way?"

His words have paid me many dividends since in time saved, energy conserved, and waste obliterated. I know of no surer formula for checking up on my own thinking than relentlessly forcing myself to answer these questions before going out on a limb.

Why am I going to do this at all?

Why am I going to do it now?

Why am I going to do it this way?

They strip every impulse of pretense, stopping me from kidding myself. They uncover the essentials of what I am planning to do. They force me to think it through.

They are a good preliminary for all kinds of enterprises, but they have especial force for a salesman.

Sales are first made in the mind of a salesman or they are never made at all.

A successful sale starts with an idea. This idea takes form in the mind. Once shaped in a preliminary way, it is ready to be examined. This is when we apply our three questions to it.

For example, you say to yourself: "I haven't seen Tompkins lately. It might be a good idea to call on him. He might be ready to do business."

You have projected a preliminary idea of a possible sale. You proceed to examine it.

Why do it at all?

Is there a truly valid reason for calling on Tompkins? Or, is it just an impulse? Am I thinking about calling on Tompkins because it will give me an excuse for not getting down to some other work I ought to be doing but would prefer to postpone? Is there some genuine service I can render Tompkins? Or, am I going on a chance? Am I going to call on him just because I would like to have the commission on the sale, and for no other reason? Is there something to be gained from the call apart from making the sale? Does Tompkins' account need a little warming up? Exactly why should I call on Tompkins?

I make up my mind that I should call on Tompkins, and I decide why. I am going with the intention of making a sale. Now comes the next question.

Why do it now?

Is a call on Tompkins the most productive one I can make today? Or, is there somebody else I can approach to better advantage? Is this the best time of the year or the month to call on him? Why did I happen to think of him? Did I read something in the paper or hear something that brought him to my mind? If so, does this make a call particularly timely? Have I something special to offer him? Just why is a call on Tompkins the number one priority right now?

I review what I know about Tompkins, his business, and my relationship with him. I think about possibilities of more advantageous timing. If all these considerations point to an immediate call I decide to see him at once.

I am going to call on Tompkins *now*, and I know why. This brings up the third question.

Why do it this way?

While I have been thinking about the first two questions I have been automatically framing an approach to Tompkins. I have visualized his needs and thought about what I have to offer to meet them. I have an idea of what I shall present to him. A preliminary outline of my presentation is already taking shape.

I now pull this to the front of my mind. Knowing what I know of Tompkins, what is the best way to present what I have for him? Is there one aspect of it which will get his attention more favorably than another, and so offer the most effective opening? Is he the kind of man who likes to gossip a little before getting down to business, and, if so, what story can I have ready for him? Has he some game or hobby he enjoys, talk about which will warm him up? What about his family? What are their names? Has there been any change in his family I must remember? On the other hand, is he the kind of man who gets briskly down to business, with no nonsense, so that I must be prepared to plunge into my proposition as soon as I sit down?

With such questions I balance what I want to accomplish against what Tompkins himself is like and his business needs. I shuffle and reshuffle the personal and business elements of my coming interview until I am convinced that I have found the most promising pattern of action. I tailor my approach to Mr. Tompkins to assure the kind of interview he will approve and enjoy. I am ready to render him a service which I sincerely believe he needs and will buy.

I now know my reason for going to see Tompkins. I know why today is the day to see him. I know why I think my visit will benefit him, and I am prepared to tell him why in the best way possible.

My mind being at ease on these points, I am mentally prepared to concentrate my energy on achieving my purpose. I have made up my mind that the sale will be made.

The salesman thinking is the salesman giving himself an edge.

Chapter 5

Planning vs. The Six Thieves of Time

THE SECOND line along which positive thinking moves is inherent in the first. When you ask "Why do it this way?" you are asking "What is the best plan I can devise to accomplish my purpose?"

This is a question which applies not only to an individual sale, but to the organization of all your resources to attain your total ambition. It is only by planning, careful and disciplined, that a salesman can be sure of handling himself and his career to achieve the richest possible results.

Planning is the best of all techniques for self-management.

Planning means providing yourself with three essentials of success:

A goal—a specific ambition you intend to reach;

A chart—a map of the steps necessary to reach the goal;

A time-control—a schedule to prevent waste of that commodity so precious to a salesman: Time!

Once you set your goal, map your course, and adopt your timetable, you have taken the first steps toward neutralizing your own inertia. Your self-respect will rise to prod you to live by them. The ear in which your excuses for evading them will sound hollowest will be your own. Planning enlists the best in yourself to serve your own highest interests.

Set yourself a specific goal.

How often have you heard it said of people: "He is not going any place"? It is the summary of a failure. If you do not want this to be the verdict passed on you, face the fact that the man who does not know where he is going ends nowhere.

You are a salesman. What are you going to be earning ten years from now? If you don't know you are stacking the cards against yourself in the great gamble of success. Not until you know your intention for ten years from now can you judge your progress now. You cannot decide whether you have gone far enough today until you can figure today's advance against the total distance you must cover to reach the destination you have set at the time you anticipate.

Hunt and Hillary finally scaled Mount Everest because they knew how far they had to climb every day. Their eventual goal set each day's standard. They made a success of each day by reaching that day's goal. The sum of their day-by-day successes added up to their final triumph. They never quit on any day until that day's distance was covered, and each day's advance was determined by the total distance to the final goal. That is planning. The man who sets himself to climb the Everest of salesmanship can afford to leave nothing to whim or mood. He sets a definite goal. He plans every day's work to carry him that day's share of his progress toward this goal. He makes a success of every day, not resting or quitting until its quota of work is done.

There is all the difference in the world between the man who says: "Well, I guess I have done enough today," and the man who says: "I need at least one more sale today to keep up with the goal I have set myself." This man makes the extra call—that little extra call every day which means two hundred and fifty every year, and registers its effect in extra accomplishment.

A good resolution not translated into a definite plan is like a pie crust—made only to be broken.

Planning is a man bossing himself. Nobody in this world lives without a boss. The difference is that some live all their lives bossed by somebody else to his advantage while the others are bossed by themselves to their own. The man who plans takes his life in his own hands to manage it to serve his own purposes.

He begins by setting a goal. He passes naturally to the second phase of planning. He figures out how to get to it.

Map the steps to your goal.

Whenever sports writers name the All-Time Baseball Team, they put Ty Cobb, Babe Ruth and Tris Speaker in the outfield. Tris Speaker was a natural fielder, probably the greatest ball hawk who ever lived. He was not a natural hitter. When he first began to play he was weak at the plate. He had, however, set his goal: he was going to be a big-league player, come what might. This settled, he mapped his course. Day after day through long winter months he took out his bat and ball, and got anybody he could persuade or hire to pitch to him. He had his plan. He stuck to it. It worked. For more than ten years he challenged Cobb every season for the batting leadership of the American League, won it once, and ended with a record which stands among the highest lifetime batting averages in the books.

Suppose you have decided to set your goal at an income of $25,000 ten years from now. What are the steps you have mapped to reach it? Let us say that you anticipate making $5,000 in your first year. How do you get from there to $25,000 in ten years? A little figuring will tell you. You do it by increasing your sales each year by twenty per cent over the previous year.

You are no longer vague. You know where you are going,

and you know where you have to be every month and every year if you are to arrive at your goal on time.

No sailor ever brought ship to port without a chart.

Your chart covers your total activity. You know very well that you are not going to pick $5,000 the first year off the trees. You have to know how to earn it. You have to work at what you know. So you arrange your time to have periods devoted to studying salesmanship, others to learning about the product or service you are going to sell, others to finding and learning about your customers, and, of course, regular hours for work at selling itself. You establish a schedule which balances each of these activities against the others, and provides also that you will be continually improving yourself through the whole ten years so as to assure that twenty per cent gain annually.

This brings us to the third and most demanding phase of planning.

Plan your time to maximum advantage.

The watch on a salesman's wrist is in the right place. It is the pulse and monitor of his business life. Every salesman must live by the watch, not by the calendar.

Killing time is not murder; it is suicide.

The only way not to kill time is to keep it occupied. The only way to keep it occupied is to plan what you are going to do with it. Only you can plan it. Only you can work your plan. Insistence on making your plan and the will to carry out your plan combine to turn time into achievement.

Analysis of department store operations reveals that a department store has to stay open forty hours a week to stay solvent. Do you have any idea that a salesman can stay solvent on less, not having the advantage of the merchandising facilities they possess? A salesman, actively employed in selling for eight full hours a day five days a week, must know every day what he is going to be doing every minute of every hour.

Every half-hour you are not actively on the job your shop is shut as definitely as a department store would be if the manager turned the key in the lock. Nobody can buy from you while you are sitting around wondering what to do next.

This illustration from a department store is helpful as far as it goes, but it does not go far enough. It needs to be supplemented. In practice a salesman has to pinpoint time much more precisely than a store.

He deals in minutes. A crucial interview may take only twenty minutes. In any case it should be as brief as possible. To fill every one of those minutes, and to waste as few as possible between calls, demands careful time control.

The wise salesman is vigilant. He is not held up by the thieves of time.

The number one thief of time is transportation.

Two calls on prospects living three hours' travel from each other consume as much time as six calls on customers living closer to one another. This is simple arithmetic, but the big sums will never come to the salesman who does not practice it.

The regular rule of every salesman should be so to plan every day that he will spend the minimum amount of time on travel between calls. Spend the day in the same neighborhood if you are working in a city. Spend the day in neighboring towns if you are covering a country area.

I recognize that life does not always bow to rules, and that there are days when other considerations have to take priority over geographical proximity. You may have times when two critical calls have to be made even though making them entails a lot of travel. What must be done has to be done, but take such a situation as this to be an exception. It is relatively rare, and a successful salesman will learn from experience how to keep it from occurring. Because it may happen is no reason for thinking it must happen, and when it does happen the salesman should be on guard against its leading him to be careless about planning the next day.

Manage your time so as to spend as little of it on travel as possible, but don't waste the time you do have to give to traveling. Take work with you. You can get a lot of your reading done while you are traveling. I have a friend who has to do a great deal of riding on airplanes. One winter he read the three volumes of *The Decline and Fall of the Roman Empire* on these journeys. That may or may not be a rewarding book for salesmen, but it does illustrate the amount of reading a man who plans to use every minute can get done while on the road. There is no need to sit with folded hands on a train, bus, or subway.

A great deal of work can be accomplished on them if you plan it.

The salesman who drives a car may say that this is impossible for him. So it is, but I would like to say two words to him also. First, train your mind to think about your work while you are driving; don't daydream. Second, if your car breaks down, don't economize falsely or waste time supervising a mechanic doing something you know nothing about; hire another car and get on with your business.

The number two thief of time is unpreparedness.

The man who knows least about a subject will always take the longest time explaining it. The salesman who knows least about his product and his prospect will always take longest to make his point. The man who is most thoroughly prepared will always need the briefest time to present his case.

President Arthur Twining Hadley of Yale was the man who warned visiting preachers at the university that "no souls are saved after the first twenty minutes." I am willing to give him credit for compassion on the students, but I also have a sneaking suspicion that the good prexy knew that he was compelling his visitors to prepare more thoroughly by putting the limitation of time on them. Compressing an idea into a brief but adequate presentation is a far more exacting job than floundering around in it by the hour.

Prepare your presentations. Know what you are going to say. Don't waste your own and your prospect's time wandering fuzzily around in a forest of words looking for the right one. Have it at your tongue's tip before you knock on his door.

The Duke of Wellington not only defeated Napoleon at Waterloo, but ran England for thirty years afterward like a beloved but crusty old uncle to the Empire. In his blunt way, he once said: "Call on a business man only on business; transact your business, and go about your business, in order to give him time to finish his business."

In other words, don't waste two businessmen's time—yours and your customer's. Say what you have to say as briefly as is consistent with saying it effectively, and stop talking when you have no more to say. If you are so well prepared as not to waste your prospect's time you will waste none of your own.

The number three thief of time is an irregular schedule.

The only way a self-employed man can hope to put in a full working day is to act as his own time clock.

Make it a rule known to your wife, your friends, and your neighbors that you are on the job at eight-thirty sharp and stay on the job until five o'clock regularly. Otherwise, you will find yourself buying the groceries, running errands, picking up other people's odds and ends, and becoming the neighborhood handy man instead of a working salesman.

Your working hours should be as inviolate as those of a factory worker every day five days a week.

Unlike a factory worker, you may frequently find it necessary to work evenings, Saturdays, and an occasional Sunday, so as to be in the right place at the right time. This should make no difference to your regular hours. Nothing should interfere with them, for one very good reason. Once you break your routine daily schedule for any excuse you are in a fair way to neglect it altogether. Laying off until ten today will make it easier to postpone starting until eleven tomorrow.

Be tough with yourself about your working day. Be tough with your wife about it. Be tough with your cronies about it. Be tough with your neighbors about it.

You have chosen to be a salesman, not because you want more leisure but because you want more out of life than limited pay for limited hours. You work just as regular hours as any worker—plus, and that plus depends altogether on your own incentive holding you to a regular schedule.

The fourth thief of time is waiting.

It has been said that punctuality is the thief of time. One of the most baffling problems of a salesman is to find himself on time for an appointment only to be kept waiting by his customer. Valuable time passes while he cools his heels.

Here are three suggestions about this.

First, as far as possible, find out before making an appointment at what hours your customer is least likely to be at his busiest, and make your time fit his. Usually a man's secretary makes a point of protecting him. She will be impressed by your thoughtfulness if you express to her your desire not to harass him when he is most tied up. She is generally more than willing to co-operate in fixing a time for an appointment when he is less under pressure.

Second, if you do have to wait, don't turn it into an endurance contest. Give your customer the courtesy of a fifteen-minute delay, but no more if further waiting will upset your own schedule for the day. Leave a polite word that you appreciate the fact that he is busy, that you do not wish to inconvenience him in any way, that you will be back to see him at such and such a time, or that you will call him for a more opportune appointment. Then be on your way. Don't let the other fellow waste your time.

Third, if this call is so decisive that for one reason or another you feel that you must wait, get out the reading or the work you have with you, and spend the time profitably. Turn waiting time into working time.

The fifth thief of time is irrelevant talk.

This also can be quite a problem. There are some customers who are brisk and ready for business the minute they shake hands, but there are others who are more leisurely souls with a fondness for sitting back and having a talk before they get down to business. Between these extremes are all the intermediate gradings.

Obviously, you cannot cut the leisurely talker short. You have to give him his head for a while. But do not let yourself get involved. You may be as interested as he is in politics or baseball or the movies, but a selling interview is not a park bench. Keep your attention on business, and, at the first tactful opportunity, get the conversation on the track of a sale. As you gain in experience you will find yourself growing more skillful in this.

The sixth thief of time is lunching alone.

There is one trouble with lunching alone which has nothing immediately to do with time but may later result in loss of time. When a busy man lunches alone he is likely to order carelessly and bolt his food too quickly. Don't do it. A lump of ill-prepared, ill-digested food in the stomach can spoil a whole afternoon's work as surely as dirt in the gas line slows down a car. I make it a rule if I cannot eat properly not to eat at all. Hunger is healthy; indigestion is not.

Best of all, plan to have lunch with a customer—a compatible one who will not induce indigestion by his presence. I know a salesman who says that when he dreams of heaven it turns out to be a place where he can take one customer after another out to lunch all day long. Lunch provides a pleasant setting and a customer who can give you all his attention. It is one of the best of all times to make a sale or lay the foundation for one.

It is a particularly good time to meet the customer who likes the leisurely approach to business. He can indulge his interests through the soup and meat, and you can have him for yours through the dessert and the smoke.

The seventh thief of time is desk work.

Many a salesman covers his unwillingness to get up and get going by saying he has desk work to clean up. He dawdles over his desk.

There is one definite way to steer clear of this.

Plan your day from getting up to going to bed. A very successful salesman I know follows this schedule. It is worth your while to study it. He is up at 6:30 A.M. By 8:30 he is at his desk, the morning paper out of the way. From 8:30 to 9:00, he reviews the calls for the day, and arranges whatever papers or other materials he needs in connection with them. At 9:00 he starts out to make calls. He calls from 9:00 to 5:00, including his luncheon engagement. From 5:00 to 5:30 he makes up the day's record. From 5:30 to 8:30 he relaxes and has dinner. From 8:30 to 9:30 he does his required reading for the day. From 9:30 to 10:30, he plans the next day's calls. At 10:30 he goes to bed for eight hours' sleep.

If you are a commuter, you have time on the train to get some of your reading done. If you have to take parts of some evenings to make calls, you have Saturday and Sunday out of which to take the three or four hours needed for your professional reading.

This kind of rigid planning will safeguard you against that great pitfall—kidding yourself that you are working when you are only killing time.

Never let any excuse whatever prevent you from being on the specific job of actual selling eight hours every day.

Never turn to your reading until your day's records are all up to date.

Never fall down on doing some professional reading every day. You need it as a doctor needs to keep up on his medical journals, or a lawyer on his law periodicals. When you sit down to dinner on Saturday night, be sure you can tell yourself that you have completed the homework you assigned to yourself for that week.

Does this sound like an iron discipline? I will offer you this compensation. The more definitely you hold yourself to it, the more quickly you will fall into habits which will make it run smoothly and give you a sense of mastery of your craft.

It is the unorganized man who is always behind in his work and harassed by details piling up on him.

Time is the salesman's wallet—carrying as much wealth as he puts into it.

Chapter 6

How to Get the Best Out of Yourself

The straightest road to inspiration is preparation.

The third line along which creative thinking moves has a close connection with the second. As you plan, and watch yourself reacting to your plan, you learn a lot about yourself. Thinking leads to self-exploration, self-discovery, and sef-expression.

I was once in the company of Mischa Elman when somebody took the great man's violin into his hand, and began to turn it over and over as though examining it. Elman said: "You know violins?" The other man answered modestly that he knew a little about them. Then Elman took the violin from him, and began to talk about it. He knew who made it and when and where. He knew who had owned it since. He took his bow and demonstrated how the strings had to be touched to get the richest music out of them. It was not just a violin to him. It was that particular individual instrument with a character, almost a temperament, of its own. We listened fascinated. The violin seemed to come to life in the maestro's hand. Elman finished by saying so simply that it was childlike: "An artist has to know his instrument."

The salesman's instrument is himself—his own will, his own temperament, his own mind, his own body. If he is to be a master salesman he must know himself as an artist knows his instrument.

It is an exciting adventure to become acquainted with one's self—to know when one works best, what stimulates one most, what one's weaknesses are, and how to get the most out of the combination of one's powers.

Sir William Osler, the famous teacher of medicine at Johns Hopkins and Oxford, used to say that all people are either larks or owls, the larks rising with a song to greet the rising sun, the owls coming to life only after dark. Contemporary psychologists talk about extroverts and introverts, the extroverts finding their ways to satisfaction by exposing themselves to the praise and blame of others, the introverts by probing themselves. H. G. Wells could write for two hours only at one time, and then had to get out and play tennis or work off his enormous physical energy in some other exercise. G. B. Shaw could sit at his desk and write for hours. Sir Winston Churchill, owl that he is, likes to call a conference for eleven o'clock at night and work through till four in the morning, a practice dismaying to his colleagues who belong to the order of the larks. Henry Ford got his best ideas while his hands were busy with mechanical work. Edison often sat immobile for long periods, his mind totally concentrated on the problem at which he was working. Einstein had an assistant write his equations on the blackboard. Most other physicists like to work at the blackboard themselves.

Each of us has his own quirks and oddities. The man who knows himself will know how to put these as well as his talents to work for him. One of the most successful salesmen I know never rides to a call if he can walk, for, he says, walking stimulates him. Another, equally successful, loves to drive a car, the purr of the powerful engine under his hands communicating a sense of power to his whole person. I have one colleague who can concentrate on study better if he can hear music quietly playing. Another demands absolute quiet if he is to do his best mental work. Still another has such powers of concentration that he can work efficiently in the midst of a busy office, break off for a question or a telephone call, and return to his paper or book without missing a beat.

The man who intends to get the best out of himself stands as a spectator at his own side, watching himself in action, catching his own faults, appraising his own talents, knowing his own foibles, discovering his own most effective stimulants to effort, all to the end that he may get the best results from the instrument with which he has to carve out his own success.

This calls for the highest kind of honesty—self-honesty, rejecting any kind of self-pity or self-deception. It is self-study in the interest of positive achievement.

Self-knowledge and self-management are the right and left hands of self-control.

As we get to know ourselves we develop a skill in discriminating among our own ideas. All sorts of ideas pop into the heads of all of us. Some are good, some not so good, and some no good. The mere fact that they come to us does not make them necessarily good or bad. Every man has to be his own editor, weighing ideas, acting on some, modifying others, and rejecting a great many.

For myself I put this into a picture phrase. I know that all sorts of birds fly over my head. but that is no reason for letting them build their nests in my hair.

Thinking is self-judgment. We test our own impulses. We need to do it all the more if we happen to be the kind of persons whose minds are unusually active and inventive.

I have two friends in the same company. One of them is chairman of the board and the other general manager. Watching them work together is fascinating. The general manager has a hundred news ideas a day. The chairman of the board listens to them. He says: "Ralph can get more ideas than anyone I have ever met. Ninety per cent, at least, are no good whatever, but somewhere among the ten per cent is one absolutely brilliant idea. I earn my pay finding that brilliant one." The salesman has to be his own chairman of the board, sifting his imaginative impulses with judgment to discover the creative ones.

At Drew University is a college called Brothers College, built and endowed by Leonard and Arthur Baldwin, brothers who were partners from the time they trapped their first muskrat in Tonawanda, New York, as boys until they became multimillionaires as men in New York City. Arthur bristled with ideas as a porcupine bristles with quills. Leonard was judicial. What Arthur proposed Leonard weighed. Arthur always referred to Leonard as "The Judge." Few of us are so fortunate as to have a brother to balance us in this way. The best we can do is to know ourselves as well as they knew each other, to be as honest with ourselves as they were with each other, and so to be both promoter and judge for ourselves.

It takes the hardest kind of hard thinking to develop both imagination and discrimination, but there is one immediate dividend. When you have thought a proposition through, you are in a position to express it effectively. You know its ramifications. You can state it in your own way. Your words will have the depth, the sincerity, and the eloquence to carry conviction.

The salesman who goes out knowing that he has put his ideas through the mill of his mind will be sure that he has rejected the chaff and is ready to offer nothing but the whole grain. Convinced of its value, he will be prepared to overcome the doubts of others.

The sale thought through is already half fought through.

You will sometimes get brilliant ideas. That is, you will—if you think hard enough. Brilliant ideas incubate in hard thinking.

A misleading fact about our most brilliant ideas is that they usually hit us suddenly. They seem to come by surprise out of nowhere. Julia Ward Howe woke up in the middle of the night and wrote the entire "Battle Hymn of the Republic" on a pad she kept at her bedside. It seemed as though a sudden inspiration dictated it to her word for word. Obviously, it was much more than this. She was deeply involved emotionally and intellectually in the question of slavery. Waking or sleeping, her mind was on it. This profound concentration brought out of the depths of her personality this stirring song.

The seeming suddenness with which a brilliant idea bursts on us is the boiling point of thoughts long on the fire. It is neither accident nor inspiration.

I will tell you how this works with me. It may help you to discover how it can work for you.

In the early days of my selling I found myself with an opening to the biggest prospect I had ever had. I made an appointment to see him, but I could not figure out just how to make my approach. I had all the facts. I found out all I could about him. I prepared thoroughly. But I could not shake off the feeling that my presentation did not quite click. I needed one idea to pull the whole thing together. I was like a child with a jigsaw puzzle unable to find the last piece that would complete the picture. The evening before my appointment I went over and over my problem, worrying it like a dog worrying a bone. I was still baffled when, worn out, I had no alternative but to go to bed. I fell into a deep sleep. I woke up in the morning, my first thoughts coming back to my difficulty. I had no answer. Then, as I was shaving, the answer came into my head, as clear and whole as though I was reading it from a paper.

I do not pretend to understand how my mind was working while I was asleep, but I know very well it would not have come up with the answer if I had not put in the hard work I did.

I have learned a lesson from this. I now know that if I work hard enough to formulate a problem clearly my mind will find the solution.

William Zeckendorf, the New York real-estate wizard, says that ninety per cent of solving a problem is knowing what the problem really is. "Once you find the right question, you will come up with the right answer," he declares. I could not agree with any statement more.

The second kind of experience I would like to mention is this. My best ideas have sometimes come to me in the course of interviews. I have gone to them thoroughly prepared, as I thought, yet, under the pressure and excitement of selling, I have been suddenly hit by an inspiration. A seemingly new sales point has occurred to me, one more convincing than any I had shaped. This does not mean in any sense or in the slightest degree that I think any salesman can rely on sudden flashes of brilliance. What it does mean is that the mind thoroughly alerted to a situation never ceases to work on it until it is brought to a successful conclusion. Under the stress of urgency, the active mind is capable of producing a new and valuable idea.

A bulb will flash its light only when connected with a wire already alive with electric current.

The flash of brilliance comes only to the man prepared to spark it.

We have talked about a man knowing his mind, working out his ideas, and producing brilliant ones. Fortunately, we do not have to go through life depending on our own minds only. We can draw on the reservoirs of other minds. The experiences and thoughts of others are available to us in books, speeches, and conversations.

A wise salesman never ceases the active search for guidance from those expert in his field. I have already urged systematic reading, and the use of every available minute to keep up with it. Any good salesman will carry with him always some material to which he can turn for learning.

Plan your reading. Read regularly. Read professionally. Read widely. Reading enables us to learn from others at their expense. It saves the wear and tear on us of trial and error, and helps keep us from making avoidable mistakes.

Any fool can learn from experience—it takes a wise man to learn from others.

I once drove with a friend of mine across the United States— an experience every American ought to give himself once. I soon found that my friend had one idiosyncrasy. He hated to ask anybody the way. He always felt he knew. No matter in what strange place we might find ourselves, miles from anywhere he had ever been, he still knew. You can imagine what happened. We ran into unnecessary detours. We found ourselves at dead ends. We came to rivers without bridges or ferries. We reached the end of long and tiring days still looking for some place to lay our weary heads. I must say the trip was enlivened with the unexpected, but I vowed a deep vow that thereafter I would travel with no one who was not prepared to ask the way of every attendant at every gas station where we stopped.

Others have traveled your way before you. Their experience is gold for your taking. To profit by the wisdom of others is a mark of a thinking man.

The mind that does not welcome visitors will always have the "vacant" sign showing.

The priceless outcome of hard thinking is self-confidence manifest in a positive mental attitude toward life and work.

You know. You know that you do not know everything, but you do know something. What you know, you are prepared to act upon, confidently, skillfully, productively.

1. You know why you have confidence in yourself. You know your instrument.

2. You know why you have confidence in your product. You have sold yourself.

3. You know why you have confidence in your ability to sell

it. You not only know, but you know that you can convince your customer that you know.

4. You know you can learn from every experience. You are sufficiently in control of yourself so that you neither brag of success nor excuse failure, but turn both into self-improvement.

Constructive thinking forges active confidence.

Your confidence is not complacency. It is an urge to growth. Because it is positive, it seeks expression. It spurs you to act.

We turn now to consideration of the salesman as he carries out the plans and program laid out.

Chapter 7

Seven Keys to Successful Prospecting

THINKING PLANS your work. Acting works your plan.

Sales move on two feet:

1. Finding prospects.
2. Seeing them and making sales to them.

Most salesmen would be glad to succeed by hard work if it did not take so much effort.

Who is a prospect?

A prospect is a man in a personal or business situation which makes him a probable buyer of what you have to sell, having a need which you can satisfy, money enough to pay for what he buys, and a door which you can open.

He is not just a name. He is a name you are convinced presents an opening for a sale. Anyone can collect names. The question is, what's in a name? A prospect is in a name when it stands for somebody who represents a likely chance for you to do business with him. To find such names, to keep on finding them, and always to have enough of them in reserve is the first essential step toward sales.

Refining names into sales works in much the same proportions as refining ore into precious metal. The output of a refinery of given size and efficiency is decided by two factors: the *amount* of ore refined, and the *quality* of the ore.

If ore containing one per cent of precious metal is run through the refinery, a hundred tons of ore will produce one ton of precious metal and no more. If ore containing fifteen per cent of precious meal is run through it will produce fifteen times as much with the same amount of effort.

A salesman who calls on a hundred names with a potential of only one per cent sales will make no more than one sale. The salesman who calls on a hundred names with a potential of fifteen per cent will make fifteen sales. Time spent in selecting names to increase sales is time richly invested.

Seeing people is not enough. Success flows from seeing the right people.

Let me say two things at once about prospecting.

1. Prospecting calls for active, creative effort.

To find the people you can serve, you should make it a point to meet all kinds of people. This calls for making friends with people, keeping old friendships in good repair, getting acquainted with new people, learning people's needs. And it means keeping a prospect file up to date of those people who are potential customers.

2. Prospecting must be continuous.

Even the best of salesmen have to drive themselves to keep their prospecting continuous.

The successful salesman on the road shows his regular samples to his regular customers, and finds himself all too easily taking the easy way, seeing them and nobody else. He has to prod his eyes open to see new prospects in familiar neighborhoods or new developments in and around well-known cities.

The salesman of personal services may get careless about prospecting because he has a file that looks full today, only to find himself paying the deferred penalty for today's neglect ninety days from now.

I have found that prospecting is the hardest of habits to form. I am not sure it ever does become a habit. Only vigilant self-direction assures continuous prospecting.

Contacts sprout contracts.

A wise salesman organizes his whole job around a live prospect list.

Now comes the question: how and where does a salesman find prospects? This is a specific question to which there are specific answers. Experience has uncovered seven effective ways to find live prospects.

The successful salesman carries seven keys to his working file.

1. Personal friends and acquaintances are potential prospects.

My friend Fred Wilson is a highly successful salesman of farm machinery in Illinois. He was born on a farm and attended the state university. He told me that the first step he took when he decided to sell was to write down a list of all his relatives, friends, acquaintances and classmates who were farmers. He then went over the list, asking himself this question: "Which of these would I gladly see if he came to tell me he was going into business, and would like to talk to me about being able to serve me?" In this way he drew up his first list of prospects— "natural" prospects, as we sometimes call them.

Note that he did not call on all his acquaintances. He did not call on any to beg them to help him. He picked those whom his product would serve. He was not exploiting friendship. He merely took the sensible step of approaching first those people who were most approachable.

Any salesman can get a good start by getting together a list of people he knows who can be helped by what he has to sell, thus giving himself the chance to present his case in the beginning under the most favorable conditions possible.

Personal friends can also introduce you to potential prospects.

Every individual is a center of influence. You can borrow your friends' influence to give you a favorable introduction to other people.

The more prestige your friend has, the more valuable his recommendation of you will be.

When you ask a friend for such an introduction, be honest and explicit with him. Tell him exactly why you want to see the potential prospect and what you intend to present to him. Get his approval on the way you are going to proceed. Learn from him all you can about the man you are going to see.

Also remember, the friend who helps you deserves to be thanked by you. See him after you have had your interview.

Let him feel that you count him among the reasons for your progress. Find pleasing ways of expressing your gratitude.

Personal friends are a salesman's springboards—good for the first plunge, but not intended to keep him afloat.

2. Cultivate the art of making new friends.

Many a salesman is stuck in the mud waiting for an imaginary ship to come in when he should be building his own armada— a fleet of friendships.

Friendships take patient building, but building them is the most satisfying and rewarding occupation in the world.

A salesman can begin building these friendships at once. The only capital he needs is good will. The only tools he needs are understanding and effort. The materials are already on hand— himself and other people.

The way to get started is easily stated.

Help others and you will help them to like you.

Have no doubt about this: Most people want to like you. All they are waiting for is to have you show them that you want to be liked and can be trusted. They will welcome what you do to help them like you.

I was in the Cromwell Drugstore one Saturday afternoon when a young man came in with two boys who were wearing hats they had evidently just bought at the circus in Madison Square Garden. They were so full of excitement that I could not resist talking to them. Before long I gave each of the boys a little toy from among the knickknacks I always carry in my pockets. When they left the drugstore their father and I exchanged cards. It turned out that he was vice-president of a sizable manufacturing company. I called him the following Monday to tell him how I had enjoyed meeting him and his boys. Our chance acquaintance ripened into friendship. As an indirect result of this casual meeting his company has placed with me a group policy running into tens of thousands of dollars.

Go to bat for people and they will sign on your team.

Go out of your way to be friendly. It is when you get off your own track onto the other fellow's that you meet him. When he finds you going his way, you make it easy for him to go your way.

My hobby is making friends. I don't happen to be the kind of man who plays golf or goes to ballgames or collects stamps or goes off painting on Sundays, although I know better men than I am do all these things. I collect people. I like people. I want them to like me. The biggest kicks I get out of life come when I can do something to help people, and I have never found the opportunity lacking. I have built my business on making friends.

No sentence ever written about me has given me greater pleasure than one in an article Sidney Fields wrote in his column "Only Human" for the New York *Daily Mirror*: "Elmer is that rarity in business, the friend who is there when he is needed, whether it is for an apartment, a job, a loan, an introduction to a celebrity, or just a good ear."

A client of mine said the same thing to me half-humorously the other day: "You know, Elmer, you're a funny guy. When anybody else calls on me, I catch myself saying, 'I wonder what he wants,' but when you come around, I find myself saying, 'I wonder what he's bringing me this time.' "

I like that kind of a welcome.

Be a friend, and you will have friends. The gold in the golden rule is the only kind I know that multiplies in your hand the more of it you give away.

Friendships float good fortune.

3. Find nests of prospects.

Every client of yours works somewhere. In most cases he works alongside other people. When you call on him you have an opening to serve those who work with him in the same office, or factory, or institution. If you can get them interested in what you are selling, you have a nest of prospects.

Each of them individually may not be a heavy purchaser, but all of them together in one place at one time may represent a profitable operation.

One of the most interesting of these "nests" that I know is in Times Square. A few cosmetics salesmen make a good living by going from dressing room to dressing room in the various theaters selling make-up. They meet a lot of prospects in a situation where the prospects are most aware of their need and are earning money to pay for what they have the impulse to buy. This is profitable for the salesman because what he lacks in volume in individual sales he more than makes up in total volume for the total time spent.

Ingenuity like this will find for any salesman groups profitable for him. Nurses in a hospital, teachers in a school, stenographers in an office building, workers in a factory are examples. The Good Humor man near a school during recess is working a "nest."

Howard Bellows was a young worker in the Firestone Buggy Works in Columbus, Ohio. He was at a ballgame which was dragging along. His attention wandered. He looked at his score card, and at the crowd around him. Then he had an idea. Advertisements on the score cards would get attention from people in ball parks during slow periods in the game. He went to the manager of the Columbus club, and bought the score-card concession for five hundred dollars. He had no trouble selling seven hundred dollars worth of advertising. He was in business.

He did not stop at that. He studied his "nest" of ballgame spectators. One cold day in 1900, he sold the first hot dog at the Polo Grounds in New York. The rest of his story is as familiar a part of a ball park as the diamond.

Where people meet sales mount.

4. Newspapers supply leads to prospects.

My friend Angus Macdonald is a big man whose territory is a big state, Texas. He does everything on a big scale, including selling and saving.

The first thing Angus does when he enters a town is to buy the local paper. Then next thing he does is to read it through.

"The local paper," he says, "is a community's calling card. It tells me where everything in town is happening, who is doing what, how business is getting along, and what is the hot local gossip at the moment. I get from it good leads on who needs my products, and, when I call on them, I can talk to them about what is the big local interest."

Angus' idea works in New York as solidly as in Amarillo.

Newspapers write about people. They report changes in people's affairs which create new needs. Where there are new needs there are chances for sales. Removals, promotions, new businesses, weddings, births, engagements, anniversaries, housewarmings, accidents—all create demands which an alert salesman can meet.

I make great use of newspapers, not only to get leads but also to cement friendships. Whenever I see an item about a friend I clip it. I mount it in a way that makes it easy to preserve. I send it to him with a brief note of congratulation.

A little time, a little paste, and a few stamps give him a little pleasure. Remind a man of your interest in him and he will retain his in you.

News give clues.

5. Satisfied customers produce new customers.

One customer recommending you to another starts a living chain which, prospect for prospect, produces the finest results.

It has been my privilege for many years to serve Walter Winchell, not only the brilliant pioneer of a new kind of news reporting, but also a great salesman for products in which he believes. "The WW program is the best buy any firm could possibly make from every standpoint," wrote one sponsor to him. "From a merchandising standpoint of the show and yourself to the dealers, from a standpoint of cost per viewer as well as per listener, and from the interest standpoint, you are a great salesman."

My fruitful and pleasant years of association with Winchell have grown out of an introduction to him by a happy customer.

A. J. Kobler was owner of the New York *Daily Mirror* when I approached him with a suggestion for group insurance designed to help him solve a labor situation with which he was working. After long negotiations which, in spite of Mr. Kobler's interest and friendliness, were sometimes almost heartbreaking for me, I finally produced a policy satisfactory to all concerned. Mr. Kobler became my firm friend. He it was who introduced me to Winchell, to Dan Parker, the sparkling sports writer, and to many others whose friendship I have treasured through the years.

The more live contacts you have, the more you get. They keep you in the field. You are exposed to more people. You pick up more leads.

Every time a prospect becomes a customer you need a new prospect to take his place. Your satisfied customer can help you find him.

This works both ways. Once I have a customer I become his booster. Every advance in his business means more business for me. Because my clients know that I boost them they boost me.

I would never be able to count the number of clients who have been introduced to me by customers who count me their friend.

The sincerest commendation is a recommendation.

6. Present customers open the way to bigger prospects.

Good prospecting not only means getting more and more prospects, but also continually raising the level of your prospects. A new salesman may have to begin with modest accounts but the good salesman always has his eye out for bigger ones. Raising the general economic level of his selling naturally lifts his resulting income.

This does not mean that he becomes careless about his small accounts. Quite the contrary. One of the greatest satisfactions of my life has been to see my small accounts grow into big ones. When I first worked with Bond Stores it was a struggling company bucking the difficult conditions faced by all men's clothing stores in the twenties. Today it is one of the biggest stores of its kind.

Serve every customer to the full extent of your power, and those who rise will lift you with them.

He who wins the love of a boy will be rewarded with the friendship of a man.

However, to be successful, a salesman has to be consciously, persistently, purposefully determined to raise the average level of his sales by finding prospects in higher brackets.

This means he has to dig for the right names. Then he has to evaluate them properly. There can be no rest from this. But there is one asset which can help.

That asset is prestige.

Prestige is the triumph of reputation over obscurity.

The other day I found a lead into the office of the president of one of the biggest manufacturing companies in the country. When I got through to him on the telephone, and gave my name, his first words were: "Oh yes, of course I know your name. My nephew has told me some fine things about you." This nephew was the head of his own company, a smaller one than his uncle's. I had done business with him, but had no idea that he had ever mentioned me to the older man. But it was this nephew's good word which gave me the prestige, making it easier to open the door of one of the biggest employers in the nation.

Make every transaction, no matter what its size, the finest possible example of a perfect sale. You may be sure word will get around that doing business with you is a pleasure.

Aim higher all the time, but keep in mind that you are neither an arrow nor a bird. You are not going to be flung on high, nor are you going to soar there. You are going to climb step by step, and the people who will give you a leg up along the way are those with whom you have business afoot.

Prestige is the community's balance sheet on personality.

This may sound trite, but it is still true that prestige can also be gained by the plain practice of good citizenship. The man who dutifully accepts his civic responsibilities in church and synagogue, in Parents-Teachers Associations and in Boy Scouts, in community affairs and social organizations will win the confidence of his associates. He will find himself on boards and committees with the most influential of his neighbors. He will meet them in conditions favorable to a good reaction. He will open doors to doing business with them. Time spent in sincere public service has a way of bringing unexpected returns in favorable consideration from powerful individuals.

Those who help the many will find many of help.

7. Community changes supply new prospects.

This ties up with what I said about newspapers, but I want to make a special point here.

There is no saturation point for sales in the United States. We can never say that any community or the nation as a whole has been so completely supplied with anything that there is no room to sell more of it.

We are a nation on the move. New businesses and old businesses going to new locations keep people moving. Thousands of individuals move of their own accord. No matter where you live there is somebody new going by your window every day. Population shifts keep markets continually open to new exploration.

To meet the population shifts new developments are opening around all our cities. Seventy-two per cent of the growth of our twelve largest metropolitan areas between 1940 and 1950 was in the suburbs. When Famous-Barr Co. of St. Louis built a great branch in nearby Clayton, then hardly more than pasture land, people said they would lose their shirts. Today Clayton is flourishing, and every big store in St. Louis has a branch there.

The live salesman will be at least as flexible as the great retailers. Every new real-estate development is a challenge to a new timetable and new contacts.

We are a nation increasing in population. We add an Omaha to our population every month—an average increase monthly of 225,000. As long as there are more and more people, there are, needless to say, more and more potential customers.

The average age of our people is rising. There are four times as many people over the age of sixty-five in our country today as there were in 1900. This means an enlarged market for all kinds of goods and services aimed at the mature customer.

Economists predict an increasing national income. Our standard of living is rising. New sources of power and improved production practices mean more goods to sell and more wealth to share. In an expanding economy, a live operator will never lack prospects.

The swiftest salesman can never outrun opportunity in the United States of America.

Chapter 8

How to Plan and Prepare for Sales

EXPECT TO MAKE *sales, but do not expect them to make themselves.*

Like many others, I have made thousands of sales. All of them have followed the same general pattern, but no two have been identical.

Every day is a new day.

Every sale is a new sale.

Each one is distinct from every other one.

Each one demands its own individual approach.

No sooner had I written this than I began to doubt whether it was always true. What about sales in five-and-ten-cent stores?

The only way to find the answer was to go and see. I put on my hat and went to Woolworth's. What I saw there confirmed what I have written here. Crowds of people looked at identical articles, but no two people saw them in exactly the same way. No two had exactly the same manner, or, I may add, manners. Some were gruff, some jocular. Some took what they wanted from the counter, others waited for the salesgirl to pick it up. Some had the money ready, others groped for it. Every customer had something unique about the way he tackled his purchase.

Whether in the mass or face to face, each sale is individual.

Yet a sale is a sale, and all sales have a lot in common. The successful salesman, therefore, figures on two aspects as he plans his sales: he figures out what all sales have in common, and he prepares to take advantage in each call of that which is unique to that call—the factor of the individual person and the individual situation involved.

Calls are like men's suits—all conform to one master pattern, but each has to be cut to an individual fit.

Let us begin by establishing the master pattern of a successful call. The object of a call is to lead a prospect's mind from where it is when you meet him to where it will happily consent to the proposition you want him to buy.

When I analyze the progress of a successful sale, I find myself charting it through seven points:

1. The point where a client's mind is when you meet him.

Respect this. He has had a lot of things on his mind before you arrived. Only in exceptional cases will he be able to turn his full attention at once to what you have to say. The first step is to establish contact with him.

2. The point where you win his favorable attention.

This is getting his mind to establish favorable contact with yours. Note the word "favorable." You can get his attention by punching him in the nose, or by being rude to him, but these will not help you.

3. The point where he becomes interested.

This comes when you have held his attention long enough to show him that you can meet a need of his of which he is aware.

4. The point at which he begins to ask questions.

These may be objections. That is a good sign. Remember: no man objects to anything to which he is indifferent. A man will not kick about price until price has begun to interest him.

Questions are the sure sign that you have brought him to the point where his interest is becoming active.

5. The point where his reaction is positive and favorable.

He now agrees with you in theory. "I guess you've got something," he says.

6. The point where he accepts your proposition.

He now not only agrees with you theoretically, but practically also. You have the consent not only of his mind but also of his will.

7. The point where he signs.

This is when consent hardens into decision. He commits himself. The sale is consummated.

A call which does not build a sale is like a dry well—all bore and no oil.

This is the pattern we would like to have all calls follow. Now let us see how calls can be studied and planned so as to make them as much like this as possible.

1

Prepare for every call.

This is the first and great commandment of calling.

Spur-of-the-moment calls lead only to hit-or-miss sales.

If you have lurking in the back of your head the idea that a planned call is artificial and will not sound natural, get rid of it pronto.

John Wesley, the greatest of English evangelists, who probably saved England from going through something like the French Revolution, used to say that he never preached a sermon well until he had delivered it twenty times.

All of us have read some of Washington Irving's writings. He reads as though all he had to do was to sit down and pick up a pen, and the words flowed like water from a spring. Yet a friend once found in his study fourteen revisions of page 14 of a book he was writing. What seems effortless when you read it was the result of revision after revision.

You may find it hard at first to believe that what is prepared carefully will sound natural. But if you think about it you will see why it is so. It comes down to this. You will be at home with what you know thoroughly. You will be at ease precisely in proportion as you are at home with what you have to say.

The call into which you put most of yourself will turn out to be your most natural call.

What does preparation for a call involve?

1. *Preparation is the antidote for nervousness.*

Facing the time to call on a prospect you are probably nervous. This is good. I repeat. This is good. The time to begin worrying about yourself is when you get too cocksure about your calls.

Caruso was so nervous before every performance that, even after his throat had been sprayed and he was all ready to go on, he paced up and down in the wings smoking cigarette after cigarette. Only because he was so keyed up could he be sure that every faculty of his was on total alert for his performance.

But the minute he stepped before the footlights and sang his first note, all nervousness vanished. Why? Because once in action he knew exactly what he had to do. He was prepared.

The salesman prepared for his interview will have the same experience. He will know his opening words. He will not fumble. He will launch himself and sail on an even keel.

The salesman who sat up last night preparing today's call will not have to stay awake tonight worrying about what went wrong.

2. Preparation makes the sale before the call.

This sounds like putting the cart before the horse, but selling is no horse-and-buggy operation. It moves by psychological impulses which have their own dynamics. One of these is that a man who is himself convinced has a head start on bringing another man to his conviction.

I once asked Harry Gould, president of the Aldine Paper Co., how he made a crucial sale which I knew he was counting on to do a lot for him and his company. He said: "I knew I had to make it. I worked on it, until I knew I was absolutely confident. Before I left the office I was sure I was going to make it. I made it because I planned it that way. I couldn't be turned down."

Every successful salesman knows this experience. He is so completely convinced that he is going to make a sale, and so steeped in it himself, that no doubt has any chance to survive his confidence.

*Confidence is to persuasion what the feather is to an arrow
—the wing that carries it to the bull's-eye.*

3. Preparation provides the content of a call.

It puts into order, form, and words ideas which would otherwise be left floating vaguely in the mind. This takes five operations:

a. You decide what you are going to talk about.

b. You put down on paper a systematic outline of what you
want to say, using key words for the main points.

c. You fill out this outline, going over each idea to be sure
you are covering every aspect of it.

d. You memorize what you have written—if not word for
word, certainly idea for idea, until you can recite them like a
multiplication table, running no risk of forgetting any of them.

e. You rehearse what you are going to say.

I have a friend who once had to make a speech in which he
had to remember to comment on each of such diverse things as
water, electricity, metallurgy, aeronautics, science, and architecture. He made sure he would not overlook any of them by
framing from their initials the word, WEMASA. With this simple mental guide, he spoke extemporaneously for twenty-five
minutes.

A salesman ought to be able to give his sales talk standing on
his head if he has to. Right side up or upside down, know your
sales talk backward and forward.

When you know it well enough, tear up your outline and
throw it away.

The salesman who only pops off will pop out.

4. Preparation puts your talk into your client's language.

A fisherman does not bait his hook with what he likes but
with what the fish will snap at.

Your customer is not a fish to be hooked, but he is a person
to be interested. You will get nowhere with him if you talk
over his head, under his head, or anywhere else except to his
head.

This means that before you go to see a prospect you know
what his problem is, and what causes it. This is what he has
been thinking about. You will make connection with him by
meeting him there.

Coleman Jacoby, a Broadway wit, went to see a psychiatrist

about possible treatment. After a little talk, Jacoby asked: "Can you help my problem?" The psychiatrist answered: "I shall need to see you twice a week for at least six months." "How much will it cost?" asked Jacoby. "Twenty-five dollars a visit," said the doctor. "Well," said Jacoby, "that answers your problem. Now what about mine?"

Every client of every salesman is asking that question in every interview. "What about my problem?" The salesman truly prepared has the answer.

What is more, he can state it in language the client can understand. Every craft has its own lingo, and, among themselves, men of a craft use words familiar to them but strange to others. A salesman needs always to be on guard against using technical language with clients. Translate your particular gobbledegook into English.

Don't try to impress people with the profundity of your thought by the obscurity of your language. Whatever has been thoroughly thought through can be stated simply. I heard an example of this once. A great scholar defined a scholar by saying: "A scholar is a man who has decided to find out all he can about what is what." That's simple enough! It has the kind of simplicity which shows that a man has spent time figuring out just what he wants to say.

The more work you put into preparing a sale the more simply you will be able to phrase it, the more easily your client will understand what you are talking about, and the more readily he will agree.

The presentation that scores is the one which brings its message home to the customer.

5. Preparation will provide visual aids.

Good planning will carry to every call something to catch a prospect's eye as well as his ear.

The advantage of the visual aid rests on two proved facts:

Of all the information the average man absorbs, eighty-seven per cent comes through his eyes, nine per cent through his ears, and four per cent through his other senses.

The average man remembers one-fifth of what he hears, two-fifths of what he sees, but four-fifths of what he both hears and sees.

Men made signs before they made words. They drew pictures

before they wrote books. Children still learn their letters from pictures, not pictures from letters. The eye is the gateway to the brain.

What sells tabloids by the millions? Pictures.

Man is the only picture-making animal, and he loves the pictures he makes. Henry Luce turned this fact into a magazine empire. Hollywood organized it into a world-wide industry. Television has made it an integral factor of home and culture. The camera has created out of it a universal hobby.

Cultivate the knack of seeing pictures in your sales. Dress your presentation in eye-catching designs and colors. Dramatize every call with chart and diagram.

You may not be sure a client is really listening while you talk to him, but once he looks at what you show him you know you have his full attention.

He who makes pictures of his presentations will color his canvassing with extra sales.

6. Preparation improves the ratio of sales to calls.

The number of sales a salesman makes will always depend on the number of calls made by him. Nothing can change that. But the wise salesman keeps careful record of the ratio between the calls he makes and the sales he consummates.

He will know his "closing ratio."

This ratio gives him a scientific basis for evaluating his calls. It supplies him with a stimulus to improve the ratio itself. It spurs him not only to work hard, but to work smart—to get ever-improving results from the efforts he makes.

A continuous reckoning of what has succeeded and what has failed in a series of presentations provides a systematic guide to the preparations of every new presentation.

Any man who comes up to his own idea of greatness must have started out with a low standard in the first place. No surer safeguard against complacency exists for a salesman than checking on his own effectiveness by watching his closing ratio.

If it remains the same, he is on dead center, badly in need of giving himself a shot in the arm. If it is declining, the sooner he faces it and does something about it the better.

Preparation for every call in the light of what your sales ratio reveals is the way to keep going up—and the live salesman knows that the only way he can afford to have his sales ratio go is up.

The most deceptive trap on the road to improvement is the pitfall of "good enough."

2

This section of this chapter may seem like only a postscript to the first. I am isolating it for one reason: to give all the emphasis I can to the fact that its point is so important it deserves to shout on its own.

A half-prepared call is like a half-baked cake—found out as soon as you get your teeth into it.

I do not know of any truth more definitely and often brought home to me as I watch men at work than this: Thoroughness is the hallmark of the outstanding operator in every field of human endeavor.

I once knew a fine aviator who lost a cross-country record which would have won him fame and fortune because, when he overhauled his plane before starting, he overlooked one rusty nut.

Among my close friends is Louis Nizer, recognized as one of the greatest trial lawyers in New York. He has a brilliant mind, but this is not all. I have never ceased to be amazed at the concentrated preparation he puts into every case he tries. During its processing and trial he withdraws almost entirely from society, hardly sleeps, and so lives with the proceedings that he can quote immediately any detail of the case and the record. He makes sure he knows more about the situation than either the defendant or the plaintiff. Except in one case, which turned into a battle of giants, he has always been confident that he knew more than the opposing lawyers. Preparation is to his mind what a strop is to a razor, sharpening it to its finest cutting edge.

He meets Carlyle's definition of genius as "the transcendent capacity for taking trouble." Somebody else has called it, "the capacity for taking infinite pains."

As thoroughness underlies all genius so it supports all great salesmanship. I think that this has to be said with extra firmness to salesmen because we are usually extroverts by nature, eager beavers happier in expansive moments than in coping with details.

Thoroughness calls for iron self-discipline.

Know your client's needs better than he does. Know your own facts as no one else knows them. Know your competitor as he knows himself. Know your own service as a surgeon knows his skills.

3

Thorough planning calls for paper work, but the good salesman takes with him as few papers as possible.

Train your memory.

Work your memory.

There is no magic about memory. It is rooted in giving attention to what you want to remember. It improves with practice. You can find a dozen guides to training memory. All of them work for the man who works them.

I have often said that I do not sell insurance, I sell everything else, including myself. The theory behind this I put into this sentence: "When you think of Elmer Leterman I don't want you to think of insurance, but when you think of insurance I want you to think of Elmer Leterman."

The most effective single tool for selling yourself is a trained and working memory.

A trained memory is friendship's prompter, flattery's errand boy, efficiency's secretary, and confidence's guard.

The client who counts you as his friend is pleased when your memory warms your greeting by prompting you to inquire familiarly about his family and interests. The client who knows you more casually will be flattered when your memory brings his name and affairs to your mind. Memory changes a casual meeting into a personal contact.

The efficient client, all business when you meet him, will give you his sincerest admiration if, when he asks questions, you, without embarrassment, can answer him accurately on the spot.

A reliable memory will guard your confidence in yourself, saving you many fears and much time.

In every situation it will call up from within you that which will most please your client.

In the mirror of a salesman's trained memory every client meets himself and is pleased with the reflection.

Part of the planning for any interview with a prospect previously seen is to call to the forefront of memory all the information learned about him. This will suggest a pleasant opening, and prevent asking again questions he has already answered. It will freshen in your mind the names and facts which will ease the interview along at a familiar pace.

The classical example of this use of memory was Jim Farley's handling of Franklin Roosevelt's first two campaigns. As he traveled between stops he systematically recalled the men he was going to see. When he arrived in any town he had at the tip of his tongue the names, the nicknames, the marital status, the children's names, and the particular political situations of those greeting him. He made of every formal reception a friendly reunion. He oiled the political machine with the emulsion of a ready memory.

Not only can a trained memory make a planned call a fruitful experience. It can also turn a chance meeting into a productive interview.

I was shivering one early winter morning at the Columbus, Ohio, airport. A fellow passenger approached the gate. He looked familiar, but I could not place him. Fortunately, just as he reached me, his name dawned on me. At once I remembered that I had tried some months before to sell him a policy, but had not succeeded.

I approached him and introduced myself. "Oh, yes," he said, "I've been intending to call you, but didn't get around to it." We sat together on the plane. Before we reached New York my sale was all but made.

He afterward told me that the cold that morning had him down. Having somebody call him by name was like coming into a warm room. I have heard him report this story twenty times to strangers. This is the kind of impression a trained memory will make again and again.

Charles Dudley Warner said everyone talked about the weather but nobody did anything about it. The man with a trained memory carries with him a faculty which can make the climate of any visit fair and warmer.

A trained memory is an unlimited drawing account on the bank of good will.

4

Before we leave the general subject of planning calls I want to add a special word about one special call—the one you make after you have decided it is no use to make any more.

This extra call is the one that amazes by its sales.

The champion is the fighter who goes one more round.

A proud San Franciscan was once showing a country cousin that city's magnificent bridge. "It is the longest bridge in the world," he boasted. He went on from there, pulling out all the stops of his native history. Superlatives fell around him like leaves in autumn. At last he stopped to catch his breath. The country cousin then got in his word. "That ain't a bridge," he said, "it's just a lot of little bridges fastened together."

That is the way bridges are built. It is the way sales are made. The last link is the call that ties all the others together.

If you have let your bucket down into the well only to have it come up dry, don't kick the bucket, lengthen the rope.

Make this part of your planning: When you have reached the point of desperation, when you have done all you can and are all washed up—make one more call!

The step which eventually wins the race is the one which carries the runner across the finish line.

The answer to a rebuff is a rebound.

Chapter 9

Eight Ways to Put "Sell" into Calls

CONTACT WITH a customer begins with the salesman's first effort to bring himself to his prospect's attention. This means that the salesman will use every device he can to have his name first come to his prospect in such a way as to give him an immediately favorable impression of it.

One way for a name, like any other word, to get a good reputation is to be in good company. The words *guest* and *ghost*, for example, have the same origin. One kept company with warm, earthy people, and the other with pale, unearthly visitors. The result is that *guest* is a friendly word and *ghost* a chilling one. Words are known by the company they keep. So are names.

1

A salesman plans his introduction to a new client with this in mind. He makes it easy for his prospect to give him a favorable reception when they meet.

There are five proved ways to introduce your name favorably:

1. Through an introduction from a mutual friend.

Most people proceed on the basis of the familiar expression: "Any friend of Joe's is a friend of mine."

2. Through testimonial letters from well-known people.

The word of a man of acknowledged status carries weight. "If the Judge says you are all right, I can take his word for it."

3. Through news stories favorable to you.

I was recently invited to a reception for a well-known man. I knew I would meet there some people I should like to know better. Before the reception I wrote everyone on the guest list a letter enclosing photostats of articles about me. The result was that when I was introduced around everyone knew my name. Each introduction had an extra dimension which fixed me in their minds.

4. Through use of a curiosity-arousing device.

Just the other day I found in my mail a card on which was printed this sentence:

> FRIENDSHIP FILES ARE THE RESULTS OF
> YEARS OF SCIENTIFIC STUDIES COMBINED
> WITH THE EXPERIENCE OF YEARS.

"Now," said the card, "count aloud the *F*'s in that square. Count them *only once;* do not go back and count them again."

I immediately counted them. So did everybody to whom I showed the card. (There are six *F*'s. If you counted three, so that card said, you are of average intelligence; four, above average; five, in a class by yourself; six, a genius.) Regardless of its value as an intelligence test, this was an excellent curiosity-arouser, and the Bois-Smith Co. of California deserves honorable mention for using it.

A live salesman will be always on the lookout for such catchy attention getters. The more original they are the more effective they will prove to be as introductions to new friends.

5. Through a carefully prepared letter.

Frankly, this is often a difficult approach but it can be effective.

How hard it is to write a pulling letter may be gathered from the fact that *The New Yorker* makes a special feature of quoting opening lines from what it calls, "Letters We Never Finished Reading."

National magazines know from experience that on cold circulation mailings they will get an average return of about two per cent, and on mailings for renewals about forty per cent.

Letters individually prepared for specific prospects may have a higher drawing power than this, but the average salesman will be well advised to frame his letter carefully and make it warm, friendly and intriguing. Also, he will need to bear one thing in mind all the time. Mailing calls for getting new names continually. He will spend a lot of time with classified lists, professional lists, directories, and every other kind of publication in which names, names, and more names appear.

2

We pass to a different kind of contact when we come to the telephone. Here we have a salesman speaking in his own person into the ear of a prospect.

The end in view of a telephone call is an interview.

No one ever hangs up a telephone after a talk with a stranger without a definite impression of the kind of man he is. Knowing this, a salesman picking up the receiver to call a prospect for the first time will alert himself to make the best impression possible.

Telephone companies spend a lot of time and money to select and train people who will greet the public with "the voice with a smile." A wise salesman will take a leaf from their book.

On the telephone your voice, not your face, is your fortune.

A favorable and effective use of the telephone may be developed around the following guides:

1. Speak clearly in a conversational tone, your mouth about an inch from the instrument. Avoid shouting. Never be abrupt.

2. Listen carefully and courteously, so as not to miss or misunderstand what the other person is saying.

3. Smile as you talk. This will give your voice brightness and convey the idea that you are happier talking to your prospect than you would be doing anything else you can imagine at that time.

4. Keep a paper and pencil handy for making notes, but do not rustle the paper or do anything else distracting.

5. State your name and connection distinctly, using the name of a mutual acquaintance, if possible, to identify yourself.

6. Be ready to talk at once; never call and then keep him dangling on the other end of the wire.

7. Make your statements brief. What you want is an interview. You can tell your story when you see him.

8. When the prospect agrees to an appointment, repeat the time and place, thank him, and hang up.

9. Whether he makes an appointment or not, be courteous and cordial. Hang up the receiver carefully without slamming it, and reserve any comments on him until you are sure the receiver is back on the cradle.

10. If you are calling a list of prospects cold, do not be easily discouraged by turn-downs. Six appointments out of an hour of cold calling is average.

Use the telephone, but don't get telephonitis. Telephonitis is the disease of the man who sits in his office and makes calls instead of getting on the road to have interviews. The telephone is a means to an end with a new client. The end is to see him.

A telephone is like a car—good for getting you places, but no substitue for going there.

3

The personal call is the high light of the sales profession.

You come to your prospect's door. As soon as that door opens his face-to-face dealing with you begins.

A man's first interview with you is like his first oyster—it decides whether he will ever try a second.

A good salesman will plan to make a good impression in the first thirty seconds.

Chesterton once said that Heaven will forgive us the clothes we wear or do not wear. I trust so. But a prospect is likely to be less merciful. Clothes may not make the man, but they have a good deal to do with making a prospect's impression of him.

You do not need to aspire to making the list of the ten best-dressed men, but I suggest you memorize a bit of Shakespeare:

> Costly thy habit as thy purse can buy,
> But not express'd in fancy; rich, not gaudy;
> For the apparel oft proclaims the man.

Not to put too fine a point on it, dress so as not to call attention to your clothes; neither as loud as a refugee from the race tracks nor as sober as an undertaker, wearing a tie as part of your clothing, not as an advertisement of your passion for modern art; your shoes polished and your shirt clean; your hair cut and groomed, neither long like a horse's mane nor trimmed like a poodle's coat.

Look like a man on business.

A priest quite properly dresses as a priest. A clown wears a clown's costume. Don't start your client guessing what you are. Go looking like a businessman, and he will treat you as one.

Greet him cordially but not too effusively.

He knows that you have come to make a sale, and are happy to have the chance. He will expect and welcome an honest expression of your respectful appreciation of the privilege of an interview. But, at the first meeting, don't go beyond this. Don't grovel. Nobody has any respect for a sycophant, particularly the man a sycophant flatters.

I once saw a man humiliated as I hope never to see another demeaned. He was such a yes-man that his patron called him in my hearing his errand boy. If this man had stripped him naked he could not have robbed him of more dignity.

Temper your cordiality with respect for yourself, and you will gain his respect for you.

When you sit down, sit up.

Take a chair near your prospect, and sit straight in it. If you are careless or sloppy, he will automatically transfer his bad impression of you to your product, and make up his mind that it suffers also from the defects he sees in you.

I think a special word of warning is in place here, for I have noticed this curious fact. The more eccentric in dress and manner a customer may himself be, the more he expects those around him to be decorous and proper. This is the same psychology that applies to some generals. The general or admiral who designs for himself the most unusual costume is usually the one who most insists on regulation dress among his subordinates. I suppose that the only way such people can get all the satisfaction they want out of their own eccentricity is to have everybody around them be conventional.

At any rate, do not think that some peculiarity in your prospect's demeanor will justify taking liberties with your own. When you are received by a man without a coat or tie, remember he will be the one most observant of your tie and the cut of your coat.

A salesman's manners are like a ship's lines—they are the evidence of his class.

4

Once seated, you are ready to talk.

Every experienced talker memorizes ahead of time two sentences of every talk he makes—the first and the last. Begin with the first. Get into it.

Perhaps it is a long time since you read *Alice in Wonderland*, and you may not think of it as a sales manual, but the King in it had one word of wonderful advice:

"Begin at the beginning, and go on till you come to the end; then stop."

A train of thought which does not run between terminals gets off the track and runs amok.

Let me suggest four signal lights for keeping your talk on the right track and headed for the desired destination.

1. Talk to your prospect as a human being.

His name is on a card in your files, but he is not something you pulled out of your cabinet. He is flesh, blood, head, and heart.

Hand him more than the bare skeleton of an idea. He will enjoy finding a little meat on the bones.

The average American has five interests as much a part of him as his five senses. They are himself, his home and family, his job, his health, and his recreation.

Every good sales talk will touch him either by direct reference or illustration at one of these points.

One of my associates once sold insurance to a man in Newark, New Jersey, who had made a lot of money but for years would not let an insurance salesman into his office. Let us call him Mr. Harris, which was not his name. Outside his business, Harris had one passion. He loved to gamble. When my associate go to his secretary he said to her: "Please tell Mr. Harris I would like to see him about a wager."

He was ushered in. "Well, young man," said the other, "what's your bet?" "I'll bet you $100,000 against $1,500 you don't turn in your chips in the next twelve months," said my associate.

Harris roared at this daring approach, and took the bet, at the same time taking my associate to his heart. Their friendship turned into one of our most profitable connections.

There are no unimpressionable customers—only some who have not yet been touched where they come to life.

2. Get his interest by being interested in him.

We all take pleasure in hearing anything that interests us, from the batting average of Willie Mays to gossip about a man and a maid. If you find your prospect nodding while you talk, don't prod him, prod yourself. His attention is wandering from you because your interest is wandering from him.

You are there to meet his need and solve his problem.

Your three key words are Profit—his profit, Prestige—his prestige, and Security—his security. As long as your talk proves you interested in these you need have no doubt about his interest in you. This is what Abraham Lincoln called "the drop of honey which will catch his heart." We can do no better than to let the Great Emancipator have the floor on this point:

"If you would win a man to your cause, first convince him that you are his friend. Therein is a drop of honey which will catch his heart—and which, say what you will, is the greatest highroad to his reason—and when once gained, you will have little trouble in convincing his judgment of the justice of your cause, if needed that cause is really just."

Genuine interest is the sunshine of sales, warming the seeds of acquaintance into the fruits of friendship.

3. Be sincere.

Never underestimate the power of plain facts.

Say what you can back up, then back up what you say.

One lunch time at the Algonquin we had a visitor who talked loud, fast, and fluently on all subjects. He had a theory about everything. At last, one of our regulars, Martin Quigley, publisher of *Motion Picture Herald,* managed to interrupt him. Quigley pointed out one fact which exploded our visitor's theory of the moment like a pin applied to a toy balloon. There was an embarrassed silence.

"The most devastating thing a theory can encounter is a fact," said Mr. Quigley quietly.

Be sure of your facts. Be exact. Be specific. Never dodge a fact. Never let your imagination camouflage one.

Know more about your product than you tell. Talk from depth. Let every word you say have behind it the buoyancy of facts which you can cite if challenged. Facts are the core of every sale. They are the foundation stones of all long-term business relationships. They are the vitamins of your customer's confidence in you.

It is better to count ten before you speak than have somebody else count it over you after you have spoken.

4. Be concrete.

What does being concrete mean? It means creating a picture which your client can see, touch, taste, smell, and feel.

I once heard a great preacher describe a ripe, dewy dish of red, lush strawberries dripping with rich whipped cream. As we walked home after the service my wife said to me: "Mmm! I can still taste those strawberries. My mouth's watering." That is what being concrete means.

Visual aids can be concrete, but a salesman should practice also the art of word pictures. Every good product is better sold by examples than by arguments. A man can take into his hand only what he can grasp. One good illustration will help him to grasp more than a half hour of generalities.

Translating advantages into the concrete is a test of brains.

Supposing you are selling canned vegetables. You may be scientifically exact when you tell a housewife that a can contains twelve ounces of beans. But I guarantee she will show a livelier interest if you say simply: "One can serves four people."

Theodore Roosevelt made his whole foreign policy concrete for everybody with a single sentence: "Speak softly and carry a big stick." Nobody needed an interpreter to explain what he meant.

Persuasive examples are to naked facts what clothes are to a beautiful woman—decoration designed to emphasize appeal.

5

Assuming that your presentation has been effective, your customer now begins to show interest. He starts to talk.

1. Let him talk.

Every great salesman is a good listener. The best time for a salesman to want to say nothing is when a customer wants to say something.

He will probably begin with an objection. Welcome it. I remind you of what we have already said. Objections are sure signs of interest. Nobody kicks unless he feels a prod.

Like everybody else, your customer does not want to feel that somebody else is selling him something. He wants to think that he is doing the buying. He wants to express himself.

Don't answer him too quickly. He is thinking out loud. Given a free rein, he is as likely as not to talk himself out of his own objections more thoroughly than you could ever talk him out of them. A salesman gets in a bad way when he is so worried about objections, and so busy answering them, that the customer never gets a chance to buy.

No man is ever unfavorably impressed by another who lends him his ear.

2. Never underestimate a prospect.

He is your prospect because you decided he was a man worth doing business with. He would not be this if he were not a man of accomplishments. Listen to him respectfully. I have known a lot of salesmen who thought their customers were nitwits, but I have never known a successful salesman who thought his were.

As a practical matter, along with the will to listen, develop a skill in putting questions to him which show that you are giving him your full attention and weighing what he says.

A respectful listener not only makes a good impression—he stands a chance of learning something.

3. Know when to be silent.

Churchill once spoke of a certain occasion as presenting "a very fine opportunity for keeping quiet." A salesman will meet many such opportunities.

If your customer introduces some controversial political or social topic outside of the business at hand, ignore it. Never heat up an argument. The hotter the argument the colder the prospect. If you feel your own anger rising, say nothing. Anger is only one letter away from danger.

Quarrels are like green apples—better left unpicked.

If you run into a prejudice, let it lie. Reasoning against a prejudice is like fighting a shadow, exhausting to the fighter and without effect on the shadow. No prejudice was ever reasoned into a man, and no reasoning will ever get it out of him.

Calvin Coolidge, who was an expert in the art of silence, once sagely remarked: "If you don't say anything, you won't be called upon to repeat it."

6

While you are silent you are not idle.

You are sifting the questions and objections of your prospect. What you want to know is whether there is some key factor in the situation presenting a real hurdle to the sale. If there is, your client will sooner or later get around to it.

This key objection is your business. Meet it head on, and answer it honestly.

A man pushed to a bluff has nowhere to jump except into the sea.

You will not be weakened but strengthened in making your own case if you are fully alert to the strength of the other fellow's case.

Abraham Lincoln usually began his final pleas in court by summarizing his opponent's contention. Many an eye witness has told how he trembled while Lincoln did this. Lincoln summed up the other side so masterfully as to make it seem unanswerable. He was often more convincing than its own lawyers. Then, having put his opponents in the strongest possible light, he turned to demolishing them. The essence of his method was to select the one central and crucial core of the dispute. He was quite willing to give away six points to carry the seventh when the seventh was the decisive one.

He won, not because he nursed the idea that his opposition was weak but because he was so clear about where it was strong that he could meet it with the greatest possible effect.

Recognize that some of your customer's objections may be valid. No product or service, including yours, is perfect.

For example, your product may cost more than something else almost equally good. As John Ruskin said: "There is hardly anything in the world that some man cannot make a little worse and sell a little cheaper, and the people who consider price only are this man's lawful prey."

The crux of the sale in such a case is value, not cost—a distinction for you to hammer at, refusing any sidetracking into talk of price cutting.

While meeting an objection of this or any other kind which has substance, be firm but not blunt.

Tact is like air in the tires, cushioning men over the rough spots of differences on the road to agreement.

Wise old Benjamin Franklin wrote:

I made it a rule to forbear all direct contradictions to the sentiments of others and all positive assertion of my own. I even forbade myself the use of every word or expression that imported a fixed opinion, such as *certainly, undoubtedly,* etc., and I adopted, instead of them, *I conceive, I apprehend,* or *I imagine* a thing to be so and so; or *so it appears to me at present.* When another asserted something I thought an error, I denied myself the pleasure of contradicting him abruptly and of showing immediately some absurdity in his proposition; and, in answering, I began by observing that in certain cases and circumstances his opinion would be right, but in the present case there *appeared* or *seemed to* be some difference etc. I soon found the advantage of this change in my manners; the conversations I engaged in went on more pleasantly.

Don't let your prospect detour you into a by-path. Keep your eye steadily on your goal, and steer for it. If you must tack to meet a shift of wind, be resourceful enough to get back on the course without loss of time.

Answer every valid objection as briefly as possible, and in such a way as to advance the progress of the sale.

Be busy as a bee, always giving the customer the honey and keeping the sting to yourself.

At the same time, do not give him an easy way out. There is a point in every interview when either he will sell you the idea that he is not going to buy or you sell him the idea that he is.

Hold steadily to your main theme—the prospect himself, his needs, and your ability to meet them.

If you are making your presentation in his office, so manage the interview that he remains seated. You can get up to show him papers or to draw sketches or to do anything that will help, so long as you rise of your own volition and can sit down again when you choose. But once he gets up, you have to get up also, and this means that you are on your way out.

Manage yourself, and the interview will manage itself.

7

When he reaches the point of displaying a positively favorable reaction, don't get overconfident and overplay it.

Steering through his objections is like piloting a ship among rocks and shoals. Steering in the presence of a favorable reaction is like docking a ship, and many a ship has come to disaster because of a turn of the wheel at the last moment smashing it into a pier.

You can still talk yourself out of a sale in the time it takes him to turn a favorable reaction into a firm decision.

Be positive. Make no further explanations. Your one job at this point is to encourage his own impulse to swing him to a decision from within himself.

Say no more than you have to say, and let every word you do say ring with confidence that he is doing himself a good turn.

His favorable reaction sets the timing for the climax of your opportunity.

Let me take a few lines to clarify that word *opportunity*. It comes from the days before modern harbors when a ship had to wait for the flood tide before it could make port. It pictures a ship *ob portu*, that is, standing over against a port, waiting for the moment when it can ride the turn of the tide to harbor. The captain and the crew are ready for that one moment, for they know that if they miss it, they will have to wait for another tide to come in. Shakespeare has turned this background of the exact meaning of opportunity into one of his most famous passages:

> There is a tide in the affairs of men,
> Which, taken at the flood, leads on to fortune;
> Omitted, all the voyage of their life
> Is bound in shallows and in miseries.
> On such a full sea are we now afloat;
> And we must take the current when it serves,
> Or lose our ventures.

When the tide of an interview turns favorable, reject all doubt, and ride it to decision.

8

That decision brings the sale to harbor and ties up the deal.

A lot has been written about "the psychological moment" to close a sale. I know only one such moment. It is when the customer is ready to sign.

There is only one magic in salesmanship—the magic of the signed name.

In rare cases a customer is ready to sign as soon as you arrive. When you run into him, cut out the trimmings, and make the sale.

I once went to see two wealthy brothers. They welcomed me into their luxurious living room and sat me in a straight-backed chair. They then sat in two armchairs facing me. With the stage set to suit themselves, one of them said: "Well, what do you want of us?"

I summoned my courage and went into my presentation. They listened and said nothing. At last I got to the end, and stopped. They looked at me for a minute, and then burst into laughter. They had put me through my paces, but, before I had arrived, they had agreed to buy two $100,000 policies—one for each.

Once in a while it really does happen. Usually, a closing requires more finesse. And that finesse has to be largely controlled by the type of customer.

Some men are direct. They make up their minds, and that's that. The wise way to handle a closing with them is to come frankly to the point. There is no sense in beating about the bush with a man who is out in the open.

More often, an indirect approach is more successful. Every salesman requires the techniques of an indirect closing.

At some point in the interview he unobtrusively pulls out his order blank and places it where it can be plainly seen. This accomplishes two purposes. It avoids the awkward pause which would come later if the salesman had to go fishing for his order blank. And, it gets the customer used to looking at it, so that he will not be frightened by it when the time comes to sign.

Then, as soon as the customer has agreed to the main points of the sale, the salesman acts as though assuming that the sale is as good as made. He begins to refer to the order blank, pointing out what it provides, and writing in the appropriate information. This is done naturally, giving the impression that both customer and salesman are collaborating on making it accurate.

Co-operation in filling out the blank leads smoothly into the customer's signing it.

When he reaches for his pen, keep on talking. Don't let your mind wander. Don't think about your commission. Think only of the service you can render your customer, and your brain will get you into no trouble.

Avoid saying, "Sign here." People have built up a resistance against "signing here." Say something like: "I would like to have you sign the way you usually sign your name," or, "Please be sure to write your name just as it appears above."

If the occasion calls for immediate payment of money by the customer, ask for it. There need be no hesitation at this stage. You can say: "I'll go over the order once more while you write your check," or, "Now, if you give me your check, I will attach it to the order, and see that it goes through promptly."

Don't relax.

Don't let down at the end.

A sale well made is like a portrait well painted—an achievement reflecting luster on both parties concerned.

Chapter 10

Service Pays off in Sales

There is a world of difference between starting out in the morning to sell something and starting out to serve somebody.

Will Rogers once swung his lariat and cracked: "Salesmanship—that which makes you buy something you don't need when you ain't got the money to pay for it."

This is a perfect definition—but not of salesmanship. It is the definition of ballyhoo.

I will let "Dad" Fuller, the brush man, come up with the answer to Rogers with this statement of his activity: "I studied the housewife's needs and made a brush for every need." He was a salesman.

Fuller started out as a young man to sell brushes he himself made. One day, early in the game, he was nearly knocked off his feet when one housewife took a quick look at his brushes, and, before he had a chance to get into his spiel, pointed at a long, black one, and said: "That's the one I want."

Fuller himself was not too sure just what this particular brush was good for. Happily for him the woman asked: "May I try it?" She at once pushed the long brush between the flanges of a radiator, and the dust flew from where no other brush would reach.

That was enough for Fuller. He at once gave up designing sales for brushes and began designing brushes for sales, which means brushes to serve. Having designed them, he did not wait for the world to beat a path to his door. He built an organization to beat paths to all the world's doors.

He created something to meet a need and took it to the people who needed it.

That is what "service" means in the lexicon of salesmanship.

"The ideal of service is the basis of all worthy enterprise," say the Principles of Rotary.

Angus Mitchell, President of Rotary International 1948–49, says that this places a responsibility on each individual to build mutual respect and understanding in his daily affairs.

The past fifty years have seen a new light dawn on American business. It realizes that there has to be more to business than mere money-making, and that its own health in the future depends on its subordinating avarice to building the community.

Great salesmen from August A. Busch Jr. of Anheuser Busch to Ted Lewis know their own biggest boost is what they contribute to making everybody happy.

The salesman who hopes to succeed as one active unit in this vast community of interests that we call American business will accept this same principle as his own guide.

This was the secret learned by many of the great sales personalities of our time who got their introduction to selling by meeting customers face to face. C. E. Hires went from door to door in Philadelphia selling his first root beer. King C. Gillette rang door bells to show his razors. H. J. Heinz pushed a wheelbarrow along country roads from farm to farm to sell his ketchup. Bruce Barton, Arthur Godfrey, Billy Graham, and Eric Johnston got their starts at the nation's back doors. They began with the customer living his own life in his own home.

My old friend, Victor Emmanuel, chairman and president of the Avco Manufacturing Corporation, is facing a new kind of demand. His customer is the United States Government buying electronic and atomic missiles. To help this customer get exactly what he needs, the Avco Corporation has organized its own department of scientific research to extend to "important frontiers in atomic energy and related fields a fundamental part of current and forthcoming corporate operations." This, on a large scale, is the application of the principle that the product's best argument is its service to the customer.

The real selling points of any product or service are in the prospect himself—in his financial situation, his family relationships, his business outlook, and his organization.

You are in the wrong place for your sale unless the man sitting with you is the best argument for it.

1

Service is deed meeting need.

A doctor is out of place paying a professional visit unless the patient needs him and he knows why. The truly professional salesman takes the same attitude toward a client as a doctor toward a patient.

He first of all analyzes his client and his need. This corresponds to diagnosis.

He takes pains to see this need in the setting of his client's total situation. This corresponds to a thorough physical examination.

In the light of his client's need and total situation he advises him what will help him. This corresponds to a prescription.

He continues to keep an eye on him and serve him after the sale. This corresponds to a regular check-up.

Sales ability gets a customer; service ability keeps him.

2

A need realized is like hunger—the beginning of a desire.

The doctor may prescribe pills, but he knows that the essential ingredient of any prescription is the patient's own will to live. The wise doctor stimulates the desire for health.

In the same way, the salesman is not selling things, but what the things he sells will do for his customers. Part of this process is to persuade them to want what they need. As the doctor sparks the body's natural drive to health, so the salesman sparks the impulse of his prospect to buy what will help him and give him pleasure.

On Eighth Avenue in New York is one of the most fascinating places I know. It is Al Cohn's Magic Shop filled with all the bright, bouncing and bewildering objects which are a magician's stock in trade. But curiously enough, Al does not make his living chiefly from these. He makes it from teaching.

For two hundred dollars a customer can take one of three courses—in card magic; in manipulation of small objects such as balls, coins, and cigarettes; or in mental magic. Because what people want is not the things themselves but the fun they can get out of fooling their friends, Cohn numbers among his alumni such well-known figures as Orson Welles, Milton Berle, Linda Darnell, and Peter Arno as well as doctors, lawyers, and business executives of all kinds and ranks.

Cohn never sells any object directly. He demonstrates whatever a customer wants to see. He does not dispose of gadgets. He sells what can be done with them.

Uncle Sam wisely does not sell United States Bonds—he sells the college education they will buy for the youngster in the home.

The clothing salesman does not sell clothes—he sells a good appearance and a smart look.

The shoe salesman does not sell shoes—he sells foot comfort and pleasant walking.

The furniture salesman does not sell furniture—he sells a home with the look and comfort the homemaker will enjoy.

The book salesman does not sell books—he sells the company of great writers, the possibility of knowledge, the pleasures of reading.

The toy salesman does not sell toys—he sells the delight of children in play.

The diamond salesman does not sell diamonds—he sells the pride of a woman in wearing them.

The bank does not sell a savings account—it sells the trip to Europe the money will buy.

Lindy's Restaurant on Broadway enjoys a high reputation for its good food, but this does not explain the lines of people standing on the sidewalk waiting their turns to get in. The restaurant's windows are filled with pictures of celebrities inscribed to Leo Lindy. Publicity quotes remarks made in Lindy's by famous people. Customers throng the place to get a glimpse of well-known personages.

The clincher in any sale is satisfying some aspiration of the person sold. This is why a salesman's facts must be presented in human terms. He aims his facts at the head, his service at the heart.

What a man desires he will enthusiastically embrace.

3

The sale that wears well fares well.

It was a custom of the Chinese in the old days to pay a physician as long as he kept them well, and to quit paying him when they fell sick. The subtle wisdom of the East perceived that the best service would be rendered by a man serving perpetual well-being rather than by one under temptation to exploit times of difficulty.

In our kind of society this may not be a practicable way of dealing with the medical profession. But the wisdom behind it applies with full force to a salesman. The most successful salesman is the one serving and encouraging the continuous and permanent well-being of his customers. He is never so dazzled by the prospect of one quick sale that he loses sight of his customer's long-range interest.

One of the great sales stories of the United States grew out of one man serving a long-time need.

When John Wanamaker entered the retail business, prices were flexible. Customers and clerks bargained and haggled over purchases. Wanamaker saw the unsatisfactory results of this. Neither customers nor clerks liked it. Customers could not be sure that they had paid a fair price. Two or more customers comparing notes would find that they had paid differing prices for identical objects. The public had no confidence in retail sales.

Wanamaker make a momentous decision. He set out to sell the public confidence. Accordingly, he established "One Price" as his policy. He put on every object a price as low as was consistent with a working profit, and he kept it there. He backed it up with a guarantee of money back if the customer could buy the same object cheaper anywhere else.

One result was that he became known as "Honest John Wanamaker." The public did business with him with full confidence.

The more far-reaching result was that the whole retail trade followed his example and was lifted to a higher plane. This was a permanent service rendered the total health of the whole community—and the community has done business more happily ever since because of it.

What Wanamaker did for retailing every true salesman will aim to do for each customer.

The customer's interest is the salesman's capital.

4

Keep your promises and you will keep your customers.

"He delivers."

The words were spoken by one of the biggest buyers in New York. He and another buyer in the same line were discussing their sources of supply. The other man had asked: "Why are you so sold on J. Q.?" The answer was brief and final: "He delivers."

No excuses. No big talk. No alibis. No disappointments. No uncertainties. No delays.

When J. Q. said, "Next Thursday at 9:10," my friend the big buyer knew he could open his gates at 9:10 on Thursday and J. Q.'s truck would roll in.

That is service!

Tall stories sire short associations.

I have an acquaintance who is probably the sweetest-talking salesman in our great metropolis. His tongue can take wings on any subject from toilet supplies to luxury cars. Birds, hearing him, stop singing to listen. Eagles fold their wings to watch his imagination soar.

He has just one trouble. He gets drunk on his own eloquence. He carries himself away. Nothing seems impossible as he listens to the music of his own voice. He promises anything. In the dull, gray aftermath he has to go back with another kind of bird. He has to eat crow. His collection of canceled orders resulting from unfulfilled promises would paper Grand Central Station.

There are better ways of stopping your mouth than putting your foot in it.

Curb your tongue.

Niagara Falls is one of the seven wonders of the world, but it does not produce power until it is harnessed and channeled. Only a disciplined tongue talks with authority.

Promise your customer all the service you can give him. But —deliver what you promise.

The worst buy in the world is an alibi.

5

The way to reach the heights is to stay on the level.

The other day a young slicker of a salesman, full of tricks, called on an old hand in his line. The younger man probably thought of the older one as an old fogy twenty years behind the times. He began to spin his yarn. My old friend listened for a few minutes, and then stopped him.

"Young man," he said, "you might as well quit playing your angles on me. I've been in this business longer than you have been alive. I know all the angles. I can hear them coming before you shape your mouth to spring them. For the good of my business I quit playing them a long time ago, but that does not mean I have forgotten them. Now, tell your story straight, and I'll tell you whether we can do business."

That young slicker was lucky. My friend talked up to him. A lot of prospects think what he said without saying it. Many a salesman has found the door of the biggest man in his field closed to him on his second visit, and has wondered why. Big men do not give time to those trying to put something over on them.

A square deal is always the right angle.

No wiser word was ever spoken than that the truth sets us free. The salesman who sticks to the truth is free from worrying about whether he can remember what he said the last time. He is free from fear of contradicting himself. He is free from anxiety about his bluff being called. He is free to concentrate on selling his product.

The customer who is confident he is getting the truth is also free—free from preoccupation with whether the salesman is playing tricks on him. He does not have to devote half his mind to outguessing a salesman, but is free to listen to the whole story. He is not entangled in suspicions, but free to give his whole attention to the merits of the deal.

The man who clips customers cuts his own life line.

The bond which pays a salesman his highest dividends is the

bond of confidence between his customer and himself. It is a bond forged in the steel of integrity.

I was sitting with a bag jobber in New York a few weeks ago when his secretary buzzed him on the interoffice communication system. I could not help hearing what she said. Her voice came over with this message: "Mrs. Johns just called from Waterville, Maine. She ordered two gross of our new lines. She said to have nobody but Billy pick out the bags for her."

I have never met Billy. I don't have to meet him. I know why he is a successful salesman. Mrs. Johns could not get to New York to see the new lines of bags. She had to have them for the new season. She knew that she could trust Billy the salesman to act as her purchasing agent. I cannot think of a higher tribute to a salesman than that.

Billy's commission on that sale was a dividend on her confidence in him won through past service to her.

Credit for service pays off in cash.

Chapter 11

How Co-operation Boosts Sales

Co-operation is self-multiplication.

Man is no more than average among the animals in physical equipment. He has survived on the earth and made himself master of it by means of three distinctive characteristics: his spirit, his intelligence, and his power to work with his fellows.

These three are so interwoven with one another that no one of them can be described without the other two. The spirit of man comes to expression through intelligence and mutual aid. Intelligence, enlightened by the spirit, creates the tools and organizations of society by shared thinking and shared work. Co-operation as brotherhood is an expression of the spirit, and as civilization is an achievement of the intelligence.

Man is greater than the beasts because he has created a community, and greater than the ants and the bees because he has built his communities not by instinct but through the operation of his conscious intelligence.

His survival is a triumph of mutual aid. What he lacks in strength as an individual he more than makes up by what he gains through co-operation. Every man multiplies himself when he joins his interests with others and all together enrich the common wealth.

Any individual who thinks he can go it alone, defying the world and walking over everybody else, stunts his own personality and denies himself his natural allies. This truth holds for all men in all lines, but it applies with especial force to salesmanship. You will not reach the top as a salesman if you are not a team worker.

I don't care how good you are, this truth is for you.

Knute Rockne had one of the great backfields of all time in the legendary Four Horsemen of Notre Dame's 1924 team. They ran high, wide, and sure over all opposition. But Rockne knew something the sports writers did not emphasize, and which the four boys themselves might have been in danger of forgetting. Without saying a word to anybody, he one day took out his first-string line and substituted for it the third string in the last quarter of a game already won. For that quarter the Four Horsemen were stopped cold. They learned their lesson. What was winning games for Notre Dame was a whole team, not four supermen.

The superman is made by the superteam.

Co-operation is the watchword of success.

The man who teams well will find others opening his way to his goal.

1

The player who does most for his team will be lifted highest when it wins.

A perfect illustration of this came from Willie Mays and the world's champion Giants of 1954. Leo Durocher started the season with a team which had not struck fire in 1953, while Mays was in the army. Mays returned for 1954, full of enthusiasm, contagious with laughter, brilliant in the field and at bat, and, above all, with a champion's determination to win. His zest in the dressing room, the dugout, and the field was a bubbling stimulus which put a new spirit into his teammates. The fifth place Giants of 1953 became the world champions of 1954.

Who received the highest accolade? There was never any doubt. Mays was voted the Most Valuable Player of the National League with the practically unanimous approval of every fan in the country. If there had been an award for the Most Valuable Player in Baseball he would have had that without dissent.

A brilliant individual performer, he was still more the idol of the stands for his zest for the team from which his mates caught fire.

The same principle also applies in merchandising. One of the greatest merchants I ever knew was Louis Bamberger, whose store is an institution in Newark and who was himself universally recognized as its first citizen. What was his secret? A big part of it was his co-operation. His store had the finest morale I have ever seen in such a place. The explanation? Many a morning I have seen his slight figure passing through the aisles, and watched him stopping to inquire of the workers whether they were comfortable and things going well with them. He was not a proprietor. He was in every sense a co-worker.

Similarly, whenever a booth was erected in the store to collect money for some good cause, he himself always visited it to make sure the person in it had just the kind of chair and desk he wanted. It seemed incredible that so busy a man could take time for such a detail, but he never missed. He was a team worker, par excellence.

Others, among the biggest men in merchandising, also have this quality, from Bernard Gimbel of Gimbel's and Jack Straus of Macy's to Henry Belk and Michael Katz, with their great chains of stores in the South and Middle West.

No matter how successful you may get, don't let your head outgrow your hatband. You will be happier, more productive, more honored, and richer if you always maintain a lively interest in your fellow workers and cultivate their friendship.

Your boss, your fellow salesmen, your secretary, the stenographers, the shipping clerks, and the office boy are all on your team. Proper decorum in the office, honest expense accounts, punctual reports, acceptance of extra duties, and assumption of voluntary assignments, all count in bringing you the respect and support of your team.

If, by chance, you think yourself a star, and are hearing a little whisper in your ear that this is so much malarkey, and not for you, let me tell you a story I got from Grantland Rice, as he used to tell it.

"I recall a star ballplayer on the Yankees under Joe McCarthy, who was getting out of hand. He was hitting .350 and, in addition, was a brilliant fielder. He felt sure of his position, no matter what he might do. McCarthy gave him an order one day which he disregarded. After the game McCarthy called him to his office.

" 'You're a great ballplayer,' he said quietly. 'You're young and fast, and you can hit. I'll miss you in this club. You're leaving us tonight. Report tomorrow to so-and-so.'

"The young star was dazed. McCarthy stuck out his hand. 'Good-by and good luck, kid,' he said, 'and, for God's sake, take a tumble to yourself. Don't be quite so smart.' "

The man who gets out of hand ends up out of pocket.

2

The salesman who plays the three gets flush.

The three of the salesman are his employer, his client, and himself.

The best interest of your employer plus the best interest of your client equal your best interest.

If you choose to give away your employer's profits your customer will take them, but your employer will either fire you or go broke and take you down with him in the crash. If you go behind your employer's back to make a deal with a customer he may go along with you, but he will never trust you enough to cut you into anything he thinks really good.

There is a maxim of business as firm as the hills: The only man who can be trusted to be loyal to a new boss is the one who had proved loyal to his old one.

Similarly, you may be able to put over on a customer a deal which will bring extraordinary returns to your employer, and the boss may praise you for it. But you will be doing neither your boss nor yourself any good. A deal which makes it hard for your customer to meet competition endangers your own market since the only way you can prosper is for your customer to stay profitably in business.

What is more, any sharp deal you make at a customer's expense will become news in the trade. There is no way known to man of stopping word from getting around. And when it does, you will find yourself treated to a steady diet of cold shoulder.

True, you have to look out for Number One in a world of fighting and, sometimes, ruthless competition. This calls for using your wits and all your other native equipment to the limit. There is no doubt about this. Personally, I would not want it any other way. The challenge of meeting competition is one of the thrills of salesmanship which a good salesman meets with a cheer.

Use your wits. But use them so as to get as many people as possible pulling for you.

Every sale can win somebody to your side or cement ties with old friends.

Mr. A. vanderZee, Vice-President in charge of sales for the Chrysler Corporation, tells a simple story which sums up how constructive a truly co-operative sale can be:

"My watch became erratic a few months ago. A friend recommended a certain jeweler. I took it to him. When the watch was returned, I found a handwritten note attached to it. In it the jeweler explained just what he had done to the watch, why it had become erratic, and how I should wind and take care of it in the future. He added that he would guarantee it for a year.

"That was the first time anyone ever took the trouble to help me understand what makes a watch go haywire. I was so impressed that I sent all the watches in the house to him to be cleaned. And since then I have sent a half-dozen of my friends to *my* jeweler."

Co-operation with employer and customer is like heat in a baker's oven—turning dough into the staff of life.

3

Co-operation is the climate of creative selling.

So long as selling is no more than a transaction by which goods are moved from the seller's warehouse to the buyer's store it is hardly more than a trucking operation. It can be vastly more. It will be when it becomes an adventure in mutual help.

In the last chapter I wrote of how the word "service" has become a part of our contemporary business vocabulary. Alongside it has also come another phrase, "to be in conference." It may be abused sometimes as "service" is, and lend itself also to satire, but it stands for something with big meaning for business. It marks the end of one-man tyranny in management.

It means that modern business in our complex society recognizes its need for a new kind of management—a management combining executive and technological competence operating through the creative process of group stimulus and discussion.

This process is the source of all creative innovation. Our modern science, for example, culminating in the atomic age, is the work of no one man but is the result of the mingling of the ideas of many men, expressed, examined, disputed, defined, modified, redefined, and, at last, superseded by still newer ideas or syntheses of ideas which are then clarified and modified by the same procedures.

This process of shared thinking has a creative function also in business. Commerce is not a rigid, iron-clad system operating by impersonal laws in a static situation. It is a human endeavor dealing with human beings—with all their desires, hopes, aspirations, struggles, disappointments, and successes. In this kaleidoscope of constantly changing interests patterns form which benefit those prepared to meet them.

No business or personal situation of any client you serve is in its final form. Within it are possibilities of improvement.

When you sit down to sell your customer a bill of goods, you may have in mind a certain quantity. He may have in his mind what he intends to buy. You are both thinking of quantity only. But if between you there exists a mutual confidence born of prior co-operation you get into a talk which touches a deeper level. You uncover in each of you ideas of which the other was not aware.

Instead of confining yourselves to price and quantity you find yourself giving him answers out of your technical knowledge to questions he has been asking himself. You help him think through half-formed thoughts. And, as you help him, you find in your own answers suggestions of ways to help him which had not previously occurred to you.

What began as a sales interview turns into a creative experience. Each of you stimulates the other. When the talk is over, a new pattern of activity has evolved, more profitable to both of you than that with which you began.

This kind of creative experience is the most rewarding a salesman can know in his work. It has the intangible rewards of emotional satisfaction as well as producing the material rewards of greater tangible profits.

This kind of creative co-operation helped to found one of the most influential corporations of our time.

Richard W. Sears was a station agent at North Redwood, Minnesota, when he took over a shipment of watches the local jeweler refused. He sold them to the railroad men passing through his office. His success led him to enlist other station agents as his selling staff along the line. When his business grew, he gave up railroading and moved to Minneapolis.

Here he soon realized that he needed an expert in watches to insure the quality of his merchandise. He hired Alvah Curtis Roebuck. The business prospered. Then Roebuck had an idea. If watches could be sold by catalogue and mail, why not other things? They expanded.

One of the salesmen who called on them was Julius Rosenwald, a clothing manufacturer. He co-operated with them. They were impressed by his readiness and efficiency in meeting what they asked of him. He won their confidence. They consulted him freely about their affairs.

What he learned led him to see that they had good merchandise and selling ability, but that they lacked a third essential—good management. His discussions with them raised this issue, and they were wise enough to recognize that he had what they lacked. He bought into the business, and it went on to become a household name.

This is not a unique story. It could be paralleled in every field from insurance to General Motors.

Genuine co-operation can mean more sales to the same customer. It can mean recommendations from a satisfied customer to new prospects. But it can also mean more than both of these. It can move into another dimension—the creative dimension.

We are on the threshold of a new economic age based on new sources of unlimited power. Its richest rewards will go to the salesman who can sell creatively.

Creative salesmanship is the number one challenge of the expanding economy of the world of today and tomorrow.

Chapter 12

Showmanship and Low Pressure Selling

Champions do not win titles with ballyhoo.

Nature is the greatest of all showmen. Which is greater showmanship, a clap of thunder or the song of a canary? Which is more breathtaking, a flaming autumn hillside or a violet? None of us, I think, would want to choose. Nature puts on an equally good show when it flames with the light of noon or is serene under the quiet moon and the stars. It speaks to us with two voices, and the quiet one sells us on the beauty of our world as effectively as the louder one.

Let us put the same idea in another way. You are walking up the avenue, your eyes taking in the people along the way. They pass you one by one, arousing no comment. Then, out of a store, steps a striking blonde with a big picture hat, an ermine wrap thrown carelessly over her shoulder, a dress ingeniously designed to emphasize every line of her figure, sheer stockings, and highly styled shoes. All heads turn for a second look. Having taken yours, you continue on your way. Suddenly, out of the crowd, appears a woman naturally lovely, exquisitely but quietly gowned, not a sensational detail about her, but everything in such perfect taste that you catch your breath. Which of these two has the better salesmanship?

You attend a meeting. A speaker rises who piles word on word, and phrase on phrase, with a lush power and eloquence dazzling your mind and seeming almost to lift you out of your seat. He is followed by a man speaking simple words in a quiet voice which seems to probe deeper and deeper into you until some voice from within you seems to be awakened by him, and his words sound to you almost as though they are your own. Which is the better showman?

You go to the theater. The lights dim. From the orchestra, without warning, comes a crash of sound, so powerful it at once banishes all thoughts of the outer world and brings your attention to full focus on the stage. The next night you go to another theater. The lights dim. There is no sound until the audience has come to silence. Then, in the darkness, a single note rises, one instrument alone weaves a haunting spell of wistful music, quieting your faculties, creating a mood. Which theater had the better showman?

The true showman knows that he gets one kind of response from men and women to a spectacular effect, but just as real and deep a one to a quieter appeal. He does not let the idea that showmanship is sensationalism run away with him. He knows that great showmanship consists sometimes in not seeming to put on a show at all. A whisper can be as dramatic as a scream.

A smart salesman will learn this lesson from the showman. There are times when selling calls for high-pressure methods and florid stunts. But there are others, and these are by all odds the majority, when selling is best served by low-pressure methods and steady cultivation. This is why I have linked showmanship and low-pressure methods in this chapter. They may seem like an incongruous combination, but they complement each other. The trick is not to rely altogether on either, but to get both into the right balance.

Suppose we ask ourselves what we mean by showmanship. Showmanship is doing something in such a way that it will provoke curiosity. The object of arousing curiosity is to get attention. Make a man curious about you, and you will have no trouble getting him to listen to you.

I personally have had my greatest successes in selling as a result of not seeming to sell at all. Nevertheless, I do not hesitate to be different, to look different, to act differently, and to talk differently when the occasion demands. I have found that I need to be able to do the sensational thing when it is called for. But I put my main reliance on the unsensational, which is no less showmanship because it is less spectacular.

These two kinds of approach must always be considered together as the left and right hands of selling. Let's discuss first some of the dramatics of selling. Then we will come to the more substantial question of indirect selling.

1

A stunt is a bid for an ear.

I went the other day to the opening of a new Wallach's store on Fifth Avenue, of which my friend, John D. Gray, is president. John is also a director of Hart, Schaffner and Marx, the men's clothing manufacturer. The store was full of prominent people who had come to admire it as the last word in architecture and arrangement designed to serve equally the conveniences of retail merchandising and the demands of good display. Mr. Gray introduced me to many people. One of them said at once: "I've been admiring that feathered lei hatband of yours." We immediately fell into conversation. The ice between us was broken.

This incident summarizes the value of the dramatic touch in salesmanship. In that crowd I was the only man not wearing a conventional hatband. It singled me out. This man noticed it. We at once had something to talk about. My hatband could not make a sale, but it could, and did, open the way to one man's ear.

For years I have had my suits made to my own original design. I have no cuffs on my trousers, and no buttons on the cuffs of my coats. My pockets are slanted, not straight. From time to time, I wear open-weave shoes, and shirts of some special texture or design. None of these variations from conventional business dress is so obvious as to stamp me an eccentric, but they are just different enough to provide openings for conversations. They make an impression which causes a stranger to remember me. When he hears my name again, he says: "Oh, yes. Elmer Leterman. Of course. He's the man with the feathered lei on his hat, and no buttons on his sleeves." This may not sound like much, but it is better than a cut finger, and a good deal better than being a cipher who fades into the woodwork when a party is over.

I also pull stunts, and enjoy them, when the proper time comes. Some time ago a tough prospect broke down enough to say that he would give me ten minutes and no more. I was punctual, and so was he. I talked fast, and was just at my talk's end when a sharp buzzing sounded. My prospect looked around. "What in the world was that?" he exclaimed. "The alarm on my wrist watch," I said. "You said you'd give me ten minutes, so I made sure I wouldn't take more of your time." He chuckled. "Let me see that goldarned thing," he said. Wrist watches with alarms were novelties then. His curiosity kept me with him for an hour, and we did business.

Some of the best sales stories come out of such playfulness. I would say to every salesman: "Use your originality. Have the courage to do the spectacular thing when you see the need for it. It can be fun. It can be effective. It can get you talked about. It can win you a reputation."

Then I would add in the next breath: "But know what a stunt is. It is a way to get a hearing for your real message. It is not a substitute for a thorough presentation. It will win you the chance for one talk with your prospect. Whether you will ever have a second one depends on what he gets out of the first."

Stunts open the way to a sale. The only thing that sells is a complete selling job.

As a salesman, I have watched professionally the stunts of those superior salesmen in politics who rise to the level where they run for the United States Senate. They know a lot about human reactions or they would not be where they are. Some of them make a feature out of their families, providing entertainment at rallies performed by themselves and their children in concert—a show of family pride and harmony which has proved effective. Others dramatize themselves as men of the modern world by flying in airplanes or helicopters from speech to speech —they have won publicity and made good copy for newspapers and newsreels.

What impresses me, though, is this. Their sensational shows do no more than bring them audiences. Their elections depend on what they do with the audience once it is in front of them. Men are not elected for their entertainment value. Senator Kefauver made a political asset of a slur by the late Boss Crump, answering it by appearing everywhere in a coonskin cap which became his trade-mark. But the cap *on* his head served only as an introduction to what was *in* his head. It was because he convinced people that he had something under his hat that he got his phenomenal vote.

Casey Stengel in his playing days had one bad afternoon when he felt himself abused by an umpire calling third strikes on him. On his final appearance at the plate, when the umpire again called a third strike, he doffed his cap, and a sparrow flew from under it. This picturesque way of giving the umpire "the bird" is not the reason Stengel became manager of the Yankees. What it did was to make him a marked figure. People watched him. When he had their eye, he went on to prove that he had what it takes to be great. A stunt is like the spotlight on an actor, but it is the act which sets his fame.

One of the most conservative men I ever knew was Dick Scott, for years president of the Reo Motor Car Co. He was as Scotch as they come, hating personal publicity, and concentrating on the single job of stamping his conscience on every last nut, bolt and wire of his product. But Dick got so nettled at whisperings that his car was too solid to be much good at climbing that one morning he summoned the photographers and drove a Reo up the front steps of the Michigan State Capitol in Lansing. It was an act completely out of character, but it did more to endear him and his car to the public than a year's advertising could have done.

Use your stunt, but be sure your product can make the grade. In the old days in Vienna, Baron Rothschild was known not only as a great financier, but also as a lover of music and a charitable man. One day a man in financial need came to him.

"I've had bad luck. I always have had bad luck," he said.

"What is your business?" asked Rothschild.

"I'm not in business. I'm a musician. I was a member of a philharmonic orchestra, but it broke up, and I've been stranded ever since."

"Ah," said Rothschild, "too bad, too bad. What instrument do you play?"

"The bassoon."

"The bassoon!" cried Rothschild delightedly. "Wonderful! Wonderful! I love all music, but especially the bassoon. I own a bassoon which I play for my own pleasure. Come. You must play for me."

"What was I telling you, Baron?" wailed the man. "Bad luck

I have. Nothing but bad luck. Of all the instruments I might have picked I had to go and say bassoon."

It is the ability to follow up that counts. Get in to see your prospect by all means. Get his attention any way you can. But, in all conscience, know what to do with it once you have it. Cleopatra pulled a great stunt when she stepped out of the rug as it unrolled before Caesar, but her greatness lay in her knowledge of how to hold his attention once she had it.

My good friend, Neville Blond, took me into a store in London to buy a piece of luggage. A good-looking young Englishman stepped up to me, and I caught a flicker in his eye as he recognized that I was an American. He proceeded to put on a show the likes of which I have never seen again. He produced a bag. He slammed it. He tipped it. He snapped and unsnapped it. At last, he threw it on the ground and jumped on it. He was like a vaudeville comic giving an imitation of an English comic's imitation of an American salesman. His vigorous and amazing show left him all but breathless, but he managed to pant: "There you are, sir. Rugged enough to stand any kind of usage. A first-class piece of luggage. Is there anything else you would like to know about it?" "Yes," I answered, "how many suits will it hold?"

Never let your stunt obscure the service your product is designed to render. Your customer is not going to call you back to do your song and dance numbers for him. He is going to call for a second order if the first has served him well. A stunt for its own sake is as sensational—and as futile—as a guest showing up in a red coat and hunting boots at a party where there are no horses and no hounds, and not a fox within a hundred miles.

Check your stunts by the results they get in sales. There is no other safe control for them. You can be known as the greatest stunt artist in your trade, and be greeted at all conventions with big grins and slaps on the back accompanied with loud cries of "Here comes good old Charlie!" but the thing that pays the mortgage and puts clothes on the back of the wife and youngsters is a sale. Never get so absorbed in proving that you are a showman that you forget to be a salesman.

Like most of you I am a fan of Ringling Brothers and Barnum & Bailey. The big top can still send the tingles up and down my spine as thrillingly as it could when I was a boy. If I were running a circus, I would want nothing more than to run it just the way John Ringling North does. I learn something from it every time it comes to town. But let's not confuse salesmanship with getting circusy. Business should not be dressed in a clown's suit.

Look for bright ideas rather than bright colors. You are worth more to your customers if you are sound than if you concentrate on *making* sound. You can do a better job with your feet on the ground than you could ever hope to do on a flying trapeze.

A sensational stunt is effective—in its place. It can open doors. It can add spice to the day's work. It can encourage and release originality. But it is not the essence of showmanship. It is a surface manifestation of good showmanship. It is by no means the basis of it.

2

The best kind of showmanship is that which carries curiosity forward to confidence. You want to arouse enough curiosity in a stranger when you meet him for him to ask, "Who is that man?" But what you want more than that is to have him say, after he has known you for twenty years, "There is a man!"

The transformation of that first question into this last tribute is a process far more wonderful than the secret which the alchemists have been seeking through the ages. They have tried to find the philosopher's stone which will turn all metals into gold. More marvelous is the miracle of character which can turn casual acquaintances into mutual confidence. All the gold in the world cannot buy confidence. Confidence can bring gold, and a whole treasury of other satisfactions beyond the reach of gold.

I have said elsewhere that I do not sell insurance, I sell myself. I believe in myself. The biggest job of showmanship I have is to demonstrate to others that they can believe in me as I believe in myself. If they believe in me, they will have no hesitation about believing in what I have to sell them when they have need of it. The sterling stamp on all products is the fingerprint of the man who handles them. If he has proved himself worthy of confidence, he is himself their most convincing guarantee.

The most frequently told of all the Baron Rothschild stories is the best illustration of this. When a man asked him for a loan, he said: "No, I will not lend you the money, but I will walk arm in arm with you across the floor of the Exhange, and then everybody will give you credit." The touch of a hand in which people had confidence was an unspoken endorsement worth more than pen on paper. It was better than a neon sign. It was showmanship at the highest level showmanship can attain.

Let me try to put this into a picture which I carry in my mind. I think of all human relationships, in or out of business, as being like a huge grid with invisible wires that connect all of us together. This grid is energized by thoughtfulness. It works like this. You put on the grid an impulse of friendship to somebody. It reports to him, bringing him whatever friendly help you wanted to render him. But it does not stop with him. It is still alive. It continues on its way, touching other people and other events. It does not rest until it comes back in some way to you. You cannot hope to know all the combinations and effects it works on its way around the great circle, but they always bring returns of good will.

For example, two strangers were sitting in the garden café of the Georges V Hotel in Paris at neighboring tables. One of them took from his pocket a pencil of a kind that I had given to a few of my friends. The other noticed it. He had in his pocket a pencil just like it. He spoke to his neighbor, "I see you know Elmer Leterman." They fell into conversation. It so happened that the first man had just arrived in Paris, and was looking for an introduction to a certain personage there. The second man knew this personage. The introduction was quickly and easily arranged, and resulted in a transaction mutually advantageous. At the time, I was thirty-five hundred miles away, but two impulses I had started on the grid of thoughtfulness met and fused. All concerned were benefited. Both impulses came back to me freshened with new appreciation.

This is only one story. I could match it with scores of others. You may dismiss such incidents as "just coincidences." I believe they are more. I believe that when we begin to know as much about human relationships as we now know about the physical universe, we shall find out that there is a Law of Friendship in human affairs so governing our acts that every friendly deed we perform benefits those we help immediately, and returns in its own way to us with some pattern of reward. "Bread cast upon the waters shall return after many days" is a saying verified too often in my experience for me to doubt its truth.

Learn to trust friendship. Its quiet confidence is the best of all foundations for all relationships, including that between salesman and client. There is no longer any room for the idea that all people are divided into two classes—customers and non-customers. Salesmanship is not a high-pressure operation to be conducted at the top of your voice. The whole emphasis of selling is changing. The great salesmanship of the future is going to be substantial, based on long-term confidence, and getting results by low-pressure methods. We can foresee a time when men of solid temperament will be attracted more and more to selling as it develops quieter and more constructive techniques. We shall always have some flamboyant salesmen, but the day when the scientific salesman asserts himself is at hand.

Indirect or low-pressure selling has its own moments. Recently we had a friend and his wife to dinner. I had seen the man frequently, but I had not said a word about insurance to him, although I knew he was thinking about a new policy. Our dinner was progressing normally, when he suddenly burst out: "Elmer, when on earth are you going to start selling me some insurance? I've been thinking it over, and I think we need something like this." He told me his ideas. He insisted that I get up from the table, get some forms, and talk business with him. After he left, my wife, still shocked, said: "Well, I never saw you act that way before." I laughed. "Neither did I," I replied.

This man had been growing more and more curious about why I had not tried to sell him. My apparent indifference had become a challenge to him. He was going to make me sell him. He probably came to the house that night saying to himself that he had me cornered, and this time I was not going to get away. He went home, I have no doubt, highly pleased with his night's work.

I hope that I am not making this kind of selling sound easy. It is not. It calls for minute attention to individuals and for constantly novel ideas for pleasing them. It defeats itself if it becomes merely routine. It has to be constantly sparked with spontaneity.

When I say "minute attention to individuals," I think immediately of something that came to me last January. It was a small appointment book for the new year—a highly useful acquisition. I have never used it. In fact, I get annoyed when I think about it. On the cover in nice gold letters was inscribed, "Elmer G. Letterman." That is not my name. My name is Leterman. The man who sent it to me either handed the job of sending out these books to an underling and paid no more attention to them, or else he saw the error and did not think it worth his while to correct it. In either case, his gift was worthless, and irritated me into the bargain.

Another instance concerns a salesman who sent to all the people on his list attractive lipstick cases inscribed with their wives' names. He overlooked the fact that a few of his clients were bachelors—who might conceivably find uses for lipstick cases, but certainly not for ones with their nonexistent wives' names on them.

Where can you find "constantly novel ideas"? First, be vigilant in looking out for the times and opportunities when you can say the right word and do the telling act. Second, use your head to make the word and action good and memorable.

What this means, in effect, is that every salesman must be his own public relations man. What we call public relations might just as well be called indirect selling. If you read often enough that Polly Prettywit is the last word in beauty and in putting over a song, you will eventually buy a ticket for her show. *You* will go to see *her*. That is the ultimate goal of public relations. It is the goal of indirect selling.

Ask yourself what a public relations man tries to do. He sets out to create an image of his client in the public mind of such a kind that people will want to see him and his work. A salesman can take this idea over lock, stock, and barrel. By indirection and low-pressure methods, he takes time to create such an image of himself in the minds of the people he can serve that they will turn to him when they need the help he can give.

There is no better illustration of what I mean than Bernard Baruch. He is never sensational. He speaks for publication relatively seldom. His books are few. He lends his name to hardly any committees or public bodies. The image he has created of himself in the public mind is that of a benign and wise man sitting on a park bench. In a time of screaming publicity, he has dramatized an understatement. He has caught our imaginations with the picture of a relaxed and patient man. The fact remains that he has done it so well that we all take for granted that when the President of the United States wants a particular kind of advice, he will turn to Mr. Baruch for it, and get the best in the world.

This personal luster has not come to Mr. Baruch by accident. In the first place, he knows what he talks about and does not talk when he does not know. In the second place, he keeps men of brains around him to challenge and stimulate his own thinking; his confidants are such figures are Ferdinand Eberstadt, John Hancock, and Herbert Bayard Swope. In the third place, he is unfailingly gracious, friendly, and helpful in personal relationships; no man is more thoughtful and appreciative in his dealing with all kinds of people. He "can talk with crowds and keep his virtue, And walk with Kings—nor lose the common touch."

Think of Mr. Baruch, and look inside yourself. Your aim as a salesman is to create among the people who know you an image of yourself as one on whom they can rely as a friend. There is only one way to create that image. That is, to lose no opportunity to show yourself a friend, the friend the moment calls for. This takes a warm heart and a bright head.

There are primitive tribesmen in the heart of Africa who have a custom of binding their heads with strips of hide to make them grow "on a bias." Travelers tell us that the first flow of blood, after the wrappings of hide are removed, is exceedingly painful. A lot of people are in worse shape than these tribesmen. Their *minds* work on a bias. They take unaccountable likes and dislikes to people. They are always mad at somebody. They have prejudices against this group or that. To get a healthy, warm flow of human kindness into their thinking is a painful process for them. Make up your mind to do something helpful for the very next person you meet whom you dislike. You will be surprised how quickly your bias will dissolve. As you deliberately create the image you want the public to have of you, you will find yourself imperceptibly growing into it.

Doctors say that head-binding does no great harm. It is all right as long as the binding affects the *outside* of the head only. But a lot of trouble begins for any man who starts binding what is *inside* his head. A hidebound mind marks a narrow man. A narrow man is one with a permanent tourniquet on his imagination. He is interested in nobody but himself.

No better cure for a narrow mind can be found in all the world than expanding it by thinking about other people. And this is the first principle of indirect selling. The finest showmanship on earth is a needed service rendered unsought at the right time. It makes an impression deeper than carving on bronze.

I remember a young mechanic who came to our town years ago with his new wife. They had lived among us only a few months when she was taken dangerously ill. Next door to them lived a couple only slightly older than themselves. This couple helped them. The woman nursed the young bride day and night. The man devoted himself to making life as easy as possible for her husband. If this older couple had been the young couple's father and mother, they could not have served them more lovingly. The young woman recovered, and, a little while later, she and her husband moved away to take advantage of a more promising job for him.

About six months later he wrote to his friend that he was becoming a partner in a new manufacturing company, and advised him to invest a thousand dollars in it, at the same time offering to underwrite it should anything go wrong. The company succeeded from the beginning. The young mechanic was first its general manager and then its president. Today his name is familiar to everybody, and his wealth fabulous. At every stage of his advancement he has carried his older friend with him. If he were his son, he could not be more loyal to him. The man who was to the other as a father in his hour of need now finds him as a son in his age.

This story is exceptional only in the size of the fortune involved. The man who acts as a friend wins a friend. And friendship is the surest, most consistent, and most productive source of the kind of business which will survive any test and come through any storm. This is the only sort of business upon which a secure success can be founded.

Yes, be a showman. When you put on a stunt, make it good. Have the courage of your full imagination. Go all out. Do something that will ring all the bells and beat all the drums and sound all the trumpets. But, don't get so infatuated with your own stunt that both you and your business die laughing at it.

The showmanship that counts over the long haul is that which consistently displays you as one whose friendship is unwavering, who knows his stuff, and whose judgment inspires confidence.

Sure selling is a technique; masterful selling, an art.

Chapter 13

The Art of Cultivating People

IN THE picture of a typical sale with which we began we saw a salesman facing a customer. We have, by this time, had a good look at the salesman. We have said: "Salesman, know and manage yourself."

Now we come to the other person in the picture. We now say: "Salesman, know your customer."

Who is he? He is a person. This means that he is one among people. He is drawn from, and is representative of, all the human beings with whose human nature all salesmen work.

People constitute the field which a salesman has to cultivate if he expects rich rewards from his labor.

A salesman is like a farmer—his field brings him harvest in proportion as he knows and works the art of cultivation.

Jeff Howell was a young farmer in the county where I grew up. When I was a boy, he was looked upon as something of an eccentric. He was the first in the county to subscribe to the state university extension courses. The older men gave him a laugh when he attended the university winter conferences, and came home with books under his arm. "So Jeff's going to read book-learnin' to his rocks and give his cows a college education," they jeered.

A few years changed that. The Howell place took on a new look. Jeff experimented with new crops. He brought new stock into the county and improved his breed of cattle. He rotated his crops. He prospered. The older men began to say: "A smart boy, that Jeff."

They elected him Lecturer of the Grange, and then, Master. He became Lecturer and then Master of the Pomona Grange.

When he moved up to become Lecturer of the State Grange, they were so proud of him that they got together and elected him to the State Senate, where he sat as the youngest member of that body.

Jeff showed that county what the art of cultivation could do for its soil. He did not sit around and wish he was in Iowa, nor curse our sandy soil for not being the fertile valleys of the rivers. He analyzed the fields he had, and produced from them the most they could bring forth for him.

Jeff made a great impression on me when I was a lad. His lesson has stuck with me. I have never wasted much time complaining that people are not perfect. They are what they are. My job as a human being and a salesman is to cultivate them for all they are worth.

People are the most complex, most baffling, most ornery, most unpredictable, and most fascinating study in the world. I would rather work for and with them than around anything else I can imagine.

Part of the lure of salesmanship is that the salesman is all the time engaged with earth's most wonderful creation, living and breathing human beings, "the glory, jest and riddle of the world."

Practicing the art of cultivating human beings is a life work full of pleasure in its own right. But it does not stand on this alone. It enlarges its practitioner by broadening his intelligence. And it rewards him with success.

An experienced salesman develops within himself his own Geiger counter, sensitive to the precious ore in the people he meets.

People are like mines—yielding their precious metal only to those who perceive its presence and proceed to dig for it.

1

The more you know people the more you know that there is always more to know about them.

You cannot know people too well.

One of the falsest statements ever to pass into common acceptance is that "Love is blind." Love is knowledge. Love believes in the one beloved as nobody else does—not because it is blind—but because it knows him better than anybody else ever can. As the saying goes, "it sees more in him."

The cynic may take intellectual pride in scoffing at the frailties of people, but he is revealing, when he does so, that he knows them only superficially. No cynic has ever called out from men any response resulting in great achievement.

The saint has spurred men to be great by appealing to them as sons of God. The Caesars and Napoleons have led them to military heights by appealing to them as heroes. Other makers and shakers of the world have called out other great deeds from men but always by believing in them enough to give them faith in themselves. No doubter of men has ever made men great by his doubt.

Diogenes, the ancient cynic, has become a legend because he carried his lamp looking for an honest man, but Diogenes did not light from it one single other lamp to brighten another's darkness.

The salesman is in better business. He brings lamps to people who otherwise would live in shadows.

In a world where production is putting out more and more goods more and more cheaply, the salesman's job is to distribute them more and more universally, to the double end that more and more people will enjoy them, and still more inventions and conveniences grow out of them. The better a salesman knows people the more efficiently he will distribute what is produced, and the more intelligently he will influence the innovations which are to follow.

"The proper study of mankind is man," said Alexander Pope. However true this may be for others, it is most emphatically true for salesmen.

2

One sure way to know more about people is to know more and more people.

You cannot know too many people.

I have a friend who flies all over the world. By nature, he is one who withdraws into himself. For years he stuck his nose into a book as soon as he took his plane seat. This was his way of letting his seat companion know that he wanted to be left alone.

About a year after the end of the war he was on a transatlantic flight. The man beside him was a slight, quietly dressed Englishman. For some reason, my friend was moved to break his rule. He got into conversation with this man. To his astonishment he discovered that his companion was a member of an English delegation on its way to the United States to negotiate a steel deal. Three other members of the delegation were also aboard.

It so happens that my friend is in the steel business. The friendships he struck up during that flight turned into a sizable and mutually advantageous contract.

Since then he has taken his nose out of his book and enjoyed people. He has not hit another contract, but he can spin yarns by the hour about the archeologist he met returning from Gordia where Alexander cut the famous knot, the prince who was traveling incognito, the government agent of Indonesia beside whom he took a seat at Cyprus, and a dozen other fabulous companions.

His travels have taken on a new color. He knows a lot more about what is moving the events of our time. He himself, I may add, has become a bigger human being and a more welcome guest.

Because this man's work carries him to strange places, giving him extraordinary contacts, the average salesman may think this illustration unfair. But what has come to him on the airways of the world can come in the same warming and enlightening way to any alert salesman on the streets of his own town.

Know everybody!

"Nothing human is alien to me," is a line from an old Latin play. Take it to heart. No human being is a foreigner in the home land of human experience. The more human beings you know the more you will find them talking the common language of human life from which you can learn about human nature and its ways.

At a formal dinner at the Waldorf-Astoria Hotel, a man I admire very much rose to speak. The elegantly dressed ladies and gentlemen listened to him eagerly. At the conclusion of his address he asked for contributions. Then occurred one of those experiences that a man never forgets. As person after person sent his contribution to the head table, this man addressed each of them by name, usually the first name, and spoke to each some personal word about his family or about some experience of his. Within ten minutes that roomful of typical New Yorkers lost all their stiffness. The formality of the Grand Ballroom of the Waldorf melted into a gathering of neighbors.

A man from out of town was sitting near me. His eyes got bigger and bigger. Finally he turned and said to me: "This guy makes New York sound like a big country town where everybody knows everybody else."

That speaker knew people, and he knew that audience as one human being knows other human beings. He got past all the artificial fences and opened the way for a flood of communication as elementally human as the cordiality of a county fair. Whether dressed in tuxedos or overalls, people are one.

Make a point of meeting somebody new every day. Others in New York know more people than I do, but one of the big kicks I get out of life is that, when I walk the seven or eight blocks along Fifth Avenue from my office to the Algonquin every noon, six or seven people may call from the crowd, "Hello, Elmer."

Whether your crowd is on Michigan Avenue in Chicago or at the village post office for the evening mail, one measure of your progress in the art of cultivating people is how many of them call you by name.

Never be guilty of saying, "He is not my kind of man." All kinds of men are your kin under the skin.

Never be guilty of saying, "That's not my crowd." The man who shuts any crowd out ends by shutting himself in.

Even the most elegant house, if its doors and windows are never opened, is no more than a prison in disguise.

A wide acquaintance is like a great orchard—full of fruit-bearing trees.

3

In the art of cultivating people, friendliness is the master touch.

You cannot be too friendly to people.

When Charles Lamb burst out with: "How I like to be liked, and what I do to be liked!" he was speaking for an urge which is in nearly every one of us.

The old curmudgeon in your town who snarls at every approach to him has his moments, you may depend on it, when he wishes somebody would burst on him with a sunny affection to dissipate his lonely gloom. Dickens knew this, and said it so well that his Scrooge has become its immortal spokesman.

Don't carry a chip on your shoulder. Don't let anybody else put one there. The man who always has a chip on his shoulder will forever go lumbering through life.

An older man whom I greatly respect once confided in me that he started out in life with a miserable disposition which he constantly nurtured by looking on the dark side of everybody he met. He was accumulating about as big a collection of hates as could be housed in one solitary individual. Along with them, he was etching into his face a pattern of lines which looked like the signature of discontent.

One morning he got a good look at himself in the mirror. It was such a shock he decided the time had come for action.

What he worked out was this. He scrupulously set himself to write down ten names every day. Against each one he wrote something he admired in its owner. He kept this up until he turned his outlook around. He developed the habit of looking for the admirable in everyone he met. He disciplined himself to like people.

He told me that he dated the beginning of his success from this.

I believed him then, and I believe him now. Not only is life too short for carrying hatreds, but hatred itself is like a cataract on the eye, impairing true sight. We do not see people for what they are if we view them with unfriendliness.

Friendliness is only another name for being positive, and not negative, in our approaches to people. It is the quality behind seeking. You seek only where you expect to find something. You pursue the search until the treasure is found. This is being positive. And we have high authority for the saying that "he who seeks shall find."

As people open their homes only to those who come as friends, so they open themselves only to those who are friendly. A negative attitude calls forth a negative response. Only friendliness is answered by a response as positive as itself. It lets us into other people's lives, enabling us to learn what manner of beings they are.

One man's name springs to mind. Nobody has shown how friendliness can be the source of human wisdom more delightfully than Harry Hershfield. The other day I attended the meeting of the New York Saints and Sinners at which Harry was the Fall Guy. The tribute of the huge assembly to him went far beyond any of the words spoken.

Somebody described him as "Mr. New York." As I looked around at the celebrities of show business, the ranking politicians, the admirals and generals, the writers, newspapermen, and business leaders who had come to honor him, I agreed with the designation. I doubt whether any other individual has so wide an acquaintance among so many men from varied fields in our city as he has.

Harry's reputation is that of a storyteller, but these people were not there primarily because of this. They were there to cheer a man they know as an exceptional human being with a deep understanding of the human heart. People like Harry because Harry likes people, cultivates them, and understands them.

It is the man who carries with him the milk of human kindness who ends by enjoying the cream of human relations.

Learning what people are really like, he will cultivate them in such a way as to bring happiness to them and the reward of their affection for himself.

Friendliness is to human understanding what freedom is to men in society—the very atmosphere of growth and development.

4

Our acquaintances are like rings in a tree—every new one marking greater stature in us.

Everyone you meet has something to contribute to your growth. You will never run into anybody from whom you cannot learn something.

The art of cultivating people consists not so much in showing yourself off as in drawing the other fellow out. And the wonderful thing about this is that very often the finest returns come from the most unpromising-looking people, just as oil comes from territory men despised for centuries as nothing but desert.

One occasion might have given rise to a legend of our country; it missed because two great men did not happen to hit it off.

Mark Twain, sitting on his porch one day, saw a stranger turn into his gate. The man was tall, and strode up the path with eagerness written all over him. In his hand was a package. When he unwrapped it, he uncovered a strange contraption—a new invention.

Twain was all curiosity. Inventions always fascinated him. Unfortunately he had lately come a cropper on some investments in them. His answer to this inventor was, "No, I cannot go along."

"But," said the other man, "all I need is five hundred dollars, and you will come in as my partner." Mark Twain still shook his head.

The tall man gave up. As he turned away, Twain put out his hand. "I didn't get your name clearly," he said.

"Bell," replied the inventor. "Alexander Graham Bell."

I am not saying that you are going to run accidentally into tomorrow's Edison, or Morse, or Bell. But you will never run into anybody who has not something he can add to your store of knowledge and human understanding. And you can never tell when you may meet the one somebody who has a lot to add.

A few years ago I was anxious to meet the president of a certain big corporation. It was one of those times when I could not discover among my friends anybody who could give me an introduction. I did not want to write or approach him cold. If only I could find some hint as to how to get to him!

While I was still puzzling over this I ran into a traffic policeman on Fifth Avenue where he was taking a breather from his duty. He greeted me. "Good morning, Mr. Leterman," he said, "I guess this is my day. I just saw Mr. [naming the man I was thinking about] go in here," jerking his finger toward one of the big buildings.

I was instantly alert. "Does he come here often?" I asked. "Oh, yes," answered the policeman, "at least once a month. He never misses the regular meetings of his college association."

This was a clue. I looked up his college, and then went on a search for something—anything I could find which would tie into this college enthusiasm of his. When I found what I thought would do the trick, I called him. It was no job at all to get an appointment when I told him of the gift I had for him.

We have been doing business now for a long time. But I never forget that my introduction to him came from no big mogul, but from the cop whom both he and I had taken the trouble to know.

There are no "little people." Every person is one connection in the complicated network of our American business, and you can never tell where a touch on any connection will ultimately register.

Was David Sarnoff "a little person" when he was the telegraph operator who picked up the SOS from the *Lusitania?*

The man who shines my shoes is the most important person in the world to me for the five minutes I am with him. The right question may bring from him some item of information I shall find useful some day. In any event, leaving him with a friendly feeling means that he will have a good word for me to the next man, and who knows who that next man may be?

A friend of mine in the advertising business tells this story.

In the Madison Avenue building where he has his office there is an Italian elevator man who has a passion for recorded music. My friend is not particularly interested in it, but he has encouraged the elevator man to talk about it, on the general principle that it is always diverting to touch any man on the enthusiasm which brings him to life.

A few weeks ago my friend went to see one of his accounts. His client's mind was not on business that morning. It was on his hobby—which happened to be recorded music. He would talk of nothing else. My friend told me that he sat there recalling everything the elevator man had ever said to him. Pulling together the bits and pieces, he managed to appear halfway informed. "That elevator man," he told me, "was worth more to me in that half hour than all the courses I ever took in college."

Never underestimate anybody. Cultivate the ever-refreshing faculty of getting out of every person you meet the unique thing he has to contribute to you.

The cable which will carry any man to the heights is woven out of the strands of all the associations of his life.

Every single strand in the cable bears its own load of the car which carries the traveler to the mountain lookout.

5

Applied salesmanship means negotiating with people. Cultivation of people is the surest way to learn the skills of successful negotiation. Negotiation is not successfully practiced unless both salesman and customer come out of it happy with its results.

Any skill in any craft is derived from applying general principles to specific pieces of work so as to get the desired results. The salesman cultivates all kinds of people to improve his knowledge of human nature in general. He then translates this into skill by turning it into personal service through sales.

As the sculptor molds clay into an individual likeness, so the salesman turns selling into individual satisfactions. A major factor in his ability to do this is the quality which is sometimes called tact and sometimes diplomacy. These are to negotiation what spices are to food—the condiments which add savor to nutrition.

Both tact and diplomacy are mistakenly thought by some people to be closely akin to hypocrisy. I know men who boast: "I am a plain man. I have no time for frills and make-believe. I call a spade a spade, and that's that." This is all very well, and may even be admirable, but all too often I have noticed that such men do not stop at calling a spade a spade, but go on to calling it a "damned old shovel," which is quite another matter.

Tact and diplomacy are not hypocrisy. Fairly practiced, they are quite the opposite. They imply approaching a man on his own terms, and thus in the way least of all likely to deceive him.

Tact is serving truth to match the palate it is designed to nourish.

A story from the Orient on tact is one of my stand-bys.

A prophet approached a sultan and prophesied, saying: "Sire, you will live to see all your sons dead." The sultan flew into a passion and handed the prophet over to his guards for execution.

Seeking comfort, he then called in another of his seers to inquire of him the future. "Sire," and this prophet, "I see you blessed with long life, so that you will outlive all your family." The delighted sultan at once rewarded him with an elephant.

Both prophets presumably knew the truth, but the second one also knew the sultan.

Tact is tying up your message with the other fellow's experience.

In 1737 Benjamin Franklin was a candidate for re-election to the position of clerk of the Pennsylvania General Assembly. He found himself opposed by one member of such influence that he seemed likely to prevent his selection. He tried to talk to him, but he was rebuffed.

Franklin neither complained nor recriminated. He quietly went to work to learn all he could about his opponent. He discovered that this man owned and prized a certain rare and curious book. At once, he sent him a polite note asking if he might borrow the book for use as reference in some writing he was doing.

The man was so delighted to receive this recognition for what he himself held in such high esteem that he left it to Franklin immediately, and swung over to his support, thus ensuring his election.

You will notice here that Franklin let this man do something for him. Tact often calls for just this. We humans are so strangely created that what one man does for another often fattens his own ego. In Franklin's own words: "He that has done you a kindness will be more ready to do you another than he whom you yourself have obliged."

In any case, and whatever may be the means you adopt for individual situations, the art of cultivating people calls for closing all negotiations with mutual satisfaction.

I have never, to my knowedge, persuaded a customer against his will. I have very often given him all the time needed for him to come my way of his own volition. Encountering opposition, I have left my proposition with my prospect, and then, after many months, have had him call me to reopen negotiations. I would always rather wait and make a whole sale than hurry and make one with half satisfaction all around.

Don't allow yourself to hold, let alone show, any resentment when one of your proposals is put on the shelf. Court patience. She is a helpmeet well proved. She can save sales. Impatience can never fare as well.

Dr. Johnson once advised, "Keep your friendships in good repair." Here is the sustaining idea behind patience in negotiation. Never accuse yourself of failure because a sale is not made within a given time. But convict yourself of failure if, in any negotiation, you lose a man's respect and friendship.

Human relationships are, so to speak, the clothing of a salesman's enterprise. If they are in good shape all the time, he can face all kinds of ups and downs, and changes in weather and fortune, and still keep his career in good health. As soon as they grow ragged, however, changing winds of fortune will blow through their gaping holes, and his career will shiver, sicken and die.

All the way from his first introduction to a prospect to the close of his negotiation with him, whether the deal be made or not, the great salesman preserves unbroken the basic good will between them. He keeps open every road he has once entered. No prospect is ever lost to a wise salesman. He always keeps his lines of communication open to all who have come his way.

Don't gloat over getting a customer's number—just be sure you are always welcome when you call it.

This has a special meaning for salesmen because there is today a marked trend to turn to the ranks of salesmen for executive leadership in all highly competitive fields.

In one week of April 1955 two men who began their careers selling tractors and sausages respectively became presidents of their companies. Robert S. Stevenson was made head man of Allis-Chalmers Manufacturing Corporation, a $500,000,000 company. Robert F. Gray was elected president of George A. Hormel Co., the nation's third largest meat packer. Stevenson began as a tractor salesman in Kansas City. Gray started out in a job where he took orders one day and delivered them by truck the next. The dynamic factor common to both is that each made his selling a creative job contributing to growth in power.

James H. Carmine, president of Philco Corp., began selling for Philco thirty-two years ago when its yearly gross was one-hundredth of what it is now. He moved through a series of district sales managerships to executive vice-president in 1949. When, after he became president, Philco hit some rough going, he literally sold his way out of the troubles—proving once again the power of creative selling to solve a crisis in an acute situation.

Among other alumni of this presidential fraternity of creative salesmen are Charles Liscomb Jr., president of the J. B. Williams

Company, James J. Nance, president of the Packard-Studebaker Corporation, and Don Mitchell, president of the Sylvania Corporation.

The "drummer" who studies the best men in his field is on his way to playing "first fiddle."

No man is a better example of this than Alfred E. Lyon, Chairman of the Board of the Philip Morris Company. From cigar salesman to head of his company, he has always sold, and is still selling today.

When Philip Morris once slipped from 8% of the cigarette sales to 7%, he called in his sales executives. They arrived, loaded with ideas for getting back that 1%. Lyon listened for one minute. Then he swept all their papers aside.

"To heck with the 1%," he boomed. "What I want to know is: What are we going to do to get the 93%."

There spoke the true salesman. That Lyon roar was the voice of the man who sees all the people all the time.

Chapter 14

Learning About Human Behavior

THE ENGINEER *who knows what makes the engine run is the man who gets the car on the road.*

A first step toward knowing what will move any one man is to know what moves all men.

How do human beings behave in given situations?

What moves them to such actions?

What is behavior? Behavior is action resulting from stimulus. A salesman will want to know all he can about what kinds of stimuli get what kinds of results.

To know why men act as they do, and how varied appeals call forth varied responses, is to come pretty close to the heart of skillful persuasion.

Paul M. Mazur, senior partner of the investment banking house of Lehman Brothers, goes so far as to say that this is the single most important part of the equipment of the salesman of today.

"The dynamic markets of the future," he told the Sales Executive Club of New York, "will go to those whose products grow out of studies of changing United States patterns of living, and whose sales techniques are based on a thorough knowledge of human psychology."

Breaking this down still further, he went on: "We must know a great deal more about the people whom we seek to serve. This we do by basic research into the characteristics of men and women, boys and girls. We must know the basic elemental motivations of human beings at fairly primitive levels. We must know what are the basic urges of people—for we can contradict those urges only at the danger of commercial catastrophe."

Mr. Mazur calls this, "increased motivation research." In its larger aspects, it is an inquiry which has a big claim on a share of the 3½ billion dollars spent annually in this country on research.

The point I want to make in this chapter is that every wise salesman will have his own "increased motivation research" project going on all the time under his own hat.

He will not go through life echoing trite phrases about "human nature," but will be always on the lookout to get all the light he can on people in action—specific and individual people performing concrete actions in definite situations.

The man who knows what moves men will move ahead.

Two roads lead to this knowledge—reading and observation.

1

Reading with a purpose is like dropping a magnet into a waste pile—it comes up with the treasure and lets the rest go.

One way to learn how men behave is to read to find out.

One word of caution about reading. It can be among the most valuable things you do; it can also be the greatest waste of your time. Reading can stimulate thought. It can also be a device for avoiding thought.

The distinction is between reading with a purpose and reading without one. An intelligent salesman will read widely, but always with one purpose in mind—to find what light his reading can throw on human motivations.

This will not make his reading less interesting or less valuable culturally. On the contrary, he will find an added interest in it. And his purposefulness will make him more aware of what the author was trying to depict, and why he depicted it the way he did.

Take the famous "Friends, Romans, countrymen" speech of Mark Antony in Shakespeare's *Julius Caesar*. It is magnificent as a piece of rhetoric, but to know it for this only is but to half know it. It takes on more depth when we realize that Shakespeare, in that scene at Caesar's funeral, is giving us ringside seats at a great struggle between two powerful men for the allegiance of the people of Rome.

Brutus' speech in its own way is a masterpiece of appeal to the mind and emotions of the multitude. Antony, realizing the effect Brutus has made, sets out to present a different kind of appeal, emotionally attuned to obliterate this effect, and to create a pitch of excitement in which the name of Caesar will rouse the crowd like a trumpet.

In other words, Shakespeare, the greatest of all interpreters of human behavior, is giving us his picture of two powerful salesmen in action. These speeches throw light on human motivations as the greatest of dramatists knew them. We can get a salutary lesson in salesmanship from them. What is more, reading them this way will carry us to the heart of what Shakespeare himself intended to portray.

People who find such reading dry are those who read aimlessly. When the reader has an interest to be served the words he reads will come to life.

An ambitious salesman will never read idly, but always to find out how people act, and what makes them act the way they do in the particular circumstances in which they find themselves. This applies to all reading, for all writing is, in one way or another, a comment on human behavior. But a salesman can find especial help in six kinds of reading matter.

1. Psychology.

This is *the formal study of human behavior*.

It has nuggets of gold for the salesman who digs into it. I have little sympathy indeed for the so-called "practical man" who takes a scornful attitude toward "the professors." In the last fifty years psychologists have opened a whole new vista in the understanding of human behavior. This new knowledge has enormous implications for the world of business. And, fully developed, it offers us the only hope we have that our scientific knowledge of man will catch up with our knowledge of the physical sciences, and uncover motivations which can check the dangers of universal destruction.

The salesman has a part to play in this. Fewer man hours now produce more goods. The only way we can cope with this flow of goods is to provide for increasing wages. Wages can be increased only through wider sales at profitable selling prices. Our choice is between decreased employment and increased sales. Psychology can show us how to increase sales, as other sciences have helped to prod production.

The salesman who is up to date with our times is the one who keeps abreast of the findings of the study of human behavior.

In one of its phases, we may say that salesmanship is no more than applied psychology. The ramifications of this are always fascinating, sometimes amusing, and often surprising. Let me give an illustration which is not world-shaking, but which is full of suggestion for anyone who takes the trouble to think about it.

In the perfume trade it is well known that some perfumes put on the market under different labels are identical, or practically identical, in content. Merchandised under unimaginative names, these perfumes drag on the market. Given more glamorous names, their sales pick up.

Take this one step further. If they are given names that are too outspoken, they will sell less than if given names that are more subtle. Something in human nature prefers to buy allure in preference to outright sin.

A further comment. One perfume house got the clever idea of marketing one perfume which it announced was not for sale to women. If a woman was to get it, a man had to buy it for her. The comment on human behavior of this needs no underlining. I know of at least one man who has given his long-standing marriage a new bloom by stumbling on this perfume, and taking some home to his wife.

This kind of psychology can be applied to all kinds of selling. An alert salesman will count no hour lost in which he gets out of some book on psychology an idea he can translate into enhancing the service he can render.

Psychology is to a salesman what navigation is to a sailor— the science behind his sales.

2. Fiction.

This is *the imaginative interpretation of human behavior.*

When I say "imaginative" I do not mean "unreal." I mean by imagination that gift in an author which enables him to get outside himself, to identify himself with a character so fully that he can uncover his deepest motivations. Some of the most searching insights into what moves men to actions of all kinds come to us through works of the imagination. Fiction is not fact, but it is truth. It is an unveiling of truth through the eyes of genius. It is a revelation of depths of truth we would miss if somebody did not point them out to us.

What does raw ambition for power do to people? Read *Macbeth*. What does foolish parental love do to children? Read *King Lear*. What does intellectual doubt do to the will? Read *Hamlet*.

I would advise any salesman to make himself the master of one great book of fiction. Probe its characters. Probe the intentions of the author. It will sharpen your own perceptions.

Tolstoy's *Anna Karenina*, for example, is a whole panorama of human drives and their interplay upon one another. Anna herself portrays the inner struggle of a woman of beauty with her passions in conflict with her mother love and her conscience. Alexey, her husband, displays the mingled experience of a great egotist still capable of deep religious feeling. Vronsky, her lover, exemplifies the strength and weakness of one whose cynicism is at odds with his irrepressible sentiment. Levin, Tolstoy's own counterpart in the book, shows a man unable to reconcile his intellectual faith with his mystical aspirations. Stepan is the man of the world, alternately boasting and repenting of his frivolities.

To know such a book thoroughly is to carry with ourselves a searchlight illuminating the dark corners of every person we meet.

I use Tolstoy only as an illustration. Such writers as Balzac, Dickens, Goethe, and a dozen others hold the same clear mirror up to human behavior. Great writers are friends waiting quietly for the salesman wise enough to cultivate them.

Reading fiction is watching human beings in action through the eyes of genius.

3. Biography.

This is *the record of one man's behavior.*

The value of fiction comes from the writer, the value of biography from the achievement of the one written about.

Great men are a priceless possession of the race. They are persons in whom some quality comes to such powerful expression that they leave a personal stamp on all human affairs. Because they are exceptional they throw exceptional light on motivations and potentialities that are in all of us, just as the superbest paintings are the ones which help us to appreciate most the hues and designs of all paintings.

Biography has a special significance for a salesman. It is to him what case studies are to a lawyer. A law student is taught the broad principles of the law, but then comes the question: How are these applied in practice? The way he finds out is to study individual law cases and decisions. Every text book of law is supplemented by a book of case studies. Every lawyer's library is reinforced quarterly by records of the courts bringing the practicing lawyer current decisions. A biography is a salesman's case record.

Among case records, certain ones assume extra importance because of some exceptional feature in them. A biography is the case study of an especially important human being, significant because of some special achievement. The salesman reads biography for the light it throws on all behavior from the understanding of one man's life.

A biography like Carl Sandburg's *Abraham Lincoln* goes even beyond this. It is like a double feature—two stories at one sitting. It tells the story of Lincoln as Sandburg knows it. At the same time, it tells us a lot about Sandburg himself. This book provides a more enlightening portrait and analysis of one kind of American—his roots, his humor, his practical sense, his poetry, his suffering, his dreams—than could be found in a shelfful of statistical studies. If I were a young salesman, particularly in the Middle West, I would live on crackers and milk until I owned this book. Then I would carry it with me, and shun all movies until I had devoured it.

Biography is to a salesman what a long-distance camera lens is to a naturalist—a way of viewing intimately the objects of his study.

4. Autobiography.

This is *one man's story of his own behavior*.

Autobiography is special because it reveals that most human of all matters, how a man sees himself.

Every person you meet has his own idea of himself. Nothing is more welcome to him than a visit from somebody who confirms what he thinks of himself. Anything which will help a salesman to get into a prospect's mind and see him as he sees himself is to him what putting an edge on a chisel is to a carpenter.

Men who write autobiographies draw aside a curtain and let us eavesdrop on them talking to themselves. They are invaluable guides to understanding how human motivations work—both in what they say, and what they leave unsaid.

As a beginning, a salesman can do no better than to read the autobiography of Benjamin Franklin. Franklin was one of the most practical men who ever lived. At the same time, he was one of the most well-rounded of human beings. Among other things, he was a practicing salesman in a class by himself. His own record of how he learned the ways of men with men, and the ways of men with maids, puts into our hands the wisdom of a wise man at little cost. I know no bigger bargain in the world than that.

Autobiography is to a salesman what an old-timer's talk is to a tenderfoot—the wisdom of the road from the road itself.

5. Newspapers and magazines.

These are *accounts of current human behavior*.

Times have their own patterns of human behavior just as they have their fashions in dress. A salesman cannot afford not to understand his times.

The man who reads newspapers and magazines with the purpose of finding out what makes people do what they do in his world will discover in them all sorts of lodes of precious guidance.

One man murders. Another plunges into a river to save the life of a stray dog. Are they two different kinds of human beings? Or, if their circumstances had been reversed, would each have done what the other did? Can we find in the story of either some guide to what brings one man to his breaking point, or what calls up the hero in another?

Stan Musial goes into a batting slump. Joe Louis had bad nights when he only just managed to preserve his title against some second-rater. Babe Ruth had weeks when he did not hit one home run, and yet had one week in which he hit seven in five consecutive games. Does this mean that there is some rhythm in all of us when energy ebbs and flows like the tide? Or, is there some definite point at which a man grows stale? On the other hand, how long can a man lay off competition without losing the sharpness of his reactions?

Such questions crop up in all newspaper items, from the columnist's account of an eccentric standing on his head at the opening of the opera to the analyst's story of the struggles for power in the political ring. Here are human beings in action. As they play their parts on the public stage, they offer material for that "increased motivation research" of which Mr. Mazur spoke. An acute observer can find in them clues to what makes all men click.

Newspapers and magazines are to a salesman what models are to buyers—demonstrators of what currently sets people off.

6. Professional publications.

These are *expert comments on human behavior.*

The salesman who does not read widely is like a sailor at sea without a chart. The salesman who does not read professional publications is like a sailor at sea without a compass.

Professional publications point up information.

They carry accounts of outstanding successes. They report experiments and their results. They analyze markets. They forecast trends. They report on competition. They suggest opportunities. They raise warning signals. They put their own industry in the perspective of the total economy and supply suggestions arising out of the interplay of the one upon the other.

The modern professional publication does what used to be done in simpler days in the coffee houses. Merchants in given lines would meet and gossip over their cups, exchanging information, discussing their affairs. In those days, every young man looked forward to the time when he would be invited to sit with the big men of his line. The young man of today needs no such invitation: he sits down with the experts of his profession every time he opens his professional magazine.

Professional publications are to salesmen what medical jour-nals are to doctors—first aids to more expert service.

2

He who is alert to observe will be astute to serve.

A second way to learn how men behave is to observe them closely.

People used to say that Charles Dickens could walk through Petticoat Lane, the famous street in London which is crowded with barrows from which every conceivable kind of second-hand stuff is hawked, and come out able to describe and place every single item on sale.

True or false, this is a story which could be told only of a man whose powers of observation were legendary. Only such a man could possibly have given us the London of Dickens' books.

He was a novelist who had to know people. You are a sales-man who has to know people. The more you discipline yourself to become as keen an observer as he was the better chance you have to become as successful a salesman as he was a novelist.

It is an excellent thing to be wide-awake, but not much use unless you see what you are looking at. The wide-awake sales-man looks at people for the definite purpose of seeing what makes them behave as they do, whether he sees them crowding into a ball park or lounging at home.

The following key questions, always borne in mind, will help you to give focus to your observation.

What makes me behave as I do?

Every man studying human behavior has one specimen at hand—himself. He can keep himself continually under observa-tion.

Walt Whitman announced, "I celebrate myself and sing my-self." So doing, he sang humanity. He called from within him-self music which has awakened answering chords in all of us.

Each of us is humanity in a small package. We are so formed and moved that our own behavior brings insight into all men's.

Often when we are puzzled about how to approach some-body, we find ourselves falling back on this question: "How would I like somebody to approach me in a similar situation?" This makes sense. Dealing with the other fellow as you would like to be dealt with is to put yourself ninety-nine per cent of the time on the right track.

There is another phrase we frequently use. "I am not myself today." It is a curious saying. Taken literally, it is without any meaning at all. Taken in the sense in which we use it, it is unmistakably meaningful.

The man who knows himself and his own motivations well enough to know when he is himself and when he is not himself, and what makes him the one or the other, is fairly on his way to knowing what makes men behave so differently in different situations and at different times.

Observe yourself. There's a lot of humanity in you.

This takes us to the second question.

What makes my friends behave the way they do?

Close associates, observed intimately, provide all kinds of opportunities to learn how actions and reactions work in the behavior of people.

One of the keenest students of human behavior I know, and a man who has turned his knowledge into a highly successful career, said emphatically to me when I questioned him on this point: "All I know about human nature I have learned in my own living room among my own intimate friends. Whom else do I know well enough to know what gets under their skins? This bunch I know. I've lived with them through all kinds of situations at all emotional pressures. It's what I've learned from them that I apply in my business. My associates and customers are cut from the same patterns as they are."

I think he underestimates himself. He has his antennae out all the time in all sorts of situations and surroundings. But his words underline a useful truth. The people we know best are the ones with most to tell us about what moves all people at their deepest levels.

Now we go to the next circle of relationships—acquaintances.

What makes my acquaintances behave as they do?

I emphasize acquaintances as over against friends for two reasons.

First, to emphasize the importance of being continually observant. We get used to our friends, and form definite opinions about them which dull our liveliness of observation. We shall be saved from growing slack in observation if we develop the habit of looking for clues to behavior in every new acquaintance who comes our way.

Second, to emphasize the practical importance of the impressions of acquaintanceship. Most of our associations with people necessarily stop short of intimacy. We have to deal with the majority of those we meet without ever looking into the depths of their hearts and minds. We need to develop what we may call "expertness in acquaintanceship," that is, ability to move men favorably without knowing them well.

The more we observe acquaintances as we make them the surer we shall be to develop the knack of sizing people up quickly, and dealing with them satisfactorily.

The other day I introduced my friend, James O'Neill, publisher of the *American Legion Magazine*, to a group of other friends. The conversation grew hot and heavy around the diverse personalities of Dr. Oppenheimer and Dr. Schweitzer. Everybody got into it, but what impressed me most was the skill with which O'Neill sized up the others, all strangers to him, and, in his quiet way, addressed each of them in turn. Watching him in action, I had no difficulty understanding why his fellow veterans elected him their National Commander, and, upon his retirement from that office, entrusted their magazine to him.

Now let us go to the still wider circle of those whom we can observe, but with whom we never get acquainted. We see them in two kinds of situations—ordinary ones, and exceptional ones.

How do human beings behave in habitual circumstances?

I always get a kick out of observing people in their everyday life. To stand at the corner of a busy street and watch the scene is to observe a play of human actions and reactions so varied that it is inexhaustible. To sit in a bus or a streetcar and watch fellow passengers is like being in a portrait gallery, every face telling a story which I try to read.

All kinds of sidelights are thrown on human motivations, and the differences between people, by the way they act in routine situations.

What drives women to fight so fiercely over a bargain counter? Why do some people crowd on to an already overcrowded bus when another is coming in the next block? Why do the others wait for the second bus? What goes on inside the people who stand in the block-long lines waiting to get into Radio City

Music Hall? What urges make people, mostly men, cluster around a hole in the ground where a bulldozer is at work? Why do some women always go without hats, while others always wear the most elaborate they can get? What makes a man wear Argyle socks? Why are some people always punctual, and others never? Why do some people notice children, while others do not?

These are not idle questions. They, and the ones you will ask yourself when you get the habit, rise in an observant man. They keep him constantly alert, always learning about his fellow human beings. There is never a dull moment for a man with eyes to see. The streets for him are a constant masquerade.

How do people act in exceptional circumstances?

Crisis is a great unveiler of human behavior.

An automobile accident, a fire, a street fight, or an arrest will suddenly heighten the pulse of a crowd. Every individual in it will reveal in some way the kind of person he is.

No matter how small the crisis, it throws light on people.

I have one friend with whom I would trust myself in any crisis on the basis of two simple experiences. One evening we were passing the corner of Fifty-third Street and Broadway when two cars locked bumpers. A crowd began to gather. The drivers started to argue. My friend calmly intervened. He sent the driver of the first car to his wheel, telling him to ease his car into gear. Then he jumped on the bumpers until they were released.

The other incident happened at Forty-fourth Street and Sixth Avenue. An old man pulling a load on a small truck spilled his packages into the street. My friend, without a word, reloaded them so quickly that not half a dozen people knew anything had happened, and the traffic did not miss a beat.

Or, take another friend, Jack Frye, President of General Aniline Corporation and former President of Trans-World Airlines. In his younger days he tested new types of planes and was famous for his cross-continental flying records. During World War II, he was called to the emergency job of mobilizing air transport for the great effort. Confront him with any crisis, and you can count on his meeting it. All his life he has demonstrated the power of a man to rise to the demands made upon him.

Heroism may be defined as ordinary people rising to meet extraordinary situations.

What is there in so many people which calls out this special response to especially demanding hours?

Whatever it is, that master salesman of England, Sir Winston Churchill, knew it was there, and called it into action in his country's desperate hour, with his challenge: "I have nothing to offer but blood, toil, tears and sweat."

The man who observes how people act in exceptional circumstances will learn a lot he can use to advantage in all circumstances.

Observation of people develops in a salesman what experience with rod and line develops in a fisherman—a sense of handling and timing expertly attuned to each contact as it comes.

3

The ambitious actor studies the stars.

One special group of people a salesman will study is the master salesmen. The higher you look for your inspiration the more you will grow.

Young Raphael sat at the feet of Leonardo da Vinci and Michelangelo. Young James Madison sat at the feet of Thomas Jefferson. Young Dr. Cushing sat at the feet of Dr. Osler. The young salesman worth his salt will sit at the feet of Jim Farley, Thomas Watson, Norman Vincent Peale, Bishop Fulton Sheen, Milton Biow, and William Zeckendorf.

When I was a young man I made it a guiding rule never to miss a meeting at which a great salesman was to speak, nor a private occasion where I might meet one. I read every word I could find about them. I went out of my way to do no more than to see one if I knew he was going to be somewhere.

I have never lost an opportunity to observe a master of my craft. I want to know what makes such men succeed.

I admired and still admire the great men in the field of selling. I make no apologies for my hero worship. It has both inspired and taught me. Admiration is positive. Cynicism and envy are negative. Admiration drives me to try to be like such men. Envy would only leave me with embitterment. I admire admiration itself. Cultivating its springs gives a lift to the inner spirit which adds a glow to all the work I do.

Here is my advice. See, hear, and, if possible, meet every outstanding salesman in all lines. Contact with masters of your craft is one way to head toward mastery of your craft.

When I find myself in the same room with General David Sarnoff, I am alive to the fact that he is a man who can and does sell a hard-headed board of directors on investing millions of dollars in new experiments. If I cannot get something out of being with such a man, I surely must be dead from the neck up.

Expose yourself to greatness. Believe in greatness. Do your best to understand greatness.

I have known all kinds of men of prominence in all sorts of fields, from great educators to political bosses. Some of them have had good public reputations and some questionable ones. But they have all had something in common. No man can rise to leadership and stay a leader who does not have something about him which justifies his eminence.

When you are with such men, ask yourself two questions: What is the quality of personality which distinguishes him? What techniques in dealing with people can I pick up from him?

Never allow yourself slavishly to imitate anybody. At the same time, never miss a chance to get any hint you can from the behavior of any outstanding man on the secret of his power.

Any master in any field is himself a living lesson in mastery.

The duffer who hangs around the pros stands the best chance of getting the professional touch.

Chapter 15

Dealing with Individuals

"I to myself am dearer than a friend."

So wrote Shakespeare. So has every man said to himself. And behind the saying is a deep truth, deeper than the egotism which is the first impression.

The more we study human nature and human behavior, the

more and more one insight grows upon us. Every human individual is unique. This is a cardinal truth for successful dealings with individuals. It should be held in the front of the mind the way a miner wears his lamp on his forehead.

It is the foundation principle of democracy. It is the cardinal idea of free enterprise. It is a star to guide the way of any man who hopes to succeed in a free economy operating under liberty.

When you sit facing your customer, you and he are two individuals. Both of you are unique. Your meeting is unique. Full appreciation and exploration of this uniqueness will bring unique results.

Because I am now writing about individuality, I can do no better than to draw on my own individual experience to illustrate how I have discovered what it means to a salesman. I do this all the more willingly because I am sure that in my own case personal relationships explain what success I have had.

1

He who respects all individuality will have the courage to express his own.

I said in the last chapter that I never slavishly imitate anybody. This is not a declaration of egotism. It comes out of something I took years to learn, and have confirmed in all the years since. I can get ideas for my work from everybody I meet, but I do my best work when I do it in my own way.

My father was a salesman, and a good one. As a boy, I used to watch him. I knew every turn of his speech. I knew all his methods. When I began to sell, I imitated him. I used the same words and the same methods. I was like a miniature of him. But I did not get the same results.

The words did not come out of me with the same ring. The methods did not carry the same punch. What, coming from him, warmed an interview, coming from me, chilled one. At first I thought it was because I had not learned my lessons well enough. I privately practiced and memorized to make sure I was letter- and gesture-perfect. Still my selling did not come to life. What was the explanation?

It came to me one night when I was tossing on my bed after a particularly disappointing day. I suddenly sat up and said to myself: "Father succeeds because he does things in his own way —the unique way native to him. What I have to learn from him is not to imitate his ways of doing things, but to imitate his courage to be himself. I must have the courage to do my work my way as uniquely as he does his work his way."

From that day forward my work picked up. I made plenty of mistakes, but they were my mistakes. When I had a success, it was my success. Through both failures and successes I worked my own way to my own personality as a salesman.

I am the first to admit that I do not have some of the qualifications for a salesman which I read about in books. I am not a fluent talker. I do not play golf or any other outdoor game. I do not smoke. If I take half a dozen drinks a year I am dissipating. Even in Hawaii, my favorite recreation spot in the world, I never put on a bathing suit though I spend hours on the beach.

This has nothing to do with being a puritan. I am neither a puritan nor anything approaching one. It simply means that none of these things come naturally to me, and so I leave them alone. I have worked out my career in terms of what I am as an individual—limitations and all.

When I sit at the Algonquin Round Table I know very well that I have little to contribute to the learned and brilliant talk of such men as Louis Nizer, Konrad Bercovici, Jesse Lasky, Martin Quigley, and Frank Kingdon. But I do have something unique to contribute. I am a good listener. And these men don't resent having a good listener in the crowd.

I accept the fact that I cannot myself entertain adequately some of my customers who have a better education than I. But I can do things for them which they cannot do for themselves. I can sometimes arrange for them to have lunch with some celebrity. Maybe I can arrange transportation for them on ships, trains and planes in an emergency. On occasion I can get them tickets to some television show or theater which they are having trouble getting for themselves. And I do it gladly. I get my biggest kick out of this kind of thing. Nothing—literally nothing—gives me greater satisfaction than bringing together people who can be helpful to each other. This is part of me.

The other day Stanley Frankel of *Esquire* magazine invited me to his office. He was good enough, while I was there, to take me to meet John Smart, the publisher of *Esquire* and *Coronet*.

I had to be with Mr. Smart only for a minute to realize that here was a man of great personality who was expert in a field I knew little about. But he dropped one remark which showed me where I could help him with a problem that was bothering him. Immediately, I suggested how I could arrange for him to meet a few other men who could give him just the contacts he was looking for. The tone of our interview changed at once. We talked as friends, and parted with an agreement to have lunch and go deeper into what we had been discussing. Insurance? We never mentioned it. Being what I am, I never sell insurance, I sell myself.

A few weeks ago I ran across an idea. When a company out West sent its Christmas greetings to its customers, it enclosed cards of credit for the wives of all the men on its list. It occurred to me that this idea could be useful to a hotel. I passed it along to Ben Bodne of the Algonquin. This is the way I work. It comes as naturally to me as breathing. It adds up to success for me because it is the way of working which expresses me.

My field is a highly technical one—group insurance. I am not prepared in many ways for all its ramifications. So I make it a point to surround myself with brains. My partner, Norman Gortz, is all I am not. A graduate C.L.U., he is highly trained in all phases of insurance, and is now adding to his technical knowledge by studying law. His contribution to our activity is a sound judgment and trained mind which, I am only too glad to acknowledge, add immeasurably to our effectiveness. Being what I am, I know how much I need with me such a man as he is.

Don't fall in love with yourself, but respect yourself. Have the courage to do your work in your own way. Capitalize on both your strengths and your weaknesses. Follow your own judgment. Don't be afraid to be original—provided you are honestly expressing your unique, individual self. Your individuality is the key to your success.

I am not advising eccentricity. Eccentricity is merely egotism flaunting itself in defiance of public opinion. It is no sign of self-confidence, but only of self-inflation.

What I am advising is what Henry Luce demonstrated when he dared to believe enough in his own originality to found a new kind of magazine in *Time*, and what Ford demonstrated when he built a car to sell at a price the masses could pay. There is always room for originality. Mark Twain's famous remark about the weather was outdated the morning the first air-conditioner was installed.

Nothing is so stereotyped that the individual cannot find a unique touch to bring to it. Nothing has been done so well that it cannot be done better. In all work, it is not an impersonal question of *the* best way to do it, but of the way that is *best for you*. Even a typist has her own individual touch. Experiment with your own ideas until you find the method through which your individuality emerges most favorably. Then practice it until it becomes a means of self-development as well as a means of selling.

He who puts himself into his work will find himself in it.

2

He who truly knows men is like an archeologist—able to find a story in every specimen that comes his way.

The more you respect yourself the more you will find something to respect in every person you meet. The coin of respect has two sides. One is respect for our own individuality. The other is respect for the other fellow's. They are not only cast in the same metal; they are struck from the same die. They are inseparable. If either is counterfeit, the other is bound to be.

The man you meet as a customer is a unique individual just as you are. Like you, he has his own thoughts, his own ideals, and his own self-esteem. Just as you know you would not accept a personal relationship with anybody who has no respect for you, so, you may depend on it, he will not welcome a permanent association with anyone who does not respect him.

We do not need to labor this point. The argument for respect for the unique individuality of every person we meet is not based on commercial values. It is the first principle of our democratic civilization, derived from the basic teachings of religion and philosophy. The only alternative to mutual respect is exploitation of one human being by another. We need no reminder in our generation that this leads to nothing but chaos and tyranny.

From my experience as a salesman, however, I can testify that respect for the personality of a customer is good practical sense as well as sound moral philosophy. This is not sentiment. Respect gives to salesmanship a quality which adds a certain something which I found in an engineer friend of mine the other day.

He had just come back from northern Canada, where he had been prospecting for water power. He showed me scores of pictures of waterfalls, taken from all angles—from the air, from below, from neighboring banks. The more he talked about them the more enthusiastic he got. He was like a boy, although he is sixty years old. If only he could close out his career "making one big contribution to North American power!" He was shining with that boyish idealism one finds in engineers, made up half of love for the natural world and half of the passion to dominate it.

Respect for what he was working on—zest for what he could do with it. This was his combination. It is the combination of every good craftsman. The carpenter loves his wood and eagerly works it. The leather worker respects his leather, and takes his delight from fashioning it into the shape perfectly matched to its texture. The beginning of great craftsmanship is respect for its materials. What this respect is to the craftsman, respect for human beings is to a salesman.

The difference between a salesman and these craftsmen is in the second part of the combination. The craftsman studies his material to see how he can shape it into something he desires to make out of it. The salesman studies his man to see what he himself can do to serve him. He does not try to dominate his client but to adapt himself to be of service to him.

I do not want to make this sound pompous. It is quite the opposite. It puts a lift into dealing with people. It adds relish. I get sheer pleasure out of people. I like them. I am as aware as the next man that they are not angels. I am not sure that I would like angels as well. People are likable and entertaining precisely because of their crotchets and weaknesses and schemings. These do not lessen my respect for them. It only adds savor to understanding them. On one side, respect for others pays off in the fun one gets out of dealing with them.

It also pays off in the response it gets from them. Most individuals are so careless in their contacts with others that you can be sure the extra pains you take to show your respect for a man will register with him.

A few years ago, a friend of mine, Mortimer Lacy, who has his own manufacturing concern, was having his shoes shined. He is a tall, distinguished-looking man. When the job was done, the shoe-shiner said: "There you are, Colonel." Lacy laughed and said he was not a colonel. "Admiral, then," said the man. "No," said Lacy. "What are you?" asked the man. "President of the Lacy Manufacturing Company." "Yes, sir," answered the bootblack, "I knew you were the boss of whatever you were the boss of. I could tell." Lacy gave him a generous tip. But he could not get him out of his mind. He made inquiries about him. In two weeks that bootblack was off the street in Lacy's factory with a steady job.

How often have you read of somebody unexpectedly leaving a bequest to some stranger in recognition of a simple deed of courtesy? What prompts such things? Simply this: the stranger gave a sign of respect to a person whom the crowd was pushing around. When you come down to it, what is courtesy? It is showing respect.

Let me tell you of an experience which makes a point. Another man and I went to see a third man. He treated us rudely—and that is putting it mildly. When we left, my companion was furious. "Let him shove his policy in the ash can!" he said. I was not ready to leave it at that. Two days later I called on the client again, giving no sign of remembering his previous bad behavior. I treated him with respect, and what I thought might happen did happen. He went out of his way to make up for his previous boorishness. He introduced me around in flattering terms. He responded to my respect for him by acting as though he deserved it. The way to bring out the best in people is to act as though you expect it. They feel a compulsion to live up to your estimate of them.

The qualities in men which command respect are like gold in nature. Gold is seldom found in an uncombined state. Almost invariably it is admixed with silver, copper, iron, bismuth, or some other inferior metal. What is more, in its pure state it is soft and malleable—so much so that one single gram has been drawn into a wire two miles long. Consequently, when it is put into circulation, as coins or jewelry, it has to be alloyed with a harder metal to stand the wear and tear of everyday use. Few gold objects are all gold, but it is the gold in them which gives them value.

Human nature is an alloy. Few men are pure gold. The gold in human nature is mixed in various men with various baser metals in various quantities. Perhaps this is necessary to give men the harder qualities able to take the wear and tear of common life. The fact remains that what gives every man the peculiar quality that makes him human is the basic metal—that inner dignity which in all humans commands respect. The salesman who deals with every person on the basis of this respect is the one who will find the golden response. This is the living truth expressed in what we rightly call the Golden Rule.

There is gold in the golden rule for the man who does not estimate others by the rule of gold.

3

Friendship is respect blossoming into appreciation.

Every individual with whom we deal will act like other people in most ways. But he will also have his own area of individuality in which he differs from them. I have already made the point that each man's area of uniqueness is the source of his peculiarly personal contribution to the world's work and wisdom.

Now I want to approach it from the other side—what it means in terms of dealing with people. His area of uniqueness is where we deal with a man most intimately as an individual. It is his most sensitive spot. Here we touch him in terms of his own ego, his own name, his own most compelling motivations, and his own definition of his own success.

If we outrage a man where he is most sensitive we naturally hurt him most deeply, and most definitely alienate him from us. But this danger is not the whole story. Its reverse is also true. If we successfully make connection with him at the point where he responds most strongly, we get from him the warmest welcome, and bind him to us inseparably.

Friendliness deepens into friendship when we take the trouble to understand a man where he is most himself, and are alert to serve him where he will be most conscious of our service.

With me, the cultivation of friendships is a passion. What

this has contributed to my career I would find hard to put into so many words. The book of friendship is not one to be audited by an accountant. But this I can say. My work has a quality of its own because I have so many friends.

I cannot describe exactly how this quality works. Even those who know me best find it hard to pin down into a definition what my "methods" are. In a sense they are not "methods." Or, perhaps I had better say, they are methods only in the same way as a farmer's planting his seed where the sun and rain will work on it is a "method." I aim to create a climate of friendship around me. The natural processes of such a climate generate activity in their own way to produce fruits.

All my life I have cultivated people. Because it is my nature, I've gone out of my way to make friends. I have brought my friends together. I have been with them whenever I could. Immediate returns to myself have never been the deciding reason for making friends. Often I've been very happy to be among friends when I had no reason to believe that any benefit of a commercial sort would come to me. All I can say is that the genial glow of friendship has warmed into life whatever seeds of business were present. Over the years, it has brought me an abundant harvest.

About a year ago, a friend of mine who owns a chain of stores in the West came to New York. I knew that he did business with another friend who is the biggest manufacturer in the country of certain goods he sells. I invited them both to dinner, and introduced them to the head of an advertising agency and the publisher of a national magazine, whom I had invited to meet them. There was nothing in this immediately for me. There was something for every one of them.

It was to the advantage of the manufacturer to meet a substantial customer. The merchant, I knew, was considering a change in his advertising program. I also knew that the publisher was wrestling with the need for more advertisements in his periodicals. The advertising man was serving none of the others, and so, obviously, he had a chance to benefit from all of them.

As the evening progressed, the merchant and manufacturer found that they were both going to Hawaii at the same time for a winter vacation. Before we separated, all five of us agreed to be there together if we could arrange it. This was an expensive trip, and I could see no immediate return, but I knew that I was in a position, because of my long and happy association with the island, to assure them a pleasant experience there.

These four men cemented a friendship. I was in the middle of it. Can I count the dollars and cents I put into the dinner and the trip, and say exactly what each one earned? I cannot. All I can say is that bringing people together in this way, in circumstances advantageous to them, has proved an effective stimulus to my friends' businesses, and, in time, a help to my own.

You may say that you cannot take trips to Hawaii. That's not the point. Within your own province, you can help people to know each other, arrange trips to their advantage, organize car pools to the convenience of three or four men going to the same lodge, fix up compatible hunting and fishing parties. You will never lack the opportunity to prove yourself a friend no matter where you are.

Being a friend to the other fellow is the best of ways to be your own best friend. Don't misunderstand this. When I say "being a friend," I mean just that. I do not mean pretending to be a friend. I mean being a sincere friend. True, friendship is a currency having two sides, paying off for me as well as for my friends. That is its nature. But remember: counterfeit currency pays off for nobody.

About two years ago I was negotiating a $100,000 policy with a big firm. We had the papers all drawn and ready for signature when the president said: "Of course you realize that our lawyers must pass on this before we sign." I agreed, and we made a date to meet with the lawyers the following Thursday afternoon.

When I came into the room where the lawyers were I had the feeling that the senior counsel looked vaguely familiar. And I noticed that he was eying me curiously. We were introduced, and when he got my name, his face lit up.

"Leterman," he said, "of course I know you. Eighteen years ago I had lunch with you and some other men. The conversation got around to a fight Joe Louis had had the previous evening. Somebody raised the inevitable question of whether Louis could have beaten Jack Dempsey in his prime. You mentioned that you had been with Dempsey that morning. I said: 'It's always been an ambition of mine to meet Dempsey.' In a couple of days you called me, and said that Dempsey would be glad to meet me at a certain time. I want you to know that meeting Dempsey was one of the greatest thrills of my life."

I had forgotten the incident. Eighteen years! But the coinage of friendship is durable metal. I need not say that my negotiations with my lawyer friend were cordial.

Every man, like that lawyer, has some private interest or enthusiasm. To discover and serve it is one of the most fascinating aspects of living. One of the biggest lumber merchants in New York would far rather talk about a scheme he has for reorganizing the docks and warehouses of the city to facilitate merchandising than about his lumber business. A public relations man I know will be your friend for life if you will listen to him discourse on how Shakespeare could not possibly have written the Shakespearean plays. A moving picture magnate of my acquaintance is a passionate student of theology, and you can bind yourself to him with hoops of steel by humbly listening to him expound it. One of our most successful button manufacturers has made a hobby of ancient manuscripts, and the way to his heart is to sit with him over the reproductions and translations of them he has had printed.

So I might go on. One man collects old masters, and another collects the pictures that used to come in some packages of cigarettes, of ball-players and theater people. I know one man who thinks steam locomotives are the finest of all man's achievements, and another who has a barn filled with old automobiles. One of my friends eats, drinks, wakes, and sleeps with Sherlock Holmes, and another considers himself the greatest living expert on the career of Lucky Luciano.

To every man his own peculiar interest is the key. We, who deal with people, miss a bet if we are not continually on the search for these keys. They click, and swing the doors of friendship open. They give us open house to those we serve.

Friendship is like the sun—greater than all of us, yet serving each according to his nature and his needs.

4

Every ego looks for a hero—in the mirror.

Anything you can do to help a man see a hero in his looking

glass is oil for the lubrication of all your contacts with him. We are all such creatures as to want to think of ourselves as complete within ourselves, knowing our own minds, and assured that what we think or will or say is wisest, most desirable, most virtuous, most discreet, and best. This is not weakness. In most situations, nothing can profit any of us more than self-esteem, grounded in what is just and right, and managed properly. True self-esteem and social conscience are rooted in the same earth.

Joe Cook put the same idea more lightly when he said: "Of all my wife's relation's, I like myself the best." No matter how we say it, we are here dealing with a universal motivation operating in every human breast. To turn it to good account is a part of successful dealing with human beings.

Always aim to make your client the hero of every sale. If there are any congratulations coming to you for making it, you can take your bows in private. The congratulations of the moment belong to him. Keep the spotlight on him as the star of the show.

It is a gratifying light. This is why, when I take a new friend out to dinner, I make a point of going to a restaurant where the hat-check girl will say: "Good evening Mr. Leterman." Being human, I want him to feel that I am important. The restaurant that boosts me gets my trade. The man I boost gives me his.

I've learned a lot about salesmanship from two hat-check attendants. One of them used to be at Sardi's Restaurant. She not only called patrons by name, but added the extra touch of taking their belongings from them without giving them a check in return. When she handed them back their hats and coats without an error, it made them feel that their visits were such an experience for her that every detail registered unforgettably in her experience. I try to leave every client feeling that I have just this attitude toward him.

My other hat-check story is about a famous man who is a regular visitor to the White House. He never speaks about seeing the President, but he will tell at the drop of a hat his story of how a cloakroom attendant at a big reception took his coat, and said: "You won't need a check. We know you here." Why? Because she singled him out of the crowd. She made him somebody to be noted—the exceptional man. What that girl can teach us is that no matter how big a man may be, he never outgrows the power of small acts that make him feel important.

A Chrysler dealer I know always keeps his most expensive model on one certain spot in his showroom. The reason is that this is the one place from which a purchaser can get a full view of himself at the car wheel in a mirror on one of the walls. Seeing himself seated in the big, shining, luxurious, and impressive car, the average purchaser cannot resist the reflection.

The effect of that miror on a customer is one every salesman without a mirror will try to reproduce by his words and attitudes. He will help the other fellow see himself in a favorable light. To help a prospect visualize himself in the role of a wise, perceptive, and impressive man is artistry of the highest kind.

I know of one shoe salesman who got a novel idea for a window display from one of the department stores on Fifth Avenue. As he went from town to town on his next round, he demonstrated it to his customers. They blossomed out with the most striking windows in their communities. Naturally, they got all the glory. They basked in suddenly acquired reputations for artistic talent. None of these displays had a shoe in them, but the shoe salesman sold a dozen pairs of shoes for every pat on the back his customers got.

Building a client's ego can take many approaches. I have sometimes clinched a sale by saying something like this: "Your choice shows you are very discriminating. As a matter of fact, you have worked out a plan almost identical with one Elmo Roper took for his organization." Identifying himself with a great reputation, the client thinks himself a greater man.

Naturally, the most effective way to appeal to a man's self-esteem is to take the line he wants most to be esteemed for. One man may take pride in the fact that he was in the same college class with a United States Senator or a president of a big corporation. Another may fancy himself a brilliant public speaker. A third may want admiration as a church or community leader. A fourth may be ambitious to be known as a shrewd businessman.

Such ambitions could be stretched into a long list, but the point is simple. Every man has his own image of himself. Among its features are some that he finds especially admirable, if not heroic. The wise salesman will search for these, and so conduct himself as to appeal to them, and thus bolster his client's high opinion of himself.

The salesman who so conducts himself that his client is made to appear to be the important man he wants to be will enjoy a wide reputation as a man of clear judgment who sees things in their true perspective.

One kind of capital a salesman can always keep working for his interest is his client's capital "I."

Chapter 16

Dealing with a Client's Associates

People square with the circles in which they move.

No man works in a vacuum. He is surrounded by people. He is influenced by them. In most cases, he can be better understood through them. Studies of people underline the truth that his friends and associates help mold an individual.

For example, one man known to me is a hard and ruthless driver of his employees. For years I wondered how he kept his organization together. I found the explanation when I met his partner, a man of unusual gentleness. The hard man is the driving energy of their machine, the gentler man is the lubricating agent. Neither man alone could have perpetuated the business. If either had an enterprise all his own, he would have to change something about himself to make it succeed. Each, working with the other, can be just what he is, and both can profit.

These two men are probably unaware of how deeply they have influenced each other. Most people accept their co-workers without knowing how much they are affected by them. But a salesman who is alive to what motivates people will keep himself alert to the associates of his clients. He will never treat any of them carelessly.

I have already pointed out the value of a co-operative attitude toward one's associates. This is what makes for teamwork. It is a vital factor in mobilizing one's total resources. It is what puts the creative spirit into an organization. Now let's turn to the question of dealing with a client's associates.

There is one main point that needs to be stressed. Treating all the people around your clients with respect is a first aid to good relationships with your clients themselves. In the first place, the better you understand a man's associates, the more intelligently you can deal with him. In the second place, the friendlier a man's associates are to you, the easier becomes your access to him.

These relationships call for a special kind of tact. I would phrase my own aim this way: to have cordial relationships with my client's associates without ever allowing them to degenerate into familiarity. I want them to be easy, but not loose.

In most companies and offices there is one dominating personality. He is the key person—Mr. Big. Those around him live constantly in his shadow. They are incidental to him. Most of the people who call to see him treat them carelessly. Consequently, they are aware of being considered secondary people. This is not easy to take. Even the humblest worker has his ego. Consciously or unconsciously, the people around Mr. Big resent being brushed aside, or patronized, as mere impersonal appendages of the great man.

Knowing this, make it a point to greet them, or transact your business with them, in such a way as to convey respect for them and what they are doing. During the few moments when you are asking a man's secretary if he is free, keep your mind on that. Do not act as though you think her an obstacle to be pushed aside. Call her by name. Keep your attention on her. What she is doing when she announces you is an essential link in the accomplishment of your mission. The way she announces you helps to set the tone of the reception you will get from her employer. Try to convey to her that you know this, and that you appreciate her service to you.

Similarly, when a client calls in a subordinate for consultation, put some questions to him to indicate your respect for his opinion. Include him in what you say. Indicate careful weighing of what he says.

Such tactfulness has a value that goes beyond the immediate occasion. You may be sure that in almost all organizations there come times when the pressures are off, and barriers are let down a little. The boss relaxes, and talks to his secretary or his associate informally. They exchange impressions of people. The boss is influenced by what he hears. At such times you want the people who have his ear to be on your side. They are important to you. Because they carry weight sometimes, give them respect always.

1

My experience leads me to put in a special word of advice about two kinds of associates—a man's quiet partner, and his secretary.

1. Early in my career I had the good fortune to run into a big lesson which I have never forgotten. Two men, Luce and Holmes, were partners in a retail furniture business. Luce was a big man, big in every way—a six-footer with a booming voice and a hearty laugh who served on every civic committee there was. He was a natural-born public personality. Holmes was a man of medium height who wore glasses and belonged to no luncheon clubs. His one center of activity was his church, which he served as a trustee and Sunday-school teacher.

I first met these two men when I found myself competing with another salesman for some insurance they wanted. My rival was older than I. He was pretty confident that he was going to get the business—so confident that one day, when we happened to meet, he as good as said he had it, and added: "That Luce! What a man! He's the whole business! The luckiest day old Deacon Holmes ever knew was the one he met him!"

These words disturbed me. I had come to know Mr. Holmes a bit, and to respect him a lot. In fact, I had talked to him more often than to his partner. Accepting my rival's assertion that the sale was as good as in his hands, I could only tell myself that I had misjudged the situation.

To my astonishment, Mr. Holmes called me a couple of days later to tell me that he and Luce were ready to sign with me. The simple truth was, as I found out, that Luce had almost unlimited confidence in Holmes's judgment about financial matters. I shall never forget one thing he said. "You know, young man, the luckiest day of my life was the day I met Mr. Holmes" —the exact reverse of what my rival had said two days before.

If there was any difference in the weight of the two men in this partnership, the quieter one carried the extra.

My rival in that deal made the mistake of underestimating the less spectacular man in a partnership. I cannot number the times that I have seen this mistake repeated. One thing I have definitely learned is that successful partnerships are not the results of mismatings. If two men are operating together profitably, you may be sure both are adding something, and each respects the other for what he contributes.

Here are two rules I have developed in connection with dealing with partners. First, when I find myself in conference with partners, one of whom is doing most of the talking, I deliberately draw the other into the conversation. Second, following such a conference, I call the quieter partner on some pretext, usually asking him to clarify something. It is important to me to make him feel that I am dealing with him as an active participant in our negotiations.

In many cases, as in that of Mr. Holmes, this has brought delightful personal friendships. The better I have come to know this man the more he has surprised me with his versatility. I myself can now value and enjoy the qualities his partner found in him. Some of the relationships which have served me best in all ways have been with men generally overshadowed by their more publicized partners.

Apart, however, from these personal satisfactions, the practical sense of treating quieter partners with respect is obvious. In many cases they have a veto power. In all cases, they are the persons with whom their partners discuss their moves.

Few partnerships indeed achieve perfect psychological balance. Both men may share equally in the financial returns, but one is likely to think that the other gets more than his share of other satisfactions. Human nature being what it is, the less noted of the two has his times when he, or his wife, resents being overshadowed. Any salesman, therefore, who pays him positive attention and accords him honor touches him at a point where he is ready to respond enthusiastically.

A partnership is often like a baseball battery. The headlines proclaim that the pitcher won the game, but the catcher knows that it was he who called the signals. You want both pitcher and catcher working for you.

I once went to see a famous lawyer about taking a case. It had so many elements of public interest in it that it was bound to get a big play in the papers. I did not know this lawyer, but I did know that he had a reputation for this kind of case which was unrivaled. He received me pleasantly, heard my story, and at once called in a man of whom I had never heard.

This man was a striking figure. He had a massive head which was like a lion's, and one of those striking faces which recall the great portraits of the Renaissance. I quickly learned the secret of the great lawyer's fame. He had forensic talents which this second man lacked, but he relied for the basic analysis and preparation of his cases upon him. This partner of his was a scholar in the law. He was even more than this to his associate. The man everybody knew made no major decisions of any kind, even the most personal, without consulting the man nobody knew.

This kind of relationship between two men is surprisingly common. The alert salesman will be prepared for it. The lesser-known man in the association I have just described was an unusually mature and wise man. But he responded as warmly as another to the sincere respect which I went out of my way to show him.

Confidants can help a salesman sell confidence.

2. Your client's secretary is, next to his partner, in the most strategic position to further your cause with him. The modern secretary is a new phenomenon—a prodigy of the machine age. No previous time produced her counterpart. In no other country is she as powerful as in the United States. She is the child of the typewriter, the telephone, and the filing cabinet. They created a demand for new skills. She fills it.

She knows her employer in his work as no other employee knows him. She is his counselor. She is his foil. She is his memory. She is his nurse. She is his private purchasing agent. She is the guardian of his secrets. She is the sentinel at his door.

He thinks her judgment is exceptionally good, for one reason which is beyond dispute: she devotes herself to him. He and his work are important to her.

To have her good will is a substantial asset to any salesman. You can get that good will by thoughtfulness and respect in your dealing with her. The man she *respects*, she will admire and help.

We might as well get one error out of the way at once. You will get nowhere, and get there suddenly, if you make passes at her. Every cheap-Jack who comes to see her employer will start out by romancing her. Don't think you have something incredibly new to offer her in this line. She has heard it all. The most pathetic of all the conceits of a salesman is his idea that he has some peculiar charm which makes his approaches uniquely welcome to an experienced secretary. I assure you that, after the first twenty have ogled and flattered her with the same drivel, the twenty-first salesman who comes in and treats her with proper respect as an equal will be as welcome to her as a clear draught of water to a traveler in a sticky jungle.

For all I know, you are a combination of Don Juan, Rudolph Valentino, and Marlon Brando. If so, I salute you. But keep it out of your business. These gentlemen make ladies swoon. The secretary will be more useful to you if she is conscious.

Be friendly, but not overfriendly. If your client gets the idea that you are a possible rival of his for the attention of his secretary, he is likely to have a bad emotional reaction to you, making any good relationship with him impossible. By the same token, any sign that you are more interested in her than in him will necessarily destroy the main impression you want to make, namely, that your one desire is to serve him.

The fact to bear in mind always is that, when you are dealing with a man and his secretary, you are dealing with an established relationship. To respect that relationship, while at the same time giving both individuals their proper respect, is the safe guide to handling yourself wisely. It will encourage friendship while averting embarrassment.

I do not want to make this sound negative. From the point of view of your interests, the positive relationship between the employer and his secretary is what counts. As you see that, and map your approach to it positively, you can capitalize on its positive aspects for positive results. What I am warning you against is introducing disturbing factors into the boss-secretary relationship. They can have no possible effect except to interrupt the free flow of natural friendliness.

The whole question really comes down to good manners—

and in nothing is a man more fully revealed than in his manners. The secretary has a name: know it and use it, shunning all such salutations as "Babe," "Doll," "Pigeon," and the like. She has, to be sure, her own pride in her looks: discreetly bolster it, without going overboard into that overheartiness which is so obviously hollow, and hangs in the air like a sour trumpet note in a Sousa march. She has her reserve: respect it, submitting her to none of your smoking-room language or jokes. She has her private life: let her live it, without intrusion.

She, like everyone else, has her private image of herself. You will most surely have her influence working for you if you match that image with her idea of how a gentleman should treat her. My advice to a young salesman on this score is as follows: When you are in doubt about how to act, always underplay.

3. I want to add another word. Never gossip about your client with either his partner or his secretary. Their loyalty belongs to him. They will carry back to him whatever you say about him. And, such is the frailty of human reporting, it will not sound on their lips the way you thought it sounded when you said it.

Don't think you can get away with gossip by hiding behind "Confidentially," or, "I know you won't let this go any further." They offer no protection. Even though you should swear a partner or a secretary to eternal silence on the bones of all their ancestors, your words will get back to your client before the rising of the next day's sun. Gossip has unclipped wings. No bars can hold it. And, in business, it always comes home to roost on its originator.

Sometimes you will find yourself with a partner or secretary who wants to gossip. Be polite—and change the subject. Such people are dangerous. You can always be sure that the person who comes gossiping to you about an associate is on his way to gossip about you as soon as he leaves you. Never gossip. Never encourage gossip. It will never do you any good.

When your client's name comes up in a casual conversation in his absence, show yourself his admirer. The word of praise spoken when he is not present will be carried back to him by somebody, you may be sure, and it will warm him to you.

A wise salesman speaks always of an absent client as one friend speaks of another when they are apart.

2

Partners and secretaries are special persons with whom a salesman must be exceptionally tactful. But the principle which applies to them applies in its own measure to every other associate of a client. It is good practical sense to treat all of them with respect.

I cannot tell you how many times I have seen young people, in obscure positions when I first met them, who have risen to influential places in their companies as the years passed. There is no magical formula for spotting these potentially valuable individuals. Accordingly, make it a point to be on good terms with as many people as you meet in every organization with which you do business. Today's office boy may be tomorrow's purchasing agent.

Any time I choose I can walk into the office of the treasurer of one of the biggest chemical companies here in New York. The man who sits in that treasurer's chair was a boy I helped to raise. When he first joined the company as a youngster, I was negotiating a policy. I spoke to him in a friendly way, just as I try to speak to everybody. This gave him encouragement to call me for help one day. I took an interest in him. Out of this a warm friendship has developed—and it is just as warm today when he is the treasurer of the company as it was when he was its youngest accountant.

As I look back over the years of my experience, I realize something which I did not realize at all when I started out. The world of business is a world of change. Powerful companies merge, expand, or disappear. Influential men retire, or die. Younger men rise to leadership. Unexpected personalities emerge within organizations. Nobody can tell today who will be the great figures in any company or in the business world as a whole twenty years from today.

All we, as businessmen and salesmen, can be sure of now is that we are doing business with certain clients. They give us our basic stability. If we are going to maintain that stability, we must continue to keep their business, no matter what changes may occur within them. Obviously, the best way we can assure this is to be on cordial terms with all the people we can in all the companies we serve. Then, no matter who emerges as the executive from the inevitable changes over the years, we shall have a pathway to his door.

Let me put in a word of warning at this point against a common weakness. When things are going well with you, be on guard against becoming self-satisfied and arrogant. I have seen salesmen flushed with success treat lesser people, as they thought them, with contempt. Later, when these "lesser people" have come to power, I have seen the puffed-up salesmen ruthlessly deflated. Don't make enemies on the way up, and you will find friends waiting when tougher days befall you. The way to have change working for you is to have as many people as possible on your side.

I am convinced that, in dealing with human beings, men make more mistakes when they are riding high than when they are having a hard time. The reason is conceit.

Write this in your book: *The time to be most on your guard against treating other people carelessly is when you are most pleased with yourself.* When we think we need other people least is when we hurt them most. The wise salesman will keep his head at normal size no matter how his pocketbook swells. To stay friendly with everybody in a changing world is to maintain one's human relationships in sufficiently good condition to weather whatever shifts of fortune time may bring.

He who keeps all his lines of communication in good repair can always get through to the right man at the right time.

Chapter 17

Building Self-Confidence

An inferiority complex is not suicide, it is murder for a salesman.

Let me say at once that I am not going to tell you how to cure the kind of inferiority complex derived from deep emotional disturbance. That calls for professional treatment. I would no more presume to prescribe for it than I would prescribe for pneumonia.

What psychologists call an inferiority complex is an emotional dislocation paralyzing the ego to the point where it cannot assert itself in such a way as to face and handle reality. It is a basic personality flaw. I would not suggest to anybody that he try to dig himself out of this kind of trouble by his own unaided efforts.

There is no reason why he should. Experienced counselors are in practice to help such people find their way through the mazes of their inner complications to discovery and assertion of their egos. If this is a problem with you, seek out your minister, or priest, or rabbi for counsel. Go to a psychiatrist if you need his aid.

Don't hesitate to do so, any more than you would hesitate to go to a doctor. Modern psychiatry is scientific treatment of disturbances of personality in just the same way as medicine is treatment of bodily ailments. There are no humiliating implications in submitting to psychiatry any more than in submitting to the care of a physician. In fact, a modern man proves himself truly modern when he avails himself of its help once he is convinced he can profit from it.

I know a young actress who has just become a star; after years of self-doubt, she achieved self-confidence through analysis. One of the richest and most famous men in our country turned over a new leaf from playboy to valued leader of his city after getting psychiatric help. I could make a long list of executives, writers, and others who have achieved self-mastery and self-direction with the aid of wise counselors.

I stress this because I feel the obligation not to write as though pep talks will answer all our personality problems. Some of them are deep-seated. They can be overcome only by the sternest kind of intelligent effort and discipline directed by professional skill. The smart thing for anybody who needs outside help is to go and get it.

Fortunately, most of us are not in such deep trouble as that. We can overcome our sense of inferiority by our own efforts. How we can go about it is what we shall now consider.

1

A sense of inferiority makes no sense to a man making sense of himself.

I suppose all of us have been to those houses of mirrors where we have enjoyed distorted reflections of ourselves and our friends. Among these mirrors is one that makes us look a lot bigger than we are, and another that makes us look shriveled. Our minds have a way of distorting images as these mirrors do. The man with a sense of inferiority is likely to be one who always looks at other people in the convex mirror which magnifies them, while looking at himself in the concave mirror which shows him less than life size. What he obviously needs is a true mirror reflecting both his image and the others in proper proportions.

Dr. Norman Vincent Peale, whose understanding of people has made him so wise a counselor to his own congregation as its pastor and to the nation as a writer, says that a first step toward overcoming a sense of inferiority is to find its cause. "Even without help," he writes, "you can discover this by careful thought. Laying bare the origin of your low opinion of yourself usually reveals that the conditions creating it no longer exist."

Let us take Dr. Peale's advice. What are the causes of most people's—especially most salesmen's—sense of inferiority? I should say that they can be phrased something like this.

1. "I am not physically graceful, and my shyness makes me all the more awkward and clumsy."

2. "I don't seem able to get that breezy manner which other men use so well to get on easy terms with people."

3. "I'm not as wealthy as the people I go to see, and I'm tongue-tied by doubt—who am I to advise men more successful than I am?"

4. "I was brought up on the wrong side of the tracks, and am afraid I shall betray my lack of good breeding."

5. "I'm naturally a serious person, and I can't remember many jokes; even the ones I do tell fall flat."

6. "I'm not 'hep' the way some men are, and show it—so that I sometimes think people are laughing at me."

7. "I didn't get the education others did, and I haven't traveled so much—I'm afraid of getting out of my depth."

8. "I'm not naturally as shrewd as some of the men I meet, and do not wake up to what they are doing until after I have left them, and then I'm likely to find out I have the small end of the deal."

I want to say two things about all these together.

First, you may be sure that these doubts have come at one time or another to every successful man you know. The people you meet who seem to be most poised are the very ones who have disciplined themselves most rigorously against self-doubts. They have them, but they master them. Arthur Murray was embarrassed all the way through high school because he was so tall, so gangling, so awkward, and so shy that he shrank from all social occasions, especially dances. He had all the makings of a first-class inferiority complex, but he did not surrender to it. Instead, he turned it into a superior skill.

On one occasion, a President of the United States took a well-known raconteur aside before a public banquet to tell him a story. He said: "I want you to listen to this, and tell me if I'm getting it right." He was afraid he might not put it over. And another President, Franklin Roosevelt, seemingly the most confident of men, confessed that he was shaking in his boots at least once—when he found himself for the first time in the presence of the majestic Queen Wilhelmina of the Netherlands.

There is nothing inferior about sometimes having inferiority feelings. Everybody has them. The most redoubtable of people have them. Yours do not make you less than anybody else.

This brings me to my second comment. *Forget yourself.*

In every one of the illustrations I used above, the mind of the worrier is on himself. Get your mind off yourself. Focus it on the job you are doing, and the man you are selling. When the first whisper of self-doubt comes, turn your thoughts deliberately to something else. Fill the moment with a specific idea or activity. Concentrate on what you are doing, and make that good.

I remember an incident at an intercollegiate track meet I watched many years ago. There was a sprinter (I even remember his name, J. D. Jones, though I never heard of him again) who was out in front in the hundred-yard dash. Suddenly, he looked over his shoulder to see where the second man was. In that instant, he lost the race. The other man flashed by him. He faltered because his mind was divided. He lost because he took his eye off the tape. Nothing can so divide the mind and scatter concentration as self-doubt.

"The play's the thing." Your work is the thing. Don't let the other fellow's breath on your neck disturb you. Do the best you can, and that best will carry you forward.

One of my associates was a lieutenant in the anti-aircraft artillery during the recent war. While he was still in training, an inspection was called one day. In the course of it, each of the platoons of his company was ordered to assemble its anti-aircraft gun. The other platoons assembled theirs in jig time. His took more than half an hour—assembling, taking down, and reassembling, until he was satisfied the job was right. The other platoons, in spite of the presence of high officers, could not restrain themselves. They hooted with laughter at the ineptitude of his command. He was crimson with embarrassment. But the upshot was that inspection of the guns showed that his was the only one perfectly assembled. The laughter rolled the other way when he was called to the front and congratulated.

Another young friend eventually made Phi Beta Kappa in spite of the fact that he flunked his first college examination. He told me the story. At that first examination, for some reason, he became bewildered by the pens around him flying as though they had all the answers on their tips. He became so sure that everybody else knew more than he did, that he could not put down what he knew. He didn't finish his own paper. But he did learn his lesson—perhaps the most decisive of his whole college career. After that, he got his mind off himself and on to his work in every test. It is a lesson for every crisis any of us will ever have to meet.

Waste no time on pitying yourself. "I wish I were somebody else. I wish I could get up. I wish I were the world's greatest ballplayer. I wish I were the handsomest actor in Hollywood. I wish I were a Deep Thinker with bushy eyebrows and a Message for the Age. I wish I were a Tragic Figure, the victim of a hopeless passion, pale and appealing. I wish I were a millionaire."

Turn "I wish" into genuine dissatisfaction with yourself.

Turn dissatisfaction into determination to do something about it with "I will." Turn "I will" into a concrete decision with "I intend." Turn "I intend" into action with "I do."

Do. Keep on doing. Concentrate on doing. Forget yourself in what you are doing. Then you will be so busy accomplishing something that you will not have energy left to worry about yourself. Your so-called inferiority complex will take wings.

The surest of all ways of finding yourself is to lose yourself in something bigger than yourself.

2

Success is a lady who confers no favors on a coward.

Overcoming a sense of inferiority is one step, but only one step, toward something much more positive—self-confidence.

There is one satisfaction which lays the ground for the enjoyment of all others—and that is, to put our hearts into our work and do our best at it. Conscious that we are doing this, we are relieved and able to give ourselves fully, even gaily, to our family and friends and everything else we enjoy.

The only way to live and work happily is our own way. There are always people around us who think they know our business better than we do. They are full of suggestions, but the trouble is that one contradicts the other, and all add up to confusion. The only road we can walk firmly is the one we ourselves map confidently.

A lot of people in this world are spending time and energy worrying what people think of them which would be money in the bank if they conserved it and dedicated it to their work. Don't skulk around, peeping and eavesdropping, like a parasite frightened of his patron's frown. Know your own worth. Get your own work done.

One of the most interesting personalities in New York is Leo Cherne of the Research Institute of America. I have watched him since he began his career. While he was still in college, he formed a definite idea of a service he would develop when he graduated. He prepared himself specifically for it. Several men who recognized his brilliance invited him to join them at high salary to do other things, but he could not be tempted. He was so confident of his own program that he could not be pulled away from it. The more he worked on it the greater his confidence grew in it, and in himself. His career has been a remarkable triumph of consistency, both in building his organization and in his participation in public affairs. Few names today command higher respect. It has been earned by courage and determination. These have released the powers of his unusually lucid mind.

He is an example of a man taking counsel of his confidence, not his fears. There is always opportunity for such men. They do not say, "It never has been done," nor "It has been tried and failed," nor "It never can be done." They say, "This is the way I can do it," and they make it succeed.

There is no truth in the oft-repeated saying: "The frontiers of America are now closed." I put my faith in the denial of it, as stated by the great genius of General Motors, Dr. Charles F. Kettering: "There exist limitless opportunities in every industry. Where there is an open mind, there will always be a frontier."

These are days when every morning's paper brings news of some fresh advance in applied science. We live in a time of wonders—new electronic devices, new instruments of communication, new machines taking over complicated operations of the human brain, new instruments of observation, and new weapons. Every morning is the herald of something new. There are people who are frightened of this. They would like to call a halt to it. They are the ones who will fall by the wayside. Those who are going to stand and move ahead are the ones who see in every advance a new opportunity, and who have the courage to move into it.

When I think of the salesman of today, I call up the picture of John Jay Hopkins, president of General Dynamics Corporation which built the atomic submarine *Nautilus*. Here is a man who has to convince a practical-minded board of directors to invest millions of dollars in experiments as up-to-date as the striking of the clock. He lives continually on the borders of the unknown. He is the spokesman for tomorrow. He stands distinct from the pure scientist who works theoretically in his laboratory. He has to take what the laboratories find, and confront it with the practical question, "How can this be put to use to serve people and build a richer economy for everybody?"

After full analysis and discussion, he comes to his board

with a proposal to try something which has never been undertaken before. He has to be able to present this in a way which will convince his business associates, who are not as expert scientifically as he is, that it is economically sound. When I visualize him selling them on one of these multi-million dollar adventures, I see a man confident of his own judgment, a man unafraid to look both facts and men in the face.

Only such men can lead us from the world of today into the world of tomorrow. Only men of this quality in all fields can make a success of their enterprises in the transition from the present to the future. It is the salesman who has this quality who is the vital middle man of today, serving both present and future together.

What is called an inferiority complex is all too often nothing more than cowardice—surrender to fear. The coward quits under pressure. Giving cowardice a softer name is no excuse for running away from a tough situation. Every one of us encounters sooner or later times which are rough. This is when the quitters run. It is when the men stand up.

In William Faulkner's story, "The Bear," the old Indian hunter says of hunting bear and deer something which applies equally to tracking down success: "Be scared. You can't help that. But don't be afraid. Ain't nothing in the woods going to hurt you if you don't corner it or it don't smell that you are afraid. A deer or a bear has got to be scared of a coward the same as a brave man has got to be." Like bear and deer, success will not show her face to a coward. Only confidence can clear the air for her to appear.

3

Confidence is the name we give victory in the most decisive battle any man fights—his battle with himself.

Some things we have to teach ourselves in the secret places of our meditations. One of the things a man has to teach himself is that the basest of all things is to be afraid. And once he has learned it, he must forget it, so that his mind and heart will have no room in them for anything but the positive thoughts which create his success.

You may say: "This is all very fine, but how do I get this

confidence?" You will have to work it out for yourself. Here are some suggestions which can be of help.

1. Dare to believe in your faith.

Every individual's faith is so private a matter with him that I would not pretend to discourse upon it. All I want to say is this. I have friends who belong to all faiths, but they have one characteristic in common. Those who dare to believe in their faith most firmly are the ones who are most secure within themselves.

They start with a foundation; it steadies everything for them. They have confidence in themselves because they believe a power not themselves works with them. They can take the good with the bad, and the bad with the good, because they are convinced that both good and bad together are parts of a greater whole. They are unafraid of the future because they believe they have resources at their command equal to any emergency.

A man of strong faith has an unshakable underpinning of confidence.

2. Dare to believe in the future of humanity.

There are plenty of voices counseling despair. These have nothing to contribute to your confidence. It is true that we human beings are facing severe tests these days. Science has given us weapons with which humanity can destroy itself. And there are misguided men following false philosophies who are putting an anxious strain on human relations. We cannot evade these facts. But humanity has faced crises before which seemed at the time insoluble. It has not only overcome them. It has made them turning points toward new advances. We shall do this same thing with the crisis of our times if only we are not afraid.

When William Faulkner received the Nobel Prize, he said in his address: "I believe that man will not only endure: he will prevail. He is immortal, not because he alone among creatures has an inexhaustible voice, but because he has a soul, a spirit capable of compassion and sacrifice and endurance." These words speak the faith of a free man who is unafraid. True, we are in a time of twilight, but twilight not only marks the coming of night, it also announces the approach of dawn. Fearful as the Atomic Age is on one side, on the other it promises mankind a future of such plenty as the world has never known. We can have this future if only we are not afraid.

Have confidence in the future. You and I are not members of a dying race. We are heirs of generations who, by courage and honor and hope and pride, have overcome all obstacles to make the incredible climb from primitive life to contemporary civilization. The way now opens to a loftier ascent. We can have confidence in man's power to go forward.

3. Dare to believe in your country.

Professional crapehangers have been announcing the collapse of our country every month since the signing of the Declaration of Independence. It is still going. Our country has its imperfections, but we are enjoying a more abundant life than any other people in history. Our capacity to expand that abundance is still unmeasured.

I think in this connection of a famous remark of Joe Louis. When somebody asked him how he, as a Negro, could fight for the U.S.A. in World War II, he answered: "There's a lot of things wrong with this country, but they ain't none of them anything Hitler can cure." I would paraphrase that: There may be lots of faults in our country's ways of doing things, but there is not one fault which can be cured by lack of faith in the country itself.

I believe in America. I have lived in various parts of it, and have seen most of it. I have shared in its periods of booming prosperity, and I have passed with it through its greatest depression. I have been part of it in both peace and war. I have seen many changes of administration. Through all, I have felt its energy and power. I have seen it learn its lessons and correct evils. I have felt it pull itself together to meet emergencies. And I have watched it emerge from all these experiences to become the world's greatest power and the leader of the free peoples everywhere.

When you estimate its resources, you see them multiplying. Its scientists and management experts are the foremost of the world. Its people are the healthiest. Its rivers and other natural sources of power are unrivaled. It is the leader in development of atomic power, and the first among nations to experiment with this power for peacetime uses. The economic and industrial future of this country is unlimited.

Every one of us has an extra right to confidence in ourselves because we have a share in this country. We can, in turn, help to assure its future by our confidence in it. I do not pretend to be a prophet, but I'd stake all I ever expect to have on this forecast: the American economy will offer more, greater, and more varied markets for a salesman twenty years from now than even the most optimistic economist is now predicting. All kinds of innovations nobody can possibly envision now are on their way. People marvel at the advances of the past fifty years. I believe the next twenty-five years will make more progress over the present than was made in the fifty years following 1900. We are living in a country and a time which breed confidence.

4. Dare to identify yourself with men of achievement.

The great of the earth belong to all of us. And who are the great? They are men and women who have overcome weaknesses like ours to develop to a high degree capacities of the kind that exist in all of us. They are made of the same stuff as we are. To know their stories, to understand their struggles, to emulate them, and to identify ourselves with them is one way to call up the best in us. Striving to be like them, we learn our own strength, and build our confidence in our powers.

As I am writing this, Helen Keller is just starting on a tour of India, Pakistan, Burma, Indonesia, and Ceylon. The governments of these countries have invited this blind, deaf, and dumb woman to travel halfway around the world so that their peoples may look upon her. Why? Because Miss Keller is an inspiring example of heroism at its noblest—heroism refusing to bow to limitations, rising above them to create a rich and wonderful life. The rulers of the East are wise enough to know that seeing such a woman is an experience their people will never forget. They know that the thought of her will work in their people's memories as a spur to rise above their own handicaps. She can inspire a will to achievement which these nations urgently need in these days of their beginnings.

No one can know Helen Keller and ever indulge again in self-pity. I have a friend who has met her, perhaps twenty times. He never ceases to marvel about one fact. After meeting him the second time, all she had to do was to feel his hand in hers to be able to call him by name, in that slow, difficult attempt at speech of hers. Lacking sight and hearing, she has developed her sense of touch so expertly as almost to compensate for them. By means of this one sense, she lives a full life in a vivid world of people and things.

Just to think about such a woman is a rebuke to every excuse we have ever made to ourselves for not going ahead. The rebuke, in turn, becomes a spur to belief that we can do better. Greatness, thank heaven, is a contagion. As we expose ourselves to the great, a little greatness gets into us.

Whatever you think your handicap is, you can find a story of somebody who overcame obstacles greater than yours to move on to great accomplishment. Were you wounded severely in the war? Look up the story of U.S. Senator Charles E. Potter of Michigan, who, in spite of the loss of both legs, campaigned vigorously enough to carry his State. Are you deformed? Read about Steinmetz, the electrical wizard of General Electric, who was a hunchback. Do you have language difficulties? William Knudsen, President of Chevrolet and Director of War Production under Roosevelt, never lost the trace of his Danish accent, yet proved himself one of the most dynamic salesmen in private industry and public affairs of our generation.

The more we know of men of achievement, the more we realize that none of them had automatic elevators in them, lifting them without effort to the top. They got there by overcoming weaknesses and limitations. As you find yourself reflected in their weaknesses, you can also identify yourself with their struggle to overcome them. In this identification, you find confidence to believe that you too can succeed.

In all the ways of men across all the years, there is probably no scene older or more universal than the gathering of the family or the tribe at a feast to hear the old men and minstrels tell the stories of heroes. "Let us now praise famous men and the fathers that begat us." Love of heroes, and courage fired by thought of them, are as old as the human heart, and as up-to-date as this morning's newspaper.

5. Dare to think big.

Fill your memory and mind with inspiring poems and stirring passages of literature. Don't be afraid of them. They come into the mind sometimes like a great tide, lifting everything at once. Their power and splendor sweep aside petty and self-pitying moods. They leave us clean as a white beach.

When I was a boy, we used to have what we called Golden Texts. We started each day with some verse from the Bible. Recited first thing in the morning, it was intended to set the tone for the day. This was an innocent device, but a profoundly sound one psychologically. It started us on the day with a big thought. "God is our refuge and strength, a very present help in time of trouble." "God is for us, who can be against us?" I do not claim we understood all they meant, but they were good company. They sent us out into the day with our shoulders back, full of courage.

Some people may call this "corny." Let them. I am sure that warming up the mind on such thoughts is a healthier start for any day than plunging into stories of sex, sensationalism, and murder. We are "corny" enough about our bodies. We give them a good breakfast of healthy and nourishing juices and foods, waiting until later to put candy and alcohol into them. Why not give the mind the same break? Start it off with nourishing fare; the more doubtful stuff will not do it so much harm later.

I believe in the power of great words. I keep a supply of them always in mind. When I need the boost words can give, I want the finest ones there are to lift me. I am never alone. I can always turn to the best company of the ages. In their great thoughts I find the courage to believe in the best I find in myself.

Carry your private anthology in your own head. Choose your own selections. They are the right ones for you, provided they help you and become friends to you. I am perfectly aware that Kipling's "If" is not the greatest of literature, but there have been times when it was just the mental tonic I needed. And there have been other times when the magic of Shakespeare's "Hark, hark, the lark" has lifted my mood. Find the words that hit the spot with you, and live with them.

This is so much a part of me that I make a habit of putting my own experience into phrases I make and collect, and which I repeat to myself, and pass on to others in the hope that they will find some lift in them too. I call them Letergrams, and I know they are not literary gems, but I hope they can spark in people good responses. Here are some examples:

"Minds, like streams, may be so broad that they run shallow."

"Do not kill time—it has no resurrection."

"A man may fall many times, but he is not a failure until he starts saying somebody pushed him."

"When you throw dirt, you lose ground."

"Worry is interest paid in advance on borrowed trouble."

"Luck is preparation meeting opportunity."

"The one helping hand on which you can always count is the one at the end of your own arm."

"The most underdeveloped territory in the U.S.A. is under men's hats."

"Small favors flower into golden fruits."

As you have gone through this book, you have noticed that I have often tried to catch the essence of its paragraphs in sharp, epigrammatic sentences. I try all the time to keep my mind actively at work saying old things in new ways, and saying new things in old ways. It is my way of thinking myself out of ruts. And the resulting slogans stimulate me.

This may not be the exact method for you. I can only testify as to what works in my own case. But whether this method is suitable to you or not, the principle behind it is sound. Think big. Spend some time every day with great words that invite you to expand your mind and outlook. The company of great thoughts inspires great confidence.

6. Dare to hold in your mind an image of yourself as a confident and successful person.

I have emphasized again and again in this book the fact that every person carries his own image of himself in his imagination. This image is by no means a passive object. It actively influences us. It gives a pattern to what we do, and helps shape us into what we become.

Think, for example, of a striking personality like Dali, the painter. He has created for himself, I should say, the image of an eccentric genius. He dresses to display the splendor of his genius. He waxes his mustache at great length to dramatize his uniqueness. He makes bizarre productions for exhibitions to underline his eccentricity. We can only admire him for having created so definite an image, and for having sold it so effectively to his public. But the point is that he first had to create the image for himself before he could portray it.

Gene Tunney is an illustration of a different kind. He saw himself as a man apart from the run-of-the-mill members of the boxing fraternity. He proceeded to project his own image of himself—speaking with grammatical precision, dressing conservatively, studying Shakespeare under William Lyon Phelps, hobnobbing with George Bernard Shaw on the Riviera, and entering into business with the serious approach of an impressive executive. The inner image molded the outer man. He dared to act like what he believed himself to be. He now occupies an honored place as a respected leader in our national community.

What we picture ourselves to be, we end by becoming. This points to one conclusion. The thing for each of us to do is to carry within us an image of ourselves worth living up to. You can begin to be confident the minute you see yourself as a confident person.

Sidney Fields began his column on me with these words: "No one is ever sure where the legend of Elmer G. Leterman ends, and the fact begins." Naturally, I like that sentence. But there is more to it than just liking it. It makes a point. Somewhere in all our personalities there is a borderline where what we are by nature ends, and what we are making of ourselves begins. It is the borderline where our inner image of ourselves gives definition to our characters. It is like that moment when a piece of marble under the chisel of the sculptor ceases to be an unshaped mass of stone and begins plainly to be a statue.

Each of us shapes his own portrait, and the model of which we work is the image of ourselves we see in our heads. Live by the image of a confident and successful person, and the lines of that character will stamp themselves on your person.

Confidence is faith in action.

Chapter 18

The Salesman's Sixth Sense

A SALESMAN, *like a suitor, must know the right moment to pop the question.*

Manual skills, I have noticed, hang on little hinges of time

—moments recognized by the craftsman when a sudden turn of his hand will give the definite touch to what he is making. I used to watch the blacksmith in my home town. He stood over the horseshoe getting hotter and hotter in the fire until it reached an exact moment he recognized. Then he snatched it from the furnace to hammer it into shape.

I saw the same sort of timing in Venice as the glassblowers snatched the molten glass from their furnaces at the exact second when it was just right for them to twist and blow it into shape.

Ask these men how they know just when these moments arrive, and, as likely as not, they will just shrug their shoulders, and say: "We know." Timing, including recognition of the psychological moment, is an acquired skill which a craftsman develops through long practice on his materials. It is his "sixth sense."

Timing is also the "sixth sense" of a salesman. He gains it as the craftsman does—through constant practice. He develops an unusual awareness of people and their reactions through tireless contact with them and study of them. He can get it in no way but by being with them. His sensitive responses to them are what enable him to detect the psychological moments to carry them forward in the progress of a sale, and to move definitely to close it. This sense of timing is an intangible but priceless item in every successful salesman's kit.

Salesmanship would be comparatively simple if it consisted merely of slapping down a piece of merchandise, and saying, "Well, here it is. Take it or leave it." You could then take out your stop watch and give the customer thirty seconds to decide, and that would be all the timing in the case. But most sales begin at quite another pace, with "Maybe yes, and maybe no, but a little more maybe no than maybe yes."

This brings us at once to these two little words, Yes and No, which are the keys to timing. One truth a salesman must learn early in his career is that Yes and No do not always mean exactly what they say. They have many shades, and he must be aware of them. He can lose one sale by thinking there is too much Yes in his customer's "Yes," just as he can lose another by thinking there is too much No in his customer's "No."

1

A salesman cannot always take "yes" for an answer.

"Yes" can be a baffling word. I once met a very angry man. The day before I saw him he had been with the President of the United States to argue for a certain position of the public utilities in a situation then pending. As he presented his case, the President kept nodding his head. My friend thought he was having clear sailing. He left the White House sure that he had convinced his man. To his amazement and chagrin, the papers of the next day carried the story of the President's decision to do exactly what he had asked him not to do. He was furious.

This man had fallen into a familiar error. He thought the President was agreeing with him, when all he was doing was to say: "Yes, I see the logic of your argument. I get your point of view. Granted your premises, your case is sound. I follow your reasoning." This was a long way from saying: "I agree with your premises, and go along with you a hundred per cent."

A salesman will often run into this kind of "Yes." It by no means indicates that a sale has been made. Quite the contrary. At its worst, it may be no more than a polite rejection. Even at its best, it means no more than that your arguments will be weighed. It is never more than a slight opening of the door. The expert salesman will know when all he is getting is this kind of "Yes," and will never be tripped into overconfidence by it. It is a "Yes" of politeness, not of assent.

A second "Yes" goes a little further than this, and amounts to "Perhaps." It says, "You not only make a good case from your own point of view, but I go along with you to a certain extent. Some of the things you say sound good to me. Maybe I'll buy. I'll think about it."

I once almost lost a big sales because I took this kind of "Yes" too seriously. I came back to my office, and said: "Well, I think we have the Arly account tied up. They were very impressed." This was one time when my sense of timing was away off. I was overconfident, and did not follow through at once. Negotiations lapsed. A year passed before I could reactivate them. This time I did not make the same mistake. The only

"Yes" on which a salesman can rest is the "Yes" which seals the contract.

There is another kind of "Yes" which turns up frequently. It is the "Yes" of the client who hates to say "No" to your face. He says, "Yes, I'll take it." You leave him, feeling that you have another feather in your cap. The next morning he calls up, and says he has thought it over, and is sorry, but he cannot go along. Your feather droops.

Clients like this are headaches; that is all there is to it. You just have to know who they are, and deal with them individually. You have to discipline yourself to their undependability. Timing with them comes down to selling them, taking their withdrawal, unselling them on their own change of mind, and then reselling them. Usually, you end with less of a sale than the first one to which they agreed, but you take it, for the simple reason that this is the way they operate, and you adapt yourself to their pace.

A fourth "Yes" and one that can get a salesman confused, is the one which comes too quickly. I have often found that the quicker I get a "Yes," the less likely I am to make the sale eventually. The client never does hear my story. "You don't have to sell me," this kind of man says. "I'm already sold." But he is not. He has not had the time to be.

I would much rather face an initial "No" than a too speedy "Yes." It closes communication. It is harder to pierce. I would say to a young salesman: "Don't take a quick Yes for an answer. Don't let it lull you. Be all the more alert. Push beyond it to get an actual commitment. Not until you get that can you be sure that you and your client genuinely agree on what you are talking about. Continue to sell until you are sure he is really sold."

Another danger of the quick "Yes" is that it often results in a smaller sale than you should settle for. It may mean that your customer is ready to give you a lesser order than you would have gained if you had had a chance for a full presentation.

This presents a dilemma. You have to unmake his mind in your favor if you can. Yet, you want to do this without running the risk of losing altogether what he is prepared to buy. Here is where knowing the psychological moment to advance if you can, or to accept if you must, calls for awareness of the most sensitive kind.

A fifth "Yes" means "Not today." Here the client agrees with you, acknowledges his need for your goods or services, and professes his intention of doing business with you—but not now. Some other time. He will call you. Right now he is not ready.

This is a situation in which your "sixth sense" will have to tell you whether to persist on the spot. You know your man. You have to rely on your judgment as to how far and fast you can push him. Sometimes, to bring such indecisive agreement to an agreeable decision will call for long and careful cultivation.

Indecision is a frustrating mood. In the book of the Revelation, the voice cries to the church at Laodicea: "I would thou wert cold or hot." Every salesman sometimes echoes that cry. The client who is not hot enough to buy, but not cold enough to be dropped, is a trial of patience. The salesman faced by the "Yes" meaning procrastination has no recourse but to weigh the value of the time spent on such a client against its possible futility, and decide positively for himself how he will handle the case.

These "Yes's," and others of varying degrees of affirmation and denial, are part of every salesman's experience. To recognize them, and to be prepared to deal with them as they arise, is a skill. It becomes more and more expert as a salesman stays alert by keeping himself constantly in touch with people. Living contacts with people are what quicken sympathetic responses to their reactions.

My friend, Jack Seidman, has developed this sensitivity to human relations about as fully as any man I know. He is a highly successful accountant with his office on Broad Street by day. He is an equally successful "angel" of shows on Broadway by night. In addition to these interests, he has a lively appreciation of the history of human achievement, which he keeps alive by his collections of art and literature. All his activities interlock with each other, and all combine to enhance his understanding of human behavior.

I cite him here because his versatility rests upon a basic skill. When he steps from Broad Street to Broadway, he knows that the lines of the plays he reads are potentially more than just words on paper. What they are to become when spoken will depend on how they are staged and delivered. It is not the words, but what the words convey that will count.

This holds true for all words. They take on emphasis and color and tone from the speaker and the place. The same words in the same order may convey entirely different impressions in different circumstances. A salesman knows this. He develops an ear not only for what is being said, but also for what lies behind what is said and gives it its true meaning. Even the monosyllable "Yes" can mean many different things. The salesman must be able to recognize and act upon what it truly means when he hears it.

The only "Yes" which finally counts is the one flowing from the end of a pen as a signature.

2

A salesman must know how to get past a prospect's "No's."

"No" has just as many shades of meaning as "Yes." But it has one advantage over "Yes" as far as a salesman is concerned. It does not disarm him. It puts him on his mettle. "Yes" can lull him. "No" stirs him. A quick "Yes" can stop a sale. A quick "No" starts one.

A big buyer once welcomed a young salesman into his office with the words, "Son, this is your lucky day. I've refused to see twelve salesmen this morning ahead of you." "I know," said the salesman, "I'm them."

Broadway got a big chuckle out of James Melton when he first came to New York. He had made up his mind he was going to sing for Roxy. He wrote letters; they were unanswered. He made telephone calls; secretaries sidetracked them. He called in person; all the satisfaction he got was a seat in the outer office. At last, he picked up all six-feet-two of his powerful frame and planted himself outside the door marked "Private." The office staff proceeded to try and throw him out. The ensuing racket brought Roxy to his door, demanding to know what was going on.

"I want to sing for you," shouted Jimmy.

Roxy decided the easiest way to settle the incipient riot was to hear him sing. That was all Jimmy needed. He walked out of Roxy's office a member of the Roxy gang.

To Jimmy "No" meant "You've got to fight for your chance." So he did. This is the only practical answer to the flat "No."

But most "No's" are not as open-and-shut as this. They are shaded by other considerations.

Let us assume that you are past this first "No." You are in your customer's office, and talking with him. You have to meet the "No's" which come from him as he listens to, and debates with, you.

There is a decisive thing to bear in mind here. It is this. He is carrying on two conversations at the same time—one with you, and the other with himself as his mind carries on its own discussion with itself about the things you are saying. The "No's" he says out loud are just as much a part of his inner conversation as they are responses to you. To understand them, you have to hear them against this background. Let us take a look at some of them.

When you enter his office, you are saying to yourself, "I am here as this man's friend with a proposition which I think can help him." At the same time, he is saying to himself, "Can this guy do me any good?" His first answer to you is the answer to this question he is asking.

His first "No" says that he is not convinced that you have anything which will do him any good.

You do not let this stop you. You take it as a challenge. It does not stop the sale; it only shifts the ground a little. You now say to yourself, "He thinks I cannot help him, but I know precisely how I can, and I'm prepared to prove it." You are prepared. You have done your homework.

Your assurance tells him so. He now says to himself, "This guy certainly thinks he has something definite to offer. I wonder whether he really has." If he says "No," this is the question he is answering.

His second "No" says that he does not believe that you have a specific and definite proposition capable of helping him in his own practical situation.

You go ahead to convince him otherwise. This is when the presentation you have prepared will be put to the test. The salesman who has barged into an office with no more than a slick talk to make a fast sale will bog down on this "No." Now, you have to be prepared to prove to him that what you have to offer will make him more secure, more successful, and more satisfied.

Since you are prepared to do this, his "No" does not shake

you. With convincing assurance, you proceed with the sale. He is now asking himself, "Is the proposition this guy is now specifying good enough for me to bother with it?"

His third "No" says that he is satisfied to go along as he has been going, and does not want to make any change.

Here is where you put into play the extra personal touch. You have studied him and his situation individually. You genuinely believe you are offering something he truly needs. You know what you are offering so thoroughly that you can put into plain and convincing words what exactly it can do for him. Your talk becomes highly personalized.

You talk concretely about him. You paint a picture for him of how your proposition will make his operations more efficient, of where he will save money, of the way in which his profits will jump, of the additional prestige he will gain, and of the extra security he will have. You make this as true to fact as a scientist would make it, and as full of human interest as a novelist would make it.

Believe every word of it yourself. If you don't, you might as well take your hat. Your sincerity, enthusiasm, and genuinely friendly interest are what will spark his response. They will get under his skin. Your aim is to make him dissatisfied with what he has, for the sake of arousing him to want and take something better.

Your inner thought now is: 'What you have is good, and you can be proud you have created it, but you cannot be satisfied with the good when I am prepared to show you how to move on to the better." In his mind he is countering with, "Maybe there is something to what he is saying, but, do I want to make the decision and the effort for a change right now?"

His fourth "No" says "Maybe some time, but not now."

This is where you run up against that universal bar to action —the hurdle of inertia. Your response is a combination of tact and timing aimed at creating an exchange in which it will be less effort for him to close the deal with you than to sell you on his refusal.

This last "No" is like the last "Yes," before the final one. It presents the subtle obstacle of procrastination. Get the customer past the block of postponement, and you have a sale. Close the sale, and you have a friendship.

3

The salesman, like the woodsman, develops his sixth sense only as he sharpens his faculties in the field.

This "sixth sense" of timing is not born into anyone. It is acquired. It comes as a result of sharp observation and alertness of the faculties. The man who acquaints himself with people as intimately as Daniel Boone knew the wilderness will end with the same keenness of perception in dealing with them as he had of the tracks of the forests and the habits of its creatures. Boone was not born with a knowledge of the outdoors. He acquired it, and he acquired it by living in and with the outdoors. After long years, he did the right thing in any given situation almost instinctively. The salesman who gets actively into the field of his work will acquire in it something of the same resourcefulness.

Once at a national golf tournament, I made the acquaintance of several sports writers. Among them was John Kieran, then of *The New York Times* and later of *Information Please*. Sometimes we took a walk together. Again and again, Kieran would stop, and, cocking his head, would say: "Sssh, listen." Then, as some birdcall came from neighboring trees, he would say, "That is a hermit thrush," "That is an oriole," naming bird after bird. The countryside had an extra life in it for him, denied to the rest of us, not because he was born with a special kind of ear, but because years of alert watching had quickened his senses to the fugitive sounds. The same kind of alertness in human relationships can produce the same kind of sensitivity to human reactions, and this is the heart of timing.

Sensitivity to other people can be raised to astonishing degrees of perception. I once heard a famous orator mispronounce a word in the flow of a speech. It shocked me. But I was even more amazed when he looked at me, one of the hundreds listening to him, and said: "You are right. The proper pronunciation is" and corrected himself. I asked him afterward how he knew I had recoiled at his mispronunciation. He said, "When I have established communication with an audience, they and I are one. I am aware of every response among them." This man was responsive to crowds because he had lived with crowds. The salesman who practices meeting the minds of his customers will develop a like responsiveness to them.

Every one of us is born with certain faculties which can be sharpened or grow dull in proportion as we exercise or neglect them. The frontiersman developed the sharp eye for movements of wild creatures, the alert ear for the sound of a breaking twig or muffled breathing, the acute nose for an alien smell. He had to have them to meet the dangers of his life. We have exactly the same potentials in our eyes, ears, and noses, but we do not develop them because we do not live as dangerously. Men's faculties sharpen as they use them.

We have need of faculties the frontiersman did not exercise. Our lot is cast in organized communities where we rub shoulders all the time with other people. To survive and succeed, we must know how to act upon, and react to, human beings in a highly complicated civilization. Because we are by nature social beings, we have the natural faculties for this. But they develop to high sensitivity only as we exericse them. The sooner any salesman determines to make himself as expert in making his way in our crowded life as the pioneer was in his isolated one, the more earnestly he will devote himself to sharpening his responsiveness to other people's reactions, and thus be on his way to expert timing in dealing with them.

I was once with some jet flyers when a captain of their outfit, who was also an ace, came into the room. The pilot beside me began at once to talk about this captain's exploits. It was a case of hero worship. He ended by saying: "He cannot make a mistake. He knows instinctively what to do in any emergency."

Obviously, nobody is born with a literal "instinct" for flying a jet plane. It is an operation about as far removed from the natural, primitive condition of man as we can imagine. It calls for acquiring a whole pattern of behavior outside any for which nature has developed us. It means adaptation to a complicated mechanism with which a pilot must identify himself as completely as his own life is involved in its survival.

The astonishing thing is that our human faculties are so varied and resourceful that a man can do all that flying a jet plane demands, and get to the point of doing almost automatically everything needed to handle it. It becomes an extension of himself and his will. He can time it so that it is exactly where he wants it at the moment when another plane, traveling with equal speed, comes into his range for the split second when he blasts it.

Faculties which one man can train as precisely as this for his purpose another can sharpen just as skillfully for his. The salesman who takes the disciplines of timing as seriously as the jet-plane pilot does will hit his mark with equal assurance.

"Timing" and "the psychological moment" are crucial in salesmanship, but they are not the result of some sort of magic, nor of lucky endowment. They are skills acquired by self-development. Expertness in them comes only to the man who mingles with people, keeps his faculties continually on the alert, and enters into communication with others through understanding. The only way to acquire this extra equipment of the craft is through active practice of the craft itself.

No man ever learned timing from watching the clock.

PART III

KNOW WORDS AND
HOW TO USE THEM

Chapter 19

Words Are a Salesman's Tools

Words are the wings of ideas, which fly or fall by them.

Coming back to our original picture of a typical sale, we may now say that we have taken a good look at the salesman and his client. They are two men set to see whether they can so understand each other that they can arrive at a meeting of minds. The means they have to use is words. Whatever ultimate agreement they achieve will have to be defined in words. Words are the tools with which the mind shapes ideas, and they are the wings on which ideas fly.

A good workman keeps his tools keen. As a craftsman, he knows that he will not be able to add the extra touch to his creation unless his steel has a fine cutting edge. As a human being, he knows that he will not enjoy his work unless he can concentrate on it without having to distract his mind, worrying about, and fixing up, flaws and breakdowns in his working equipment.

The tools of a professional workman are both his pride and his joy: pride, because fine tools mean fine workmanship; joy, because good tools add pleasure to work. When you see a carpenter sharpening, polishing, and oiling his kit at the end of the day, you know not only that he is an expert craftsman, but also that he is looking forward proudly and happily to his next day's work. You have only to look into any man's tool bag to know whether he is a craftsman or a hack.

The salesman finds in words the same kind of pride and joy that a worker finds in tools. They enable him to say exactly what he wants them to say. Command of them gives to what he says the same authority which a sharp edge on his knife gives to the butcher cutting up a steer.

I cannot overemphasize the usefulness of words to a man who makes sales. They are the fuel and lubrication of salesmanship as gasoline and oil are fuel and lubrication to a car. A salesman with a day on the road ahead of him fills his tank and has his oil checked. If he is as smart about himself as he is about his car, he will make just as sure that his mind is as regularly fueled and lubricated as his engine.

Words are the *lubrication* of the mind because it cannot run any more smoothly within itself than its command of words allows. A man's thinking is exact only to the degree that he has words to make it so. We can think in nothing but words. When our words run out, we come to the end of our thinking; all we can do is to repeat ourselves. The more words we know, and the more explicitly we differentiate between them, the more exactly we can tell ourselves what we are selling, the more we can save ourselves from confusion.

Confusion can sometimes be not only frustrating but also embarrassing. For instance, a salesman who is not sure of the distinction between "adulteration" and "adultery" is open to serious misinterpretations. In only a lesser degree, the same sort of pitfall yawns at the feet of one who cannot distinguish between "courtesy" and "curtsy," "costume" and "custom," "dam" and "dame," "coffer" and "coffin," "assay" and "essay," and "tack" and "tact." A confused vocabulary can mean a very confused man rattling around. One way to get the rattle out of your selling is to lubricate your thinking with knowledge of the words you must use.

Words are the *fuel* of the mind because it cannot run any farther than they can carry it. You may think your product is "wonderful," but your sales interview will come to an abrupt end if all you have to say to your prospect is, "It is wonderful." I was once with a man for an evening who thought everything we saw was "crazy," which, to him, was a word meaning delightful, happy, fortunate, magnificent, tasty, admirable, and enchanting. No matter what we saw, heard, or tasted, if it pleased him, he said: "Man, that's crazy!" By the end of the evening I thought I was crazy, but not at all in the sense in which he used the word.

His limited vocabulary prevented him from discriminating among the varieties of pleasure he received from a good meal, followed by the theater, followed by a midnight show. It also limited the communication between him and me, so that, by the time the evening was half gone, it stopped altogether, although his voice went on and on. This same termination of communication will be the fate of the salesman who has not taken pains to build a reservoir of words to keep his mind in fuel.

All of us are likely to grow lazy about our speech, and to fall into ruts of expression. I should like to suggest two practices which will help develop the habit of using fresh words.

1. When you come across a word new to you, use it three times as quickly and naturally as you can. Let your ears hear you say it, and it will become a tool at your service. There is no need to be self-conscious about this. You can do it without putting on airs, or hint of being pedantic.

Do not fall into the popular fashion of apologizing about being articulate. Lazy people are prone to make vulgar sport of those who take pains to use the language well. Sometimes their coarseness may tempt a sensitive person to be apologetic about his unusual cultivation of words. If you have ever felt this, let me tell you this. In all my experience I have never known a man who started with the handicap of poor education and rose to high position who did not work just as hard to enlarge his vocabulary, correct his pronunciation, and improve his grammar as he worked at his own job. Indeed, every one of them considered this a part of his job, for all were aware that they must learn to take their places easily and comfortably among those into whose company their new eminence brought them.

Go into training from the beginning to be a pre-eminent person. Do not be afraid to be different where your difference will carry distinction. Good spech adds distinction to anybody.

You will never alienate a customer by talking to him intelligently. I mean "intelligently." This means that you will not parade polysyllables, or indulge in showy mannerisms. Avoiding such foolishness, you need never fear that your customer will not respond to the flattery of being addressed in good English which conveys exactly what you mean. You do not have to play down your own intelligence, nor do you have to underestimate his, to create a good impression.

"The good old English tongue" is probably as rich a language as men have ever had at their service. It is a heritage to enjoy and use. It is a living language full of new delights. It is still growing. In our own country, it is taking on new coloring and music from our American ways and echoes. To revel in it, discover its surprises, and handle it expertly is a privilege given to every salesman by the nature of his work.

2. When an idea comes to you, call up various ways in which you can express it. Everyone has the power to do this in some degree. Everyone can increase this power by exercise.

Let me give you a famous example, all the more valuable, I think, because it shows how one of the greatest of all poets was not above searching for the best way to express an idea. One evening, Keats was sitting writing in the same room with his friend, Leigh Hunt, who was reading. At one point, Keats looked up, and said, "Hunt, what do you think of this?" 'A beautiful thing is an unending joy.' " "Good," said Hunt, "but not quite perfect." There was silence for a while. Then Keats spoke again. "What about this? 'A thing of beauty is an unending joy.' " "Better," said his friend, "but still not quite it." Again there was silence, until Keats spoke again. "Now, what do you think of this? 'A thing of beauty is a joy forever.' " "That will live as long as the English language is spoken," said Hunt.

Now, look at that "perfect" line. It contains only two words of more than one syllable, and these, words of such simplicity that a child might use them. Of the three ways in which the poet expressed his idea, the best was the simplest. I want to emphasize this. There is a kind of man who thinks he must show his mastery of English by use of obscure words. This is not mastery but egotism. When a man knows English well enough, and works over it hard enough, the proof of his mastery lies partly in the directness and clarity of his expressions. Only those who truly know words can be sure of speaking simply.

Practice the habit of saying the same thing in different ways, and then choose that way which is best fitted to the occasion on which you have to use it. To a golfer you may want to state your proposition as offering "a good approach," to a yachtsman as "taking the right tack," to a chess player as "an irreproachable gambit," and to a gambler as "a sure bet." Design the cut of your words to the form of the minds you want to suit.

The more ways you can state your idea to yourself, the more resources you will have to draw upon when you are presenting it to somebody else. You will not repeat yourself. You will be like a diamond merchant, turning your idea over and over as he turns a stone, revealing its many facets catching and flashing light.

"His words, like so many nimble and airy servitors, trip about him at command," wrote Milton. It is a good description of a trained salesman, provided—and this is crucial—we put an emphasis on the word "command." To marshal words, to add reserves to them constantly, to be able to call from among them those best suited to particular missions, and to have all under such control that none ever run loose—this is the way of a successful salesman with his words. His vocabulary is an army, regimented and equipped to march at his will.

Such a force at one's back cannot be enlisted or trained without planning and discipline. Let us now take a look at four elements of progress toward command of words.

1

Words, like dogs, are faithful friends and good companions to those who treat them lovingly.

Words can be fun. Language was made to be enjoyed. The power and pleasure of knowing and using words are unlimited. They may be enjoyed by everybody. Words are not sycophants of the rich; the poor man may possess and take pleasure in them. They are not a privilege of the educated; the humblest may claim them all for his birthright. They are not perishable like last year's car model; they are always up-to-date and shiny for those who care for them.

Every trade and profession conducts its work with words. The salesman moving, as he does, among all kinds of people will have one thing in common with all—his words. He will get out of himself and them all the more for every extra word they share.

A smart salesman will be "word-minded." These are days when everybody is asking us to be something-or-other-minded— "air-minded," "atom-minded," "globe-minded," and the like. I suggest that, in addition to these other "mindeds," we be "word-minded." Before we die, the airplane as we know it may be as outdated as a horse-drawn Central Park cab. The atom may do a lot of strange and terrible things. But one fact we may be sure of: words will still matter. Whatever the world of tomorrow may be like, our capacity for thought and speech will be the only quality that will keep us out of the zoo.

Men live. Words live with them. Words have a life of their own. Every word has its own history. Every word is affected by the company it keeps. The man in whom this life of words comes to living understanding will be himself enlivened by it.

I have seen one word bring forty thousand people to their feet with a howl which sounded as though it came from one throat. It was spoken by an umpire at the Yankee Stadium, and it was "Strike!" Two men on base, the ninth inning of a world series game, the team at bat one run behind—that one word meant the pennant.

We cannot hope to make every word we say as dramatic as that, but we can give every word we say an extra brightness if we know the life in it. We have, for example, in our language two words which are first cousins, both deriving from the same Greek grandfather. For many years they were spelled "rime" and "rhythm." They spent so much time in each other's company that gradually the less fancy one began to take on the airs of the other, and now we spell it "rhyme." It has every right to this more splendid dress, and I, for one, get a little added pleasure out of it because it would not stand for being always the drabber relative.

Our familiar friend "apple" started out as "napple," but spent so much time in company with the indefinite article "a," that it found the only way it could live comfortably was to yield its "n" to its little friend, and so "a napple" became "an apple," to everybody's satisfaction. "An ewt" reversed the process, and became "a newt." Words have their biographies.

You may think we are not going to have much to do with apples and newts, so let me give you an illustration which will sooner or later surely come your way. It is the " 'm" in "Yes'm." This has an impressive, almost imperial pedigree; none on Beacon Hill can match it. It began as "mea domina" in the days of the grandeur that was Rome. In various places and various times it passed through "madonna," "madame," and "ma'am," to "'m." I trust you will approach the lady a little more gallantly for knowing her noble blood.

When I hear somebody say something about the TV, as he calls it, I wonder whether he knows that he is speaking Greek and Latin. "Tele" is Greek, and "vision" Latin. I know at least one man who can get into a fine frenzy over this word because he fumes that we have no right to mingle Greek and Latin in this "mongrel" way. I cannot get as excited as he does about it, but I must say that the word comes to life for him, and has an extra life for me because of him.

Unfortunately, most of us get our introduction to words in the drab process of learning the formal rules of grammar, a process guaranteed to reduce every syllable to a dry bone. But this need not permanently impair us. Part of the fun of growing up is unlearning much of what we learned in school. No inconsiderable part of that is to rediscover words as living things. It is something like finding out for ourselves that a Rockette is more than an automaton in a precision dance. The beginning of wisdom with words is to love them.

2

Words, like piano keys, are mastered by practice.

I know of no greater fallacy than the common belief that all a man has to do is to open his mouth, as he turns on a water tap, and the right words will flow in a smooth stream. Words are more like rocks than water. They have to be shaped and polished and fitted before they will combine to make a foolproof, weatherproof design. Just the other day, I read this sentence: "Miss America read the Declaration while Governor Leader made the oration." All I can say is that the audience must have been very confused. And no less a paper than the careful *New York Times* presented this startling item: "Gov. Robert E. Meyner will start the $750,000 campaign with a dinner speech Tuesday evening. It will run one month." A bit long, I should think, for even so admirable a public servant.

These illustrations show how careless use of words can confuse. It can go further. It can leave an impression exactly the opposite of what the speaker wanted to convey. For example, I once heard a Senator say: "This bill is sound, if limited." He did not at all mean to say that *if* the bill was limited, it was sound. He meant the exact opposite, that the bill was sound although it was limited. Thus a man famed for his use of words fell carelessly into saying what he did not at all mean. We all do it. But we can all be better off for being on our guard against it.

Words have a mischievous way of playing tricks on us if we do not watch them. One of my favorite men, a sports writer, once said in his column: "The horse was literally melting like butter." If it had been, he would undoubtedly have had the most sensational news item of the day. He fell victim to that gremlin of a word "literally." It is a good word to use sparingly because usually it does not mean "literally" at all, but something far short of it. When a friend tells me he is "literally dead" on his feet, I make no preparations to attend his funeral.

"Practically" is another imp among words. As commonly used, it means "not practically." When one of my archer friends from Westchester tells me that he "practically" hit the bull's-eye, I know he missed it.

I do not want to be pedantic about this. In ordinary conversation such uses of words are acceptable and not dangerous. They are likely to get us into trouble, however, in a business transaction where exact understanding is essential. Again and again, I have seen sales fouled by a salesman's inexact or ambiguous use of words which left his client thinking he had said what he had no intention of saying. In one instance, this kind of misunderstanding went so far that the client accused the salesman of out-and-out bad faith. It was nothing of the kind. The salesman was guilty of bad English.

The ideal to set up for the use of words is this: make them say what you want them to say as briefly as you can to get the full effect you intend.

Lincoln's Gettysburg address contains 266 words. Short as it is, it could have been shorter without losing any of its *literal* content. "Four score and seven," for example, is literally "eighty-seven." Lincoln, however, was looking beyond a literal effect to a *literary* one. He was in the position of the President of the nation speaking in a ceremonial capacity on one of the battlefields of a war in which it was engaged. His genius rose to the representative character of the hour with a phrasing which echoed the stately measures of ritual; and the vocabulary he used was rich with overtones of religious memory—"conceived," "dedicated," "consecrate," and "hallow." The effect is that of a recurring theme in a great symphony, a solemn bell echoing through a chorus. Yet, in the end, the speech falls to a conclusion of simple, homely words of plain American speech, "and that government of the people, by the people, for the people, shall not perish from the earth."

Compare with this another report of his words. When he was asked in the summer of 1864 whether he could not go away for a rest, he replied to the friend who had put the question: "I cannot fly from my thoughts—my solicitude for this great country follows me wherever I go. I do not think it is personal vanity or ambition, though I am not free from these infirmities, but I cannot but feel that the weal or woe of this great nation will be decided in November." Here, in what was a casual conversation, we hear the same accent and rhythm of speech as at Gettysburg. The words are Lincoln's without a doubt. But they are less formal. They express a different occasion. They do, however, say just as precisely what he had to say, and they said it to produce the effect he humbly and sincerely wanted them to carry.

Both statements are brief, but not too brief. Effect was not sacrificed to brevity. Both brevity and effect were served.

The man who lives with words as Lincoln did, loving them and mastering them, will come in his own measure to an expertness with them, enabling him to make them say just what he expects of them on all occasions.

3

Words are fuses of the emotions.

I remember from my childhood a story of an old lady who said: "Every time our dear pastor says 'Mesopotamia' I got a blessing in my heart." Don't laugh at the good soul too heartily. We all have words in our experience which act like triggers for our emotions. Your word may not be Mesopotamia, but there is some word which ignites your feelings like a fuse.

France was turned upside down by people who were swept as a prairie is by a fire when they shouted, "Liberty, Equality, Fraternity." The Jewish people have performed the historical marvel of survival in an inhospitable world because they have rallied around the symbolic word, Jerusalem. Most religions, and all nationalisms, rally to fiery names and words, which are to them more than armor and sword. In our own country, the most listless of generations can be awakened by appeal to Washington and Lincoln.

> I know a land that is sunk in shame
> Of hearts that faint and tire.
> I know a Name, a Name, a Name,
> Shall set that land on fire.

The wise salesman keeps himself alert to the incendiary power of words, and does not hesitate to use one which will ignite his client's enthusiasm.

He will remind himself, however, that fuses sometimes blow out, and words do not keep forever their same power over the moods of men. Like coins, they wear smooth, and, if kept in currency too long, lose their patterns. As the mint calls back the tired coin to replace it with a new one, so the salesman will be careful to renew the currency of his speech when words and phrases become so trite they lose their moving power. His words must be sharp with reactions of pleasure and pain, desire and aversion, surprise, hope, and fear. They can piece the head with power to reach the heart only as long as they are fresh.

I remember a spring day on Sixth Avenue. As I walked along, I passed a blind man with a cup, whose sign read, "Help the Blind." He collected a few pennies from the passers-by. As I continued my walk, I came to the corner of Sixth Avenue and Central Park South, across the street from where the trees in the Park were bright with the first, fresh green of spring. On this corner stood another blind man with a cup, but his sign read: "It is May—And I Am Blind." The words were like a stab at the heart, and dropping silver in his cup was an offering of thanksgiving.

On another day I was walking on Eighth Avenue. I saw a crowd at the window of a pet shop which I passed regularly on my way to work. I wondered what attracted them. When I reached the shop, I saw that it was having a special sale of birdhouses. But the lure was not the little houses. It was what the proprietor had put on his sign over them: 'A House to Let—For a Song."

All of us enjoy felicitous combinations of words like these. And the salesman who loves words and works with them can have the added pleasure of sometimes finding for himself the happy phrase. But, remember, the aim of the phrase is to get a favorable reaction from the customer, not to advertise the wit of the salesman. Few things can alienate more people than cleverness for its own sake.

The young doctor who had a sign in his office, "Small fevers gratefully received," was undoubtedly a bright lad, but he knew little of psychology. No fever is a joke to the man who has it. And the hint that a doctor is willing to make a little money out of it is bad taste in the extreme.

On the other hand, the sign in a sports equipment window, "Fishing Tickle," is not obnoxious. It is just plain silly. It advertises nothing except the inability of the owner to do what he hoped to do.

It takes a lot more thought to find a combination of words which strike a human and humorous note than to find a superficially clever one, but the warm word will attract where the glittering one will alienate. The man who wants to succeed with his fellow men will be on guard within himself against mere verbal play. He will begin humanizing his speech by humanizing his thoughts. As he guards the sources, the stream of his speech will flow untainted. He will not need a book to tell him that words are more effective when they glow than when they glitter.

There are salesmen who try to make their speech glitter with profanity. I have only one word to say about swearing—"Don't."

Swearing is a confession of bankruptcy in words. It is the substitution of the counterfeit for the sterling. Its effect is synthetic like that induced by drugs. It is a habit which deceives the swearer into the illusion that he is a he-man, yet leaves his listener indifferent, or repelled.

You will occasionally run into a client who revels in his own profanity, and who may find a kindred delight in your indulgence in it. But he is the exception. Most of your business will be done with people of another kind. Your profanity will not impress them. Many of them it will disgust. The best safeguard is never to swear, and then you will not have to regret having sworn in the wrong place before the wrong man.

Profanity cannot possibly add emphasis to a persuasive presentation. Stick to plain and honest words. They will never hurt your reputation with anybody.

They will also save you from falling into the practice of using the kind of stiff and glacial vocabulary which has a semi-professional sound, but no more power to touch the feelings of your client than a speech in Choctaw. "I have particularized the details to graph how we can service you." Not even Winston Churchill could say that with enough flourish to get an emotional response. It is bad English, bad thinking, and bad salesmanship.

I read a letter the other day which closed: "We shall make an inspection next Tuesday, which we trust will be convenient, after which our quotation will at once issue." I think I know what the writer meant, but I am confident that IBM or Remington Rand could put out a machine tomorrow capable of saying it better, and with more human warmth in it.

I should have to write another book to do full justice to this enticing subject of words and their warmth, but let me give a few illustrations. "Room" is more hospitable than "accommodations," "meal" than "collation," "food" than "comestibles," "drink" than "imbibe," and "eat" than "partake." "Pay" gets a more straightforward response than "emoluments," "gift" than "donation," "try" than "endeavor," "brave" than "valiant," and "show" than "evince."

This does not mean that one word is always preferable to another. What it does mean is that everything has its "dominant name," the controlling name, so to speak. "Buy," for example, is the dominant name for what it means, and when we say "purchase," we are only translating "buy" into another word. "Say" is dominant, "remark" is its translation. What Johnny steals from a jar is "jam," and "preserve" only when we don't choose to call it jam. When Father is at home, he says, "Mary, please shut the window," but on a bus or a train, he says, "Do you mind if I close the window?" He is a little more formal, and trots out a translation.

As a general rule, the dominant is the best word to use. Not always (invariably). But when you substitute a translation for it, you should know why. You may want a more careful shade of meaning. You may use it for special effect. You may want to avoid repetition of the same word. Your reason may be perfectly good. But bear in mind that you will be better served usually by the dominant, the simpler and more accustomed word.

Speak with clarity. Say what you have to say in words least likely to be misunderstood. But avoid dullness. Make your speech lively enough to ignite bright attention.

4

"Words are the dress of thoughts, which should no more be presented in rags, tatters, and dirt than your own person should."

These words of Lord Chesterfield to his son are good for framing on any salesman's desk. Sloppy speech is as inexcusable as sloppy dress. True, there are more ways than one of saying almost anything, but there is never more than one most effective way.

Suppose we play a little game. Here are three typical illustrations of saying the same thing in different ways. You choose the better in each case.

1. We note that you will let us have the necessary estimate in due course, and shall be obliged if you are able to arrange for same to be delivered as soon as possible.

Thank you. We hope that you will let us have the estimate as soon as possible.

2. Thank you for your letter of August 2nd. I am looking into the matter, and will write you again as soon as I can.

Referring to your letter of 2nd inst., I am giving the matter immediate attention and will communicate with you further as soon as possible.

3. The contents of your memo—A34-10-941—under date 13th ultimo have been communicated through the medium of our New Haven office to Messrs. Slocum, who now write us as per enclosed copy of their letter.

Our New Haven office sent a copy of your letter of November 10 to Messrs. Slocum. We enclose a copy of their reply.

A. P. Herbert, English writer and publicist, made a list some years ago of business terms which make communications untidy. Here are a few of them:

"We thank you" is written	"We beg to acknowledge."
"Write"	"Communicate."
"Inquire"	"Make the necessary inquiries."
"Tell" or "inform"	"Advise."
"We shall try"	"It will be our endeavor."
"Some" or "much"	"A substantial percentage."
"Give details"	"Furnish particulars."
"You cutthroats"	"Your good selves."

I would add a postscript to Lord Chesterfield's advice. Don't deck your speech in laces and frills any more than you would your costume. "Stylish" words are no help to a good style in writing or speaking. They have their places, but the homely, plain, natural words are the hardy ones that get the work of the world done.

The salesman who prefers the stylish word to the working one for no reason except that it is stylish will end by becoming pretentious, stuffy, and incongruous. In short, he will be a bore —even though he describes himself in his own curious way as "an exact manipulator of the forms of English speech to achieve maximum values of articulation."

"Let thy speech be short, comprehending much in few words." Make your prologue always shorter than your story. When the story is done, end it. Never thunder in the appendix.

Chapter 20

Building a Treasury of Words

Words met for the first time are like unopened letters—their value known only to those who get inside them.

When your Uncle Henry comes to visit you, and your conversation runs to automobiles, the radio, jet planes, atomic weapons, and nuclear discoveries, you exchange words and ideas all but unknown to the American of 1900. If your grandfather and his Uncle Henry should be suddenly dropped at your side, these venerable gentlemen would think you were talking something alarmingly like gibberish. Our new century has given all of us a new vocabulary.

We may go further. Since the first atomic bomb was dropped on Hiroshima on August 6, 1945, every one of us has added virtually a new language to the one he already knew. We now use such words as "radioactive," "fission," "contaminated areas," "fall-out," "nuclear," and "reactor" as though we had always known them. New words are continually entering the language; new twists are being given to old words.

Language is a living thing. This is all the more evident when we take note of the fact that when we need a new word we go back to the Greek and Latin languages to find it. Our "live" modern forms come from the "dead" languages. Which simply means that no language is ever truly dead.

"Language," said Emerson, "is never stationary. New words are constantly being formed; living words are constantly changing their meaning, expanding, contracting, gaining or losing caste, taking on moral or spiritual significance, and old words, though long sanctioned by custom, sometimes wither and die."

This process, operating at all times, has been speeded in ours. We are forced to learn new words. The question we have to decide is: shall we learn our new vocabulary in a haphazard way, or consciously build it systematically?

The Anglo-Saxons called a man's vocabulary his "word-hoard." I strongly recommend that we adopt this idea of our vocabulary being a treasury, and plan the accumulation of its wealth. Here are a few suggestions on how to go about it.

1

An unfamiliar word is like a new dish—not to be spurned until tasted.

A good dictionary is a salesman's friend. Its stories are a little brief and lacking in plot and characterization, but to the point. When a bright salesman comes across a word he does not know, he looks it up.

Once you get the habit of doing this you will need no urging to continue it. It becomes a game you play against yourself mentally with as much fascination as you play golf against yourself physically. You get so you want to improve your score, and find yourself moving into ever-widening fields of interest. You become a broader person. You enlarge your capacity to meet other people confidently.

The man with a large treasury of words will not use all of them in his selling, but every word he does use will carry an extra punch because of the reserves behind it. They will be weighted with the subtle impression of authority. The individuality which a customer finds in a salesman does not come only from hearing him say "I." It comes from a tone, an attitude, and a point of view. What registers is a salesman saying things in such a way that he himself is recognized as a force in saying them.

Just as soon as a man begins talking to us we know whether he is speaking from shallowness or from depth, just as we know whether a man is experienced with tools the minute he puts saw to wood. The workman carries his own credentials in his manner of handling his tools. Every word we speak registers the word-power behind it.

The rule for every man seeking to know words is not to depend on the training other men prepare for him, but to find his own words for himself. These are the ones in which he will express himself as he is. New words becoming every day a part of a salesman are like the daily accumulations of a rich soil. Slowly, word by word, they unite to become a depth of wise experience which enlarges all the expressions rooted in it. The salesman who speaks from this depth will have little trouble making his customer see what he is presenting if the thing itself has life for him, and he describes it as he sees it.

1. Hunting out words can be a fascinating game as we get the habit of it. There are two kinds of pleasure for ourselves in this sport.

One is getting behind the public masquerade of a word to uncover the word itself, to see what are its true face and family connections. What do you see when you come upon the word "mountebank," for instance? It literally means "one who mounts on a bench," a soapbox orator, as we would say. I have said elsewhere that a salesman must have enthusiasm. What does this word mean? Literally, it means the quality of one "possessed by a god," "en" being our old friend "in," and "thu," the Greek root for *god* with which we are familiar in the word "theology." An enthusiastic man is an inspired man, one with a flaming spirit in him.

Perhaps you ride in taxicabs, "hacks." Here is a word that comes from Hackney in England, where somebody thought up the idea of hiring out broken-spirited horses, to be ridden by people who could not handle high-spirited ones, or, to be hitched to public carriages. "Hackney" was shortened to "hack," and this became the name of both the drudge of a horse and the carriage which he pulled. When the horse disappeared, the name stuck to the carriage's successor. It also survived as a name for any kind of drudge, working with broken spirit at his labors.

"Hack" drivers sometimes "haggle." This word comes from another kind of "hack," the one we use when we talk about hacking wood. It was an old Anglo-Saxon word meaning to cut roughly with strokes of a cutting instrument. When it reached Scotland, it ran into the guttural habits of that great people, and was pronounced "hag," from which, in a way that will not seem strange to those who know the Scots, it passed over into a description of a man hammering out a bargain.

Little dramas of words, like these, can be found on every page of a dictionary. You may not have realized how one word's fortunes can carry it to altogether different extremes of meaning. The Latin word for hut was "taberna." It survives among us in both "tavern" and "tabernacle," those two perpetual contestants in the struggle of the flesh and the spirit. "Ghost" and "guest" are the same word in slightly different costume; they both mean a visitor, but strike us variously because the visitors come from different starting-places. I could fill a book—other men have filled books—with such illustrations, but these are enough to give a taste of how studying words turns out not to be a drudgery but a delight.

The second pleasure a man can get from knowing words is that, when he knows them well enough, he can take liberties with them. Woodrow Wilson used to say that no man is master of any subject who cannot take liberties with it. I do not recommend wordplay in a sales talk, but I certainly do recommend it as an exercise to keep the mind alert. It is good mental calisthenics. Just as you do not go through your morning exercises in the public view, so you play your word games privately. And, just as keeping yourself fit physically sometimes pays off publicly, so keeping your mind agile may prove profitable in the right spot.

Wit does not make a subject light, but it sometimes flashes light on a subject. Two bakers in a community once got into hot competition. One of them hired a stunt pilot to put on an airplane exhibition at the local fairground, and had signs all over the place, "This Daredevil Eats Our Bread." As the people left the show, they were greeted by his competitor's signs: "You Don't Have to Be a Daredevil to Eat Our Bread."

A friend of mine was once told by a client's secretary: "I'm sorry, but Mr. Eagle cannot see you. He has a strained back." "That's all right," my friend answered. "Just tell him I don't want to wrestle with him. I only want to talk to him."

Nobody comes up with the right word for the special moment who is not in practice, any more than a swordsman flashes the telling thrust who does not practice fencing. Accumulate words. Have fun with them. The more of them you are familiar with, the more they will dance at your bidding when you call the tunes.

2. Increasing a vocabulary does not stop at providing counters for a game out of which we can ourselves get pleasure. It also fits us to talk in their own languages to our varied customers.

Anything that interests any kind of man may turn up some time as grist for a salesman's mill. Yes, it may be "corn." One man's "corn" is another man's staff of life. Beware of the kind of snobbery which dismisses anybody else's interests as being below you.

Because you are a resident of the city, do not get the idea that everything in the country is "hayseed." Because you live with the natural rhythm and simplicities of the country, do not tag everything in the city as contemptible and evil. Wherever people are, human interests flourish. The more of these interests you know and share, the more kinds of people you will be able to meet and converse with cordially. A rich vocabulary is a universal introduction.

More than once I have found myself talking to a president of a great corporation in a skyscraper office when the conversation has taken a shift to terms used on the farm. I have had to talk to him in agricultural similes. Why? Because he was born on a farm. He thought in farm terms. I would have been awkward and at a loss at such times if I did not know the difference between "fallow" and fertile."

We "tune in" on the other fellow's wave length when we can express ourselves in words native to his own particular way of thinking. When you come upon an unfamiliar word, and are tempted to skip it because you cannot see when it will be useful to you, remind yourself that the next day you may run into a customer who uses it. You may even have to help a customer with a crossword puzzle, as I have done more than once to get an interview off to a good start.

I remember a day at a cattle ranch. The owner's youngest son was assigned to show me over the place. Unfortunately, he was the strong, silent type. I had to keep the conversation going, to the accompaniment of his laconic "Yeh's" and "No's." I was glad I knew the difference between a Jersey and a Hereford, a Brahman and a water buffalo. I dug down into my memory for every cattle word I had ever heard to support that hour and a half. I certainly gave no evidence of being a cattle expert, but my vocabulary saved me from seeming like a complete ignoramus to a man whose cattle was his life.

On another occasion I was riding in his car with a client, when, out of the blue sky, he said: "What is the plural of the word 'opus'?" When I gave him the right answer, "opera," he was immensely pleased with me. Apparently, this was a sort of intelligence test he used privately. Men's tastes in words differ as much as their tastes in drink.

Never pass a word by. Pick it up. You never can tell when it will be just the right word to unlock another fellow's approval. Turn unfamiliar words from hurdles into stepping stones by incorporating them into your vocabulary.

2

Style in the use of words is like the handle of a tool—fashioned to assure ease, balance, and effectiveness in action.

A second good habit with words is this: When you are struck especially favorably or unfavorably by anything you hear or read, ask yourself why this particular combination of words affected you the way it did.

I will illustrate what I mean by two examples, which are poles apart, but both of which affected me favorably.

In the window of an apartment on Charlton Street in Greenwich Village this sign appeared one day:

"The apartment I live in is a lemon. All my guests bring shoehorns with them for the tight squeeze, spiked shoes for balance, ear plugs for jam sessions, steel helmets for falling stars, and, after 11 P.M. earmuffs and hot-water bags."

That has style. Every word is concrete. Every phrase is a picture. It is like a tour of the apartment. It presents both its size and its shivers. Moreover, it leaves us with an unmistakable portrait of the tenant. Whoever he was, once in his life he found words to make both facts and himself come to life.

My second example is more classical.

"There is but one healing, catholic principle of toleration which ought to find favor in this house. It is wanted not only in our colonies, but here. The thirsty earth of our own country is gasping and gaping and crying out for that healing shower from heaven. The noble lord has told you of the right of those people by treaty; but I consider the right of conquest so little, and the right of human nature so much, that the former has little consideration with me. I look upon the people of Canada as coming by the dispensation of God under the British government. I would have us govern it in the same manner as the all-wise dispensation of Providence would govern it. We know He suffers the sun to shine upon the righteous and the unrighteous; and we ought to suffer all classes to enjoy equally the right of worshipping God according to the light He has been pleased to give them."

These words were spoken by Edmund Burke. They have style. They match perfectly the weight and generosity of the sentiment he was expressing. They could have been spoken with equal truth in any age. They stand alone, needing nothing before nor after them. I should count strangely insensitive any man who can read them without a quickening of his pulse.

A salesman, or anybody else who uses words, can better afford to ponder how Burke got this effect than to read a dozen jog-trotting manuals of rhetoric. This is not to say that any salesman would be fool enough to address a customer as Burke spoke to a parliament. What I am saying is that the man who knows what effect words can have, and how the masters of words have gained their effects, will be the one who shapes his own words to procure the effects he wants.

You will also come sometimes upon combinations of words which produce the opposite effect of those I have just quoted—a disgust and rejection. They too are worth examining. They can uncover dangers which you can avoid.

In a book on public speaking I found this sentence: "You have to have appeal as well as power in your voice. You've got to convince the hogs you have something for them." I put that book aside at once. This man had nothing to teach me, except what I should avoid. Both his approach and his taste were offensive. No man will ever be a first-class salesman who allows himself in his own mind to think of other people as hogs. He degrades himself, not them, by thinking of himself as a dispenser of swill.

Whenever you are conscious of an unusually vivid reaction, favorable or unfavorable, to any sentence or phrase, take a second look at it. What has proved an effective handle to an idea for somebody else may fit your hand also. What makes another man bungle may prove equally unfortunate for you.

My own pondering of effective words has brought me to one general conclusion. Words are made primarily to be spoken. I have never known a memorable phrase which could not be comfortably spoken aloud. I suppose poetry is what it is because poems are made to be recited, but I leave that to others to discuss. My own experience is in selling, and here I say confidently that my best results come when, in letters and presentations, I stick to words that can be spoken aloud. Sometimes, for technical reasons, I may have to introduce a jawbreaker, but I allow this only as an exception. A letter or presentation is not a problem in algebra to be written in special symbols, or a doctor's prescription calling for Latin, or a secret code demanding cabalistic signs. It is all the better for "sounding" well.

3

Words, like men, wear business clothes to work.

When Jacqueline Cochran was asked about her daily schedule, she began her answer: "I usually get up about 8, and read the mail and newspapers—especially the advertisements. Did you know the ads are the best part of the papers? I go through them thoroughly in order to get ideas." I recommend to every young salesman that he take a leaf out of Miss Cochran's book.

Read advertisements and business communications with the definite aim of getting the "business feel" of words. The market place has its own vernacular as truly as the drawing room or the schools. You will be understood by businessmen if you use words in the way they understand them.

I have already warned you against parroting some of the needlessly formal expressions which have become trite and over-formal. There is, however, a lively kind of business speech which is stimulating and provocative. The alert salesman can pep up his own work by using it.

Every newspaper brings a course in living words to every salesman with an eye for it. Here are advertisements which are the products of the most expert copywriters on earth. They are packed with helps for salesmen.

I make a habit of tearing from my newspaper every morning every advertisement and every statement which catches my eye. I put them in my pocket. At various times during the day, when I have the opportunity, I look at them again. The ones that ring a bell a second time I work over in my mind. I may think of some place where I can use them as they are. I may rephrase them for my own use. In some way I see to it that they serve as "fiery sparks" to my own thinking. Nobody's mind can strike fire on itself all the time. As fire is kindled by fire, so one sales-man's mind can be kindled by contact with others.

When I hit upon some catchy saying or picturesque device for advertising my own business, I send it, not only to my cus-tomers, but also to certain other people whom I know to be especially interested in such things. These people, in turn, send me what they develop along the same line. In this way I keep a swirl of novel ideas circulating around me. I am constantly in-fluenced and stimulated by the most active people in this field. My vocabulary and expression are kept alive and up-to-date.

Current advertising is to me one of the most fascinating activities in the world. Such men as my friend Milton Biow seem to me to be as full of inventive genius as the Fords and Edisons.

They have invented the modern American market. They have found a power in words to move men as surely as the internal combustion engine and electricity move machines. Without them, our magnificent advances in production would have given us goods without any place to go. They have stimulated the demand which has absorbed the supply. They are still doing it.

They do it with words. The words they use are the ones we all know. The difference is in the way they use them. Every day, in newspapers and magazines, and on the air, they give us demonstrations of how they do it. At no cost, we can see them at work and learn from them. Every smart salesman will take time every day to pick up some lesson from their work.

One thing you will learn quickly. Carefully chosen words can have more power than a thousand admirable performances of which nobody ever hears. Give a dog a bad name, and he will be always remembered by it, no matter how many women and children he saves from drowning on the quiet. The only historic act I ever heard ascribed to geese was when their honking saved Rome, but I have never heard one of them described as anything but a "silly" goose. I believe that there are learned men with stacks of proof that donkeys have more native intelligence than horses. They might as well retire gracefully. We insist on talking about a "stupid" donkey and "horse sense."

Milk—and I speak with the utmost respect of this beverage, which is a favorite of mine—is, from all I read, more dangerous than alcohol. It has to be pasteurized, boiled, graded, and I know not what, to prevent it from spreading tuberculosis and undulant fever. I never heard of anybody getting tuberculosis from champagne, or feeling that he had to pasteurize wines. Indeed, my information is that germs which thrive in milk wither in alcohol. I do not have the figures—but I would "venture a guess without fear of successful contradiction," as the politicians say, that deaths from alcoholism are a very small percentage of those resulting from diseases carried by milk.

I do not have to labor the point. Milk is fed to babies while wine, champagne and beer are forbidden in some states to men. Why? Among other things, because when a man sells milk we say he sells milk, not "bacteria-carrying liquid," but when a man sells beer or wine we say he sells "intoxicating liquors." The man who sells milk is called a milkman, but the man who sells champagne is in "the liquor traffic," an ominous phrase carrying overtones of such sinister things as the white slave traffic, opium traffic, traffic in currencies. "Traffic" has a bad name. The cow has had good publicity; the grape has had bad.

This illustration, I need hardly say, is intended to be humorous, but it points to a truth. The language in which we talk about anything helps to fix in our minds the impression we carry of that thing. Words are potent allies and dangerous enemies.

One of the most instructive of advertising campaigns has been that of the automobile industry. In the early days of the car, performance was the true basis for selling. The Model T Ford dominated this period, because it provided more performance per dollar than any other car, and nobody cared whether it looked good or not. But, once this initial period was over, all automobile engines were so expertly made that virtually the same performance could be expected from all of them. The public's interest then shifted to design. Purchasers wanted to know about looks, gadgets, and extras. Sales talk changed with this shift. Chrome and convenience became the key words. Today the pleasure a car owner takes in his car is like that which a child takes in his toys, and cars are sold partly with a toy psychology. Watch a crowd milling about at an automobile show. Their facial expressions are almost like those of children in a toy store. People climb in and out of cars to get the "feel" of them, as children climb into toy cars in a shop if they have the chance, and play with the gadgets as children push buttons.

I have a lot of respect for the automobile industry's advertising. It has moved with the times, and produced an effect which is one of the great achievements of salesmanship—all the more impressive when we remember that it has done its job against a background of rising costs, and publicity which has featured automobile fatalities and traffic congestions. Any salesman who follows the example set by the automobile industry will do a better job with his own product.

Study all advertising. Make your own analysis of it. Put your finger on what you think is especially good. Incorporate that into your own work. Take advantage of the current trends in selling to boost your own. Know the words the big men are using. Know how they are using them. Follow their example. Ride on their momentum.

4

Clarify your words to amplify your sales.

When you come upon an advertisement or a business letter or a presentation of any kind which strikes you as being too complicated and obscure, ask yourself how you would have said the same thing more simply and clearly.

As an old hunter in the jungle of words, I can practically guarantee that you will soon be on the track of four little phrases which clutter speech and writing as confusedly as climbing vines tangle a forest. They are: "in view of," "in respect to," "from the standpoint of," and "in connection with."

Do you recognize this? "In connection with your fellow citizens, your conduct should be such as to exemplify the standard of helpfulness you expect from same." It is a translation of the familiar rule: "Do unto others as you would that they should do unto you."

A newspaper writer, reporting on preliminary conversations looking toward the founding of the United Nations wrote: "The unity of view of the participants in the conversations has been established in respect to the exceptional importance at the present time of an all-embracing collective organization of security on the basis of the indivisibility of peace." All he meant to say was "All the people in conference agree that a system of collective security, in which all nations shall participate, is now essential to the maintenance of peace."

A recent advertisement in one of our New York papers ran like this: "In view of our imminent removal from our present location we are offering our entire inventory at sacrifice prices. This special event will open on Saturday at 9 A.M." Whoever wrote this was telling us: "Because we are going to move, we are ready to sell our present stock at reduced prices. The sale will open Saturday at 9 A.M."

I was happy to receive from one of my customers a letter which began, "From the standpoint of recent developments of which we have informed you, we are pleased to state that we are now in a position to discuss your proposition further, with a view to closing." How much simpler, however, it would have been for him to write: "We have now cleared the matters which have been holding us up, and are ready to talk to you about signing. When can you come to see us?"

Our difficulty with these four phrases, and a lot of others equally confusing, arises from the fact that they are so generally used, and we are so often submitted to them, that we become victims of them. They take us over without our knowing it.

This kind of thing happens in all kinds of activities. I am sure that most of the civil servants who write such appalling letters in "officialese" are not aware of having fallen victim to a lingo. It has crept up on them. The same goes for social workers. I once heard a social worker say to her fellow workers at a conference: "We shall take the next hour to redefine our functions." Nobody in the room batted an eye at this strange, not to say, droll suggestion. I picked up an engineering report once which stopped me in my tracks with a paragraph about "dezincification." And a friend of mine turned up with a prize example from orders issued to the air force of a friendly power; the gentlemen were told to pay attention to "the disinfection, de-insectization, and deratization of aircraft." (If "deratization" puzzles you, it means getting rid of rats.) These are all examples of confusing words substituted for clear ones because the people involved had fallen victim to the jargons of their crowds.

There may be some value in a special jargon for a special group. Possibly it can provide a sort of shorthand of speech. But jargons, like pajamas, should not be paraded publicly.

A salesman has no use for jargons. He calls on all kinds of people. His language is the common speech. Realizing how easy it is for him, like any other weak mortal, to fall victim to jungle English, he will set especial guard on himself. Eternal vigilance is the price of uncontaminated speech.

I have a friend who, during the war, was with one of the information services. Part of his job was to get statements from generals and other important people about activities of which they had charge. These took the form of short radio recordings which then were used for morale purposes. Each recording was limited to three minutes. Invariably, the personage would show up with a speech running anywhere from seven to fifteen minutes. He insisted he could not put his message in any shorter form. My friend worked patiently with him. His experienced hand finally produced the three-minute statement, and the personage usually exclaimed: "I wouldn't have believed it, but it's all there."

What the personage may not have realized was that his ten-minute speech would have lost his audience, while his three-minute one was sure to hold them. By simplification he got his message across to more people.

The salesman who takes the same kind of time to simplify will invest it well. He will say what he intends to say. He will say it brightly. He will say it clearly. He will hold his customer's attention. His written presentations will be brief, and the kind that are read, not pushed aside.

Taking pains with words pays. Improve your vocabulary every day. Make every word you meet surrender its meaning to you. Marshal words to do your bidding.

Chapter 21

Improving Your Use of Words

Using words is like juggling—a skill that stays only as long as it improves.

There is only one sure way to learn how to use words—and that is to use them. Hundreds of ambitious writers once gathered for a lecture on writing by Sinclair Lewis at the University of Minnesota. His first words to them were: "I thought you wanted to be writers. If you do, why aren't you at home, writing?"

We can talk about words. We can make generalizations about them. We can study other people's use of them. The only way we can bring them to serve ourselves is to use them ourselves. As we manipulate them, as we watch ourselves juggle them, as we take time to amend and improve our arrangements of them, we learn their pliability and their combinations. They respond to the personal touch.

The salesman is necessarily a man of words. He lives with words. Living with words is like living with a wife. He can go through life intimidated by them. He can go through life intimidating them. Or, he can respect them, and establish a relationship with them in which both he and they will live and work happily together.

A windbag is a man intimidated by words; they run away with him, like a horse taking its head against a timid rider. A pedant is a man who intimidates words; he keeps such a tight rein on them that they are never spontaneous, or anything but pedestrian. The truly articulate man keeps a confident hand on a firm rein; his words and he enjoy whatever pace they choose to share together. You cannot learn to ride a horse without getting into the saddle. You cannot hope to manage words without putting your hand to them.

"Any well-grounded salesman can write a good sales letter," says a friendly adviser. There is no doubt that he *can*. This is like saying that every human *can* swim. The potentiality is there. But not every human being *does* swim. Not every salesman *does* write a good sales letter. *Can* has to be transformed into *does* by *practice*.

"Reading," says Bacon, "maketh a full man, conference a ready man, and writing an exact man." It is this exactness which produces a good sales letter, a good sales presentation, and, indeed, a good sales talk. It is a quality to be gained nowhere apart from the place where a man puts words into sentences, and then examines these sentences to make sure they say what he intends to say in such a way as no other sentences could possibly say it. Every man gets his own exactness from being his own editor.

A live salesman will make sure he makes some advance in his *use* of words every day. This is a habit which fortunately grows easily upon a man who has consciously established for himself the goal of using words expertly.

1

The finest free education on earth is good talk.

Conversation is a natural testing ground for words. Many people shy away from certain words because they have never heard themselves use them. The most natural way to overcome this is to use the word in familiar conversation. You will have no trouble coming out with the exact word in a sales talk if you have accustomed your tongue to using it in ordinary talk. It will rise naturally to your lips and register its full impact sincerely.

This applies not only to the formal words of a dictionary, but also to slang. Slang is a kind of talk that comes from taking liberties with words. It invents new words. It gives a new twist to old words. It is often the speech of the young and irreverent. It has a humorous turn. A good deal of it comes from the vernacular of sports. It can be vivid, amusing, clever, and valuable. It can also be an affectation and a bore.

Slang produces two kinds of snobs. There is the snob who looks down his nose at it, and says, with a sniff, "I never use slang." There is also the other snob who thinks himself a devilish fellow because he repeats and repeats the latest tricks of speech, and looks upon any one who does not join his uproarious enjoyment of his empty wit as an old fogey. Don't be either kind of snob. The virtue of speech lies neither in scorning nor embracing slang, but in using any combination of words which makes your meaning clear.

If some slang expression seems to come naturally to you, give it a trial run in conversation. See how it lies on your own tongue. Watch how well it wears. If it helps you say exactly what you want to say, use it. But do not let it tyrannize over you. Slang is informal speech, "language that has taken its coat off," as somebody called it. This is no reason for using it when it is no more than language that has taken its trousers off. Good sense, good results, are the tests. Conversation is the laboratory in which you can apply them. Whether slang or not, the word or phrase we think we can use to advantage, we can try out in familiar talk.

I am, and have always been, a student in the college of good talk. I spend all the time I possibly can in the company of good talkers. When I have a dinner party at my house, I do not turn it into a card party. I choose people who will be congenial, and, at the same time, will stimulate each other. I like to hear them talk. I learn the proper pronunciation of words. I pick up new words. I get an ear for good sentence structure. I put in my own two cents worth, and build my own confidence in my own use of words.

I want to say two things about exposing yourself to good talk —the freest and best kind of education in the world. First, a man can select the company he keeps with a view to helping himself. No matter how small his community, it has people in it who use good English, and are glad to have an audience. Every man decides for himself whether he will spend his time with such people, or with the boys down at the poolroom. Second, a man who knows what he wants out of a conversation can pretty largely set the tone of any one at which he is present. Every conversation begins with trivialities, as a matter of course. People take time to get warmed up to each other. But, that over, there comes a time when talk can take another road. This is when it either degenerates into mere storytelling or passes over to more profitable discussion. Here is where you can turn it with a tactful touch into helpful channels. People like to discuss. They just need somebody ingenious and energetic enough to touch them off.

Among the most exciting evenings I have ever known were some in a country store serving a town of less than a thousand people in the State of Maine. The old storekeeper, the schoolteacher, the minister, the local State Senator, and a few others sat around the stove regularly, to take the world apart and put it together again. They were mighty talkers. They played a mighty game. Words were their counters. To be with them, and occasionally to venture an opinion, was an exercise in language which has proved priceless to me.

From that general store in Maine to the Algonquin Hotel, I have profited all my life from the company of literate people. Any salesman can manage to do the same. If he works from his own home, he can cultivate a circle of friends there. If he is on the road, he can pick up acquaintance with people along the way who will welcome him for the hours he is not working. In every case, a salesman will be the better for occasionally folding his legs and having his talk out with people who can help him improve his vocabulary and broaden his interests.

Good conversation is a first aid to adequate self-expression.

2

Your letters are short visits from yourself.

Dr. Johnson said of one of his acquaintances: "Tom Birch is as brisk as a bee in conversation, but no sooner does he take a pen in his hand, than it becomes a torpedo to him, and benumbs all his faculties."

This Birch has many descendants—men who are as natural as songbirds until they begin to write. Then they fumble and grope for words like owls blinking in the sunlight. It all comes, possibly, from writing English compositions in school, and being marked for them. Some people never sit down to write without looking over their shoulders for the schoolmarm ready to pounce on them. They write like men with stubbed pens, cramped over a school desk.

Any man will get away from this if he remembers one thing. A letter is "you" making a short visit to a friend. It is not a grave and weighty contribution to Literature (with a capital *L*). Yours are good letters if they are natural, carrying the individual flavor of your personality, your ways of work, and your phrasing. Letters are conversations carried along writing lines, and are effective to the extent that they strengthen personal relationships.

This does not mean that they can be tossed off easily. The time you take to compose them is time given to putting yourself in them, and the more of yourself you put in them, the more of you your correspondent will find in them. Your use of words in letters will constantly improve if you consciously work to make each day's letters more sincerely yours than the previous day's. Here are a few suggestions on how to go about it.

1. When you write, or dictate, "Mr. John Brown," call up the image of Mr. Brown, the human being. See him. He is the person to whom you are writing. Your letter will be warmer in tone if you think of him personally as you write or dictate it.

2. Be sure you know what you want to say to him. Take time to outline all the subjects you want to cover, and know in what order you want to take them up.

3. Take your time composing your letter. Forget the stories you have heard about dynamic men dictating to three or four secretaries at once. Think about what you want to say, and take pains to say it clearly.

4. Point the letter to its one purpose. If it is to clinch a sale, make it a clincher. If it is to answer questions, make it an answer. Know what message you want it to carry, and put that message into it—all of that message, and none of any other.

5. Put some of yourself into the letter. Get a personal tone into it. Remember that the man receiving it will receive a lot of others along with it. Many of them will be formal, or muscle-bound, or coy. Make your letter distinctive. Your personal touch will give it a better chance to get and hold his attention.

A young salesman, trying his wings, would be well advised to write out the first drafts of his letters. He can then go over them to cut out unnecessary words and to clear up muddy passages. In this way he will learn what are his own weaknesses. By editing on paper, he will get the knack of editing in his head, so that, as he matures, he will edit as he dictates.

It has often been said that a letter should be like a woman's dress—long enough to cover the essentials, but short enough to be interesting. This is not an easy ideal. Even as accomplished a writer as Woodrow Wilson once finished a letter by saying: "I hope you will forgive me for writing so long a letter; I did not have the time to write a shorter one."

The right word in the right place is what gives a letter its punch. The shorter and simpler the word, the more effective it is. The more disciplined we are in the choice of words, the surer will our touch on them grow to be. This touch will stamp the good letter writer's letters with his own style. Those who receive them will find him in them, for the style is the man.

3

A written presentation is a whole argument set forth to appeal to a whole man to win his total consent.

A presentation differs from a letter. It is more comprehensive, more formal, and more directly aimed at winning the immediate consent of a prospect. It is, in a way, more formidable. This is where we have to be on guard. Precisely because it is more formal, it is likely to be more stiff. We must stand guard against making it too cold.

A presentation is a letter in full dress, but we shall make a mistake if we forget that a heart must beat beneath the boiled shirt. We are selling a living proposition to a living man.

His acceptance is never the assent of a calculating brain alone. It is an act of the whole man. Therefore, while a presentation differs from a letter, it will be all the better for retaining as much of the warmth and personality of a letter as we can put into it.

If a presentation has one particular and peculiar function, it is to be "explicit." By "explicit" I mean it must enable the customer to understand precisely what the proposition is. A presentation is not aimed at impressing a prospect with your knowledge; it should be so written that he is not left thinking about you, but about what you are selling him. It is not a lawyer's brief, piling argument on argument in weighty dissertation; it is more in the nature of friendly advice turning the customer's attention to something of interest and profit to him. Its object is not to perplex and confuse him; it is to make the proposition crystal clear.

This means that it should be free from anything that is likely to distract him in any way. He should be able to get its meaning instantly at one uninterrupted reading. This puts two tasks up to the salesman. First, he must write in such a way that the reader will not run into complicated sentences; he ought not to have to read any sentence twice to find out what it means. Second, the presentation must be so written that its technical words and phrases are skillfully handled; a customer should not have to stop to puzzle out what they mean. Anything that sidetracks a customer's attention slows up his consent.

When you prepare a presentation, go over it paragraph by paragraph. Treat every paragraph as a unit by itself. Ask yourself these questions: Does it make one point, and one point only? Does it make its point clearly? Does it have the tone I want, or have I slipped into too technical or too cold a way of formulating what I have to say? Does it carry forward the effect I want the whole presentation to have? Is it right in itself, and in its right place in the whole presentation?

Do this with every presentation. Every presentation is an individual production on its own. I have read many formulas for writing sure-fire presentations. After reading and studying them all, I still have to say that I have never found one that works all the time. I have no formula. I do have a method. I treat every new presentation as a fresh challenge. I make it, in itself and for the person to whom it is going, as thorough, personal, and persuasive as I can.

This calls upon all the resources of my working vocabulary. It makes my vocabulary work for me. It makes me work my vocabulary. My vocabulary increases, and, at the same time, my ability to handle it improves.

Your aim in a presentation is to make it as exact, as clear, as well designed for its objective, and as professional, as an architect's blueprint for a building. Take pride in making it measure up to this standard. You will get the satisfaction of accomplishment out of it when you think you have succeeded. A presentation can be a technical masterpiece in the hands of a salesman who uses his words as a master craftsman handles his tools.

4

Visual aids are verbal shorthand.

Presentations are greatly helped by visual aids. These dramatize arguments. They enlist the eye. They make an impression estimated to be five times as powerful as that made by the spoken word.

The decisive thing about a visual aid is knowing when to introduce it. It does not operate apart from words, but in cooperation with them. Words must introduce the visual aid, and words must explain it. Visual aids are illustrations of the proposal. The proposal itself must first be stated. The aids have effect only after the proposal is known. Words set the timing for visual aids, and visual aids economize words.

I stress this because, in all cases, the proposal must control the visual aids, and not the visual aids the proposal.

When a salesman takes his presentation to a customer to go over it with him, he must keep control of the material if he is to maintain management of the interview. The minute a salesman loses control, the client's attention goes off on its own, and he will pay no more attention to the salesman's illustrations than to his words. In cases where a client actually takes an illustration in his own hands, a salesman is usually better off to stop talking altogether, to wait, and not to resume his story until his material is back in his own control.

A visual aid is not introduced to be admired as art work. Neither is it a substitute for a sales talk. It is what its name says it is, an "aid." It can be a powerful one, but it is never an end in itself. It is present to advance the sale. The salesman has to make the sale.

I have found that I have to do a special kind of talking when I present my visual aids. I can take the impressions they make for granted. I do not have to be detailed in my exposition. I can pass more quickly from one emphasis to another. There is a skill in knowing what to say and what to leave unsaid in the presence of a visual aid.

I have said that it is important to know when to introduce visual aids. It is almost equally important to know when to leave them. An aid has its place and function. It carries a discussion a certain distance forward. When it has done its job, the time has come to lay it aside. We must be prepared to go on. To capitalize gracefully on the impression it has made, yet not to dawdle over it, is essential to getting the most impressive results from it.

We cannot think about the relationship between words and visual aids without reminding ourselves also that words have their own places within the visual aids themselves. They appear in its title. They are printed on it to point up its significance. Indeed, in some cases, the visual aid is no more than a word, printed in big or striking type. Here is a case of a specialized use of words, calling for the utmost brevity, which, in turn, calls for the most acute kind of discrimination among words. The *right* title, the *memorable* slogan, the *bullet* word—these do not come by accident.

Seldom do they come from leafing through a dictionary or a thesaurus. They come out of the treasury of a salesman's own word-hoard. The richer that treasury, and the more effectively he has organized and worked it, the more certainly he will come up with the illuminating word. And, what is just as decisive, he will recognize it when it occurs to him.

In short, visual aids by no means dispense with the necessity for verbal skills. If anything, they create a demand for greater versatility in the use of words. The alert salesman will balance his appeal to ear and eye so attractively as to open both gateways to his customer's attention. His pictures will illuminate his words, and his words interpret his pictures.

5

A salesman who speaks in public is like a man who drives in a city—confident everywhere.

I strongly urge every salesman to practice public speaking as a part of his learning to master the use of words. It builds self-confidence. It disciplines self-expression. It calls out confidence from others. It adds authority to a man within his own organization. It wins him recognition in his trade and professional associations.

There is no surer way of finding out whether you are expressing yourself plainly and persuasively than to speak in public. I have seen some of the truly big men of industry unhappily embarrassed because they could not explain their views convincingly in public. One unfortunate, but inevitable, result was that their inadequacy shook their listeners' confidence in them. The president of a company who stammers before his assembled employees hurts not only himself but the morale of the whole organization. It would be better for him not to try to speak.

It would be still better for him to take a good course in public speaking. No matter how big or successful a man is, he can be more effective as a businessman, a citizen, and a human being, when he is able to stand on a platform and impart his ideas to an audience plainly, coherently, sincerely, and attractively.

No salesman can begin too early to acquire this accomplishment. If you are a young salesman in a rural area, join the Grange and speak up in its sessions. If you live in a college or university town, sign up for a course in public speaking. If you reside in a city, hunt out some place where special instruction in public speaking is being given, and join a class.

Don't say you have not the gift. You have. You can hold forth before three people. Addressing three hundred is different only in degree, not in kind.

Don't say that you have not the inclination. This is only a camouflaged way of declaring that you are either too lazy or too scared to try. Public speaking can be useful to you at once. Every year it can be more useful. On some occasions, if you are at all successful, it may be essential. Get started on it. It is like swimming, calling for an effort to take the first plunge, but, once that is past, preparing you for a hundred occasions when you will be glad you know how.

1. Public speaking will emphasize the habit of thorough preparation. When you know two hundred people are going to listen to you for fifteen minutes, your self-respect will drive you to prepare. You will want to be sure you have something to say which they will consider worth hearing.

2. Public speaking develops the habit of matching a message against a given time. When you know you have fifteen minutes on a platform, you will plan fifteen minutes of talk. If you run over, you will soon hear about it. There is no lesson in the economy of words comparable to that of a time limit on a speech.

3. Public speaking encourages attractiveness of style. As you talk to audiences, you will soon find that the most imposing of truths must be dressed in pleasing costume if it is to hold the attention of your listeners. Audiences will force you to learn a charm of style which you can practice profitably in all communication.

4. Public speaking will build your own confidence in yourself. I have seen amazing examples of shy and self-doubting men literally transformed into self-contained and self-confident persons by a course in public speaking. Once anybody realizes that he can keep the attention of twenty or five hundred people for a given length of time, he comes to a healthier appreciation of his own quality. If he is sensible, he does not immediately think himself an orator, but he does find that when he has something to say, he can trust himself to say it.

5. Public speaking builds a man's reputation. Plain sense well presented to many people turns each of them into a booster for the speaker. Reputation opens doors. Professional associates give extra respect to a colleague able to express an interesting development or theory. Business associates see a fellow worker in a new light when he can impress them from a platform. Public speaking sparks personal prestige.

6. Public speaking often leads to promotions and to new opportunities for personal advancement. You never can tell who may be listening to you; just the man to give you the right boost may be among your auditors. You never know when, in a conference or association meeting, the moment may come which

is made to order for a man able to think on his feet. Public speaking makes an impression. Impressions last. When promotions are made, or a new job is looking for its man, the fellow with the reputation is the one who comes to mind.

Apart from evident advantages, public speaking is a first class road to a salesman's professional skill with words. It brings its own reward by making him a better craftsman. No salesman will speak to a customer as though he were a public meeting. But every salesman who knows how to speak in public meetings will speak to his customer with more confidence and more authority as a result of it.

Chapter 22

Your Voice—How to Use It Well

A pleasing voice is like a charming herald preparing a welcome for his master.

A striking feature of modern business is increased use of the voice. Eighty years ago, men who lived fifty miles apart seldom heard each other's voices. They might be doing business together, but a fifty miles journey was a major undertaking. Negotiations were conducted in writing. They saw each other no more than three or four times a year. Then came Mr. Bell.

Today, a businessman in New York thinks nothing of calling a customer in San Francisco or London. Airplanes bring distant cities within a few hours' ride. Automobiles make the remotest village accessible. Men doing business together meet frequently, and, though separated by miles, instantly recognize each other's voices over the telephone. We live in the "talkingest" age man has ever known.

In such a world, a man is known by his voice. It can run the scale. The impressions it leaves may be as pleasant as music or as discordant as fury. Its quality and pitch have much to do with whether those we meet are happier to see us arrive or to see us leave.

An ambitious salesman will give thought to his voice. The

voice we hear ourselves using at fourteen may have developed in us without our thinking about it. The voice we are using at forty is our conscious responsibility.

Some people are fortunate enough to be brought up in an environment and among people helpful to good tone and pitch. Others find themselves in childhood competing with an elevated railroad or a neighboring steam hammer. All can afford to take time, at the beginning of a career, to learn what impression our voices make.

Each of us is aware of the variations in other voices, but we are all too likely to take for granted the charm of our own. I would like to raise enough doubt in your mind about yours for you to make sure that your voice sounds as musical to others as it does in your own ears.

Your voice is not like the number of your fingers about which you can do nothing. It is an instrument which you can tune, manage, and play to get the quality and the effects you want. Lily Pons did not suddenly surprise her parents by bursting into the "Bell Song" from *Lakmé* in her cradle. She squalled like any other little girl. The years which have taken her from that infant squall to superb glory of song have been years devoted to disciplining an untrained voice into a controlled instrument. Miss Pons reminds all of us that, in our own measure, we can take our voices, too, and make them instruments of the effects we wish to create.

Listen to a barker at a fair; he creates a specific kind of tension in a crowd by a pitch of voice he manages expertly. Close your eyes at a mystery play; you will at once recognize how the tone of the actors' voices enhances the mood of horror. Go to a reading by Charles Laughton; his voice is like an organ, now whispering, now exalted—and every other sound he makes, his sniffing and the smacking of his lips, moves with his voice to produce layer upon layer of effect on our ears. Watch the commercials on your television; an expert director has spent hours drilling a trained performer to say each word with a premeditated effect in mind. This one-minute commercial often has had as much time and care spent on it as the whole of the accompanying show.

The least sophisticated child in the country knows how the voices of the birds call across the woods in spring to start a new year's mating. The most sophisticated of industries pay big fees to have just the right voices talk about their products to the buying public. From the lonely marsh to the antennae on the Empire State Building, sounds made by creatures and men keep the busy round of the world spinning. In such a world, the clever salesman will not be careless of the sounds he makes. He will train his voice to do his service.

1

A man's voice is like his cooking—he should be sure of it himself before he tries it on others.

I had a friend who fancied himself as a public speaker. He was a rich man, and spent none of his money with more pleasure than when he gave big dinners at which he spoke. The dinners were always perfect, but we paid heavily for them when his speech came. He talked sense, but delivered it in such a rasping voice with such atrocious diction that we suffered physically and were embarrassed into the bargain.

His wife came to me, as his close friend, and pleaded that I do something to save him from this self-imposed humiliation. At first, I was at a loss about what to do, but one evening, listening to a tape recorder at another friend's house, I got an idea. I went to my oratorical friend when another of his dinners approached, and suggested to him that we arrange to have a recording of its program made. He jumped at the idea.

The week end following this dinner I went to his house with the recording. Playing it was a cruel business. I sat in pain as I watched his suffering when he heard his speech. "Do I really sound like that?" he asked. We nodded. "I shall never speak again," he declared. He does speak. He speaks well. He took himself in hand, trained his voice, improved his diction.

As a result of this experience, I recommend to everybody whose speech and diction are influential in the impression he wants to make that he get a tape recorder and listen to himself talk. Robert Burns wished that some power might "the giftie gie us to see oursels as others see us." There is no power yet that can do this for us. But we have found one that can "the giftie gie us" to hear ourselves as others hear us.

What kind of voice does your prospect hear the first time you get him on the phone? What impression does it make? What kind of an introduction does it give you? A tape recording can give you an idea. Take advantage of it.

I have a friend who has been on the radio with his own program for many years. He tells me that he has never failed to listen systematically to his records every three months. In spite of his experience and conscious vigilance, he says that every such session shows him that he falls into bad habits—lapsing into slurred pronunciations, dropping consonants, reading monotonously, and so on. He maintains that even the most trained of ears cannot truly hear the sound of the voice in the same head with themselves. They hear it, he says, from the inside, others from the outside, and he believes there is all the difference in the world. I quote him because, if I mentioned his name, you would recognize him at once as famous for his voice and diction. If he has to watch his use of his voice, I am sure you and I need to watch ours.

I recommend his method to every salesman. Check up on your voice and your enunciation at regular intervals as conscientiously as an athlete checks on his condition. Make a special point of checking on your delivery of those parts of any sales talk which you repeat often. Frequent repetition is apt to produce a mechanical and singsong kind of talking; you will not fall into this if you are aware of its danger.

When a director gets his Broadway play on the stage, he does not think his work is over. He drops in at regular intervals to see and hear the cast in action. He wants to make sure the acting is still fresh and vital. Even the most highly trained and perfectly directed cast of actors can go stale. Plays often repeated can lose spontaneity. The pitfalls of the experts are warnings to all of us. A salesman has to be his own director. He will be all the more effective in his work if he is a stern one, observing regularly and critically the quality of his voice and habits of his speech.

2

A voice is like a musical instrument, responding only to him who masters it.

Think of your voice as an instrument in the hands of a musician. Even after he knows his instrument, a musician takes time to tune himself and it before he plays publicly. A violinist does not take his fiddle out of his case and begin at once to play. A pianist does not set his fingers to the étude until he has warmed them on the scales. An organist does not call on his organ for full utterance until he has let its pipes take a deep breath. From concert master to drummer, musicians tune themselves to their instruments and their instruments to each other before they start to play. The ambitious salesman will spare no effort to make his voice as perfectly attuned to the occasion of its use as the artist his instrument.

We salesman use our voices on three kinds of occasions. Each calls for its own techniques.

1. On the telephone.

Telephones are so familiar to us that we may think we can take their use for granted, but we may not. The telephone is a singularly uneven convenience. It produces mixed emotions. Useful as it obviously is, it can also exasperate us almost beyond endurance. It has no compunctions about interrupting a train of thought, breaking into an important job, or cutting off a dictation. When it does these things, we would gladly consign it to perdition. But when we ourselves need to call somebody, we embrace it as a gift from the gods.

You know how the telephone affects you. Always bear in mind that it affects the man at the other end in the same ways. Speak to him as you would be spoken unto.

A good telephone voice can become a habit. It can become that most deeply imbedded kind of habit which psychologists call "a conditioned reflex." You have probably heard of the famous experiment of Pavlov with dogs. He gave them meat simultaneously with the ringing of a bell so often that, at last, their mouths would water when the bell rang even though there was no meat around. By steady self-discipline, you can get to the place where the ringing of your telephone bell will automatically call up your "telephone voice."

My own favorite illustration of a conditioned reflex is an electric light button. As I pass a switch, and my eyes get a glimpse of it, my hands respond without my thinking about it. I often flash on the light in a room filled with sunlight. I have sometimes automatically turned it off in a room full of company.

I see a switch, I push it. That is a "conditioned reflex," an immediate reaction without thought to an accustomed stimulus. In just this way, if we take ourselves in hand to answer a telephone pleasantly, the time will come when the minute we pick up a telephone we shall switch on the right manner and voice.

The big essential of the "right" voice is friendliness. The telephone itself is mechanical and cold. To overcome this, a good telephone voice is a little extra cordial. The telephone companies call it "a voice with a smile." This is an apt description. No matter how disturbed you may be by the phone, smile as you pick it up. Your voice will register that smile as surely as your face brightens with it.

There are people I hate to call on the telephone. They are so brusque and grumpy-sounding that I have the uncomfortable feeling that they think I am inexcusably invading their privacy every time I call them. Even as I talk to them, I can feel myself tightening up. No salesman can afford for an instant to create any such reaction as this. When any man who knows me is thinking about placing business along my line, and has a choice between calling me and somebody else, I want him to be happier about the thought of calling me than anybody else in the business. Part of sucess comes from making telephone calls sound welcome. Keep your telephone voice in good tune.

2. Face to face.

The impressions and effects you want to create during an interview are many. Your voice plays a part in creating every one of them.

First comes the greeting. Your voice is respectful or familiar in tone, depending on your relationship with the man you are addressing. It echoes with your attitude, quiet with respect, or bright with interest as you inquire after his health, his family, his golf score, or his favorite charity. It sets the tone for the interview—altogether serious, or more free-and-easy, as the case may be.

Then you get down to business. Your voice becomes earnest. It conveys the workmanlike pride you take in being able to bring him a proposition so good for him, and so thoroughly worked out that it must command his respect. Your tone tells him that you are sincerely convinced of the value to him of your proposal. It gathers more and more intensity as you pass from point to point, building the impact of your argument.

This growing intensity should register in a *deepening* of the voice. Many of us have a tendency to let our voices rise as we get more emphatic. This is a mistake. A rising voice gets thinner and reedlike, less impressive, and usually less musical. If we keep our voices down, and let them get deeper as we talk, our tones get richer. They imply self-control. They suggest reserves of power. A salesman's exposition should always carry the impression that he could say a lot more if he had to. A deepening voice helps to suggest that he is speaking from depth.

The next phase is persuasion. The voice takes on a new quality. Persuasion is emotional. The voice accordingly becomes an instrument to play on the emotions. It grows more colorful, more charming, and friendlier. It is not longer describing an impersonal proposition, but is appealing to a person. Warmth of personal understanding comes into it. It has an overtone of promise.

Persuasion runs into objections. As he meets these, a salesman keeps his voice under maximum control. He does not allow it to sound patronizing or irritated. He may think the objections ignorant, puerile, and obstinate. He may be burning up inside. His voice betrays none of this. He gives it no license to be fretful or sarcastic. It may be emphatic. It may be incredulous. It may be humorous. But it is always what the salesman wants it to be in the light of accomplishing what he has set out to achieve. His voice, even under the severest of provocations, is his servant.

When the objections are answered, the sale is either made or it is not. His voice matches both contingencies. If he has made the sale, it is warm with congratulation for the client—never loud with triumph for the salesman—the customer gets the cheers. If the sale has not been made, it is firm, but friendly, regretting the failure of the moment, but full of reassurance of mutual understanding and respect. A disappointed salesman should leave behind the echo of a positive and friendly voice.

At first, a young salesman may find something artificial, even distasteful, about the idea of listening to his own voice during an interview. He may think it will dull the brightness of spontaneity. During his apprenticeship, he may indeed pass through a period when this is more or less true. But I must emphasize what

I have said before. A sales interview is a professional practice. It calls for technically correct handling. In the beginning, these techniques may seem awkward, as a violin is awkward in the hands of a beginner, but, mastered, they do not hamper spontaneity, they release it. They bring out of the clumsy neophyte the practiced virtuoso. The salesman who begins by consciously controlling his voice in interviews will grow into the master whose voice responds at his will to serve every demand of every sale.

3. On the platform.

The use of the voice in public speaking is so big a subject that another book the size of this one would be required to cover it thoroughly. All I want to do here is to make one point about it. *Public speaking is at its best when it is most like conversation.*

I think that if the average salesman will get this clearly in mind, he will lose half his fears of talking from a platform. Talk to a hundred people as you would talk to one. Be just as simple, just as straightforward, just as sincere. You are only talking to each of the hundred in your audience one at a time.

Public speaking is conversation on parade. The voice has to project itself against a more pretentious setting. Articulation of syllables must be a little clearer, tone a bit fuller, and appeal more forceful. But these are modifications. They do not change any essentials. The voice on the platform is used as it is in conversation, only more of it is used with more scope.

But bear this in mind. *Don't shout.* Above all, don't begin by shouting. A speaker who begins at the top of his voice is soon suspended in hot air with no visible means of support. Begin in a conversational tone. As you get into your subject, let your voice deepen. Its carrying power will then be pumped into it by the bellows of your own intensity. As you become moved by what you have to say, your body will rally its powers to give your voice impetus.

This will not happen if you scream. A rising tone will put all the responsibility for your voice on your throat alone. Instead of your lungs filling your voice, your larynx will strain for effect. Your voice will rise and rise until it cracks. There is almost nothing more unpleasant than a screaming voice, and few things more ludicrous than a cracking one.

Almost as important is this. *Don't drone*. If you feel you have to read a speech, score it for emphasis. Governor Dewey's written speeches are so underlined and marked that they look almost like musical scores. He knows exactly how he is going to vary emphasis to get effects. On the other hand, a Duke of Devonshire is said once to have yawned in the middle of a speech he was making. I have often listened to droners, and wondered by what miracle of self-control they have kept themselves from following his example.

Speak up. Speak plainly. Know what a fine instrument your voice is. Train yourself to be an artist in its use. You will find pleasure in this for yourself. You will bring delight to those who hear you. You may not always make your sale, but you can be perfectly sure that you leave a better taste with the man you delight than the one you distress. Your voice can be a pleasant memory you leave with everyone with whom you deal.

Chapter 23

Now It's Up to You

THE WORLD of tomorrow is a challenge for great salesmen. The modern salesman has a unique and indispensable contribution to make to our country's success and progress. These two statements fit together like hand and glove. Both of them are founded in sober fact.

The next twenty-five years are going to be marked by a technological revolution. It will develop out of the use of new kinds of power. It will involve unpredictable changes in manufacturing and production. Already we can foresee that certain industries, like housing and transportation, must, of necessity, bring forth radically new products created by much more efficient methods. Modern technology is ushering in a new epoch.

Merchandising will have to keep pace with technology. More goods more efficiently produced will call for new methods of selling and more efficient distribution. The salesman will be the key to getting the goods to the consumer. His work will be increased, as he has more goods to sell. His social significance will be enhanced, for it will be plainer and plainer that the only way to keep the whole economy going is to keep goods moving. The challenge to his originality and courage will increase every day. His income will be limited only by his ability to keep up with opportunity.

Not only will there be more goods, there will also be more customers. The United States is not moving toward a stable population. It shows every sign of developing a constantly increasing one.

In 1954, 4,060,000 babies were born in the United States—the largest number in any year of our history. This is a fact of such importance that I would say it is the most exciting news item of the year. It changed our whole outlook on the future economic development of the U.S.A.

This is a big statement. Let us examine it.

We begin with the U.S. Census Bureau. This bureau, on the basis of the birth rate of the twenty years since the birth depression of 1932-1933, has been predicting that our population would be static in a few years, and then would begin to decline. Statistically, this was a justifiable forecast. What 1954 indicates is that statistics do not tell the whole story. Social forces have moved in to change the picture entirely.

In 1933-1934, depression years, the birth rate was about thirty-five per cent lower than 1954. This is interesting because 1954 was the year when the first children of those born during the depression came into the world. The number of marriages in 1954, reflecting the low birth rate of twenty years ago, was below average. But the number of children born to the total married population set a record.

This indicates that the low birth rate of the depression period was an isolated phenomenon. We have come through it, and are now back in what we may call a "normal" period. The historical birth rate of the country has shaken off the effects of the depression. A new generation has arisen which did not know the crash.

The rising birth rate means more young people of marriageable age during the next twenty years. Romance is one constant in a fickle world. These young people will marry and have children. Every year will see an increasing number of babies. Eight or ten years from now, the birth rate will take another big jump. Twenty years hence, it will take another.

At a conservative estimate, the population of the U.S.A. will increase by something like 30,000,000 in the next ten years, and by upwards of 60,000,000 in the next twenty years. These figures represent what we may call "the gross expansion" a salesman can expect in the number of consumers in the home market.

These gross figures can be broken down into analyses which are of interest to salesmen planning their futures. Our Negro citizens, for example, while they still have a high birth rate, have a declining one. I should expect that we may anticipate also a declining birth rate among those newcomers who now have a higher rate than the average; adjustment to our customs usually has this effect.

There is, too, the question of the relative sizes of various age groups. For instance, the numbers of children and of people over sixty-five years of age are abnormally high in comparison with past times. One interesting fact which emerges from this is that, while our population is increasing by 30,000,000 by 1965, the number of people of working age will increase by only 7,000,000.

Not all of these will be working. A marked sign of our times is increased enrollment in our colleges. We are in a period somewhat like that of 1920-1940, when our high school enrollment rose from twenty per cent of those eligible to ninety per cent. Today, colleges are having the increase. The 1954 enrollment rose to 2,500,000, an increase of ten per cent, most of it at the freshman level. At this rate, 3,000,000 will be in college in 1965. Take these from the 7,000,000 attaining the working age, and it indicates that only 4,000,000 will actually enter working ranks.

No matter how we look at these figures, they forecast that relatively fewer workers will be serving a much greater population. The salesman who is prepared to cope with this growing and changing market can look forward to decades of expanding opportunity. The man in business today will see the population

Now It's Up to You / 249

of the United States grow as much in the next ten years as it did in the thirty years from 1920 to 1950.

I have written of the expansion of the American market only. There is another. One of the greatest accomplishments of our time may well be to raise the living standards of the hitherto backward peoples of the world. A rise in living standards among hundreds of millions of people, even though it be but a fractional rise, will create a demand for goods and services that staggers the imagination. United States production and services will have to take a big share of meeting the demand. The vistas this opens for selling capital goods, heavy machinery, consumer goods, and the peculiar services we have developed to match an industrial society, are enough to make me wish I were starting all over again. A salesman prepared for new occasions is going to lack no opportunities to work his talent in the next quarter of a century.

Technological advance—increased production—more people to buy—new markets! These set the stage for an era of great salesmanship. It forecasts a world calling for great salesmen. I am not prophet enough to draw exact specifications for the cut and practice of the salesman of tomorrow. What I do know is that, if he has the right attitude and the essential qualities, the alert salesman of today will grow into the effective salesman of tomorrow. He will be alert to changing conditions, equip himself to understand them, and prove himself competent to move with them.

The salesman ready for tomorrow is marked by seven distinctions.

1. He knows himself.

Because he knows himself he disciplines himself. He is equally aware of where he is most facile and where he is weakest. He knows the dangers for him in both. He does not let his facility betray him into laziness. He deliberately sets himself to turn his weakness into strength through the cultivation of industrious habits. He makes of himself the perfect instrument of his will to serve his ideal of success.

2. He is single-minded.

He chooses his job deliberately. Having chosen it, he makes it his lifework. He puts all he has into it. He takes from others and from experience whatever they can contribute to helping him toward his goal. He allows neither himself nor others to turn his energies elsewhere.

3. He knows what he is selling.

He knows it thoroughly. He knows precisely how it will serve those to whom he sells. Behind this, he knows of what it is made, why it is made as it is made, the processes of thought out of which it has developed, and how all these combine to make it uniquely what it is. Whether it is a product or a service, he is master of it, and of all it can do.

4. He knows his customers.

He knows them as individual people. He knows their needs and their problems. He is to them as a friend and a partner, trying always to understand, to help, and to forward their interests. His vivid awareness of his customers and their situations is itself a powerful part of his education in the realities and demands of a changing market. It thus stimulates his own growth and versatility.

5. He takes pride in his work.

He puts his name to no detail which does not represent the very best work of which he is capable. His fierce pride in his own craftsmanship keeps him tuned to the minute as a violin is tuned for perfect tone and pitch.

6. He wins a friend with every sale.

He never treats human beings as statistics. He finds in every human contact an enlarging of his own understanding. This deepens his technical expertness into the profounder quality of wisdom. He ripens as he sells. And the ripening of his wisdom enables him to judge men and affairs so soundly that he can sense the deeper trends of his time, and thus keep himself prepared to forecast and meet their developments.

7. He makes the end of one sale the beginning of the next.

He is a restless man. All growing things are restless. The minute they cease to grow they begin to die. The salesman crossing the threshold after he has made a sale is the salesman on his way to the next. He makes time his servant. He makes of every experience a teacher instructing him how to make the next one better.

The future of any of us is unknown. As we look to tomorrow we can be sure of only one thing. Tomorrow will yield its prizes only to the man who has the courage to face it without fear, and the preparation to meet its demands. The man who is most alive today will live tomorrow most fully. The salesman, or any other man, can face tomorrow, whatever it may bring, with faith and hope, provided that he tackles today with confidence and ambition.

Index